ROYAL HISTORICAL SOCIETY

STUDIES IN HISTORY

New Series

RELIGION, TIME AND MEMORIAL CULTURE IN LATE MEDIEVAL RIPON

Studies in History New Series

Editorial Board

This series is supported by annual subventions from the
Economic History Society and from the Past and Present Society

PAST & PRESENT
a journal of historical studies

RELIGION, TIME AND MEMORIAL CULTURE IN LATE MEDIEVAL RIPON

Stephen Werronen

THE ROYAL HISTORICAL SOCIETY
THE BOYDELL PRESS

First published 2017

A Royal Historical Society publication
Published by The Boydell Press
an imprint of Boydell & Brewer Ltd
PO Box 9, Woodbridge, Suffolk IP12 3DF, UK
and of Boydell & Brewer Inc.
668 Mt Hope Avenue, Rochester, NY 14620–2731, USA
website: www.boydellandbrewer.com

ISBN 978-0-86193-345-7

ISSN 0269-2244

A CIP catalogue record for this book is available
from the British Library

The publisher has no responsibility for the continued existence or accuracy of
URLs for external or third-party internet websites referred to in this book, and
does not guarantee that any content on such websites is, or will remain, accurate
or appropriate

This publication is printed on acid-free paper

Typeset by Fakenham Prepress Solutions, Fakenham, Norfolk NR21 8NN
Printed and bound in Great Britain by TJ International Ltd, Padstow, Cornwall

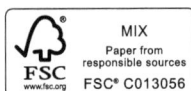

MIX
Paper from
responsible sources
FSC
www.fsc.org   FSC® C013056

Contents

List of Illustrations

Maps

Tables

Acknowledgements

A great number of people have read some or all of this book in one form or another, and their comments and suggestions have been invaluable. I would especially like to thank Emilia Jamroziak, Richard Morris, Roberta Gilchrist, Wendy Childs, Peter Coss, Erin Dailey, Eleanor Warren, Isabella Bolognese, Kirsty Day, Richard Thomason and Jeff Miller. I am particularly indebted to Stuart Palmer who helped me to check the proofs. My editor, Christine Linehan, improved the book enormously with her amendments and suggestions and Rohais Haughton at Boydell & Brewer was very helpful in seeing the book through the production stages. All the remaining faults and errors are my own.

I must, of course, express my thanks to the Economic History Society whose bursary helped me to undertake my research. I would also like to extend my gratitude more generally to all my colleagues at the universities of Leeds, Kent and Copenhagen. Above all I would like to thank Sheryl McDonald Werronen, with whom I discussed all aspects of the cult of St Wilfrid and the medieval parish of Ripon more frequently and more extensively than with anyone else. Her patience and support over the years have been essential to me.

Stephen Werronen
April 2017

Abbreviations

AoC	*Acts of chapter of the collegiate church of SS Peter and Wilfrid, Ripon, AD 1452 to AD 1506*, ed. J. T. Fowler (Surtees Society, 1875)
Chantry certificates	*The certificates of the commissioners appointed to survey the chantries, guilds, hospitals, etc. in the county of York*, ed. William Page (Surtees Society, 1894-5)
CPR	*Calendar of patent rolls*
EHR	*English Historical Review*
MR	*Memorials of the church of SS Peter and Wilfrid, Ripon*, ed. J. T. Fowler (Surtees Society, 1882-1908)
NH	*Northern History*
ODNB	*Oxford dictionary of national biography*
P&P	*Past & Present*
TE	*Testamenta Eboracensia: a selection of wills from the registry at York*, ed. James Raine (Surtees Society, 1836-1902)
TNA	The National Archives
VCH	*Victoria County History*
YAJ	*Yorkshire Archaeological Journal*

Introduction

In the summer of 1380, John de Hawkeswick and John de Clynt oversaw the casting of a new bell for Ripon Minster. The minster was a large and ancient church situated above the meeting-point of the rivers Ure and Skell in the north-west part of Yorkshire. Long ago, in the seventh century, a holy man named Wilfrid had driven out Ripon's first group of monks and founded his own new monastery. The original monks followed the customs of the Irish Church, but Wilfrid replaced them with a monastery aligned with Roman customs, loyalty to which was a defining feature of his career. Wilfrid's most famous achievement was to introduce the Roman system for calculating the date of Easter at the Synod of Whitby. Among the many churches that he founded, Ripon was one of Wilfrid's favourites and he was buried there after his death in 710. He then became the posthumous protector of his followers, proving his sanctity through miracles. The archbishops of York had high esteem for Wilfrid, who as bishop of Northumbria was one of their predecessors. They rebuilt the minster in the late twelfth century in order to provide a more suitable architectural setting for his shrine. The seven canons of Ripon, who eventually succeeded Wilfrid's monks, continued to prize his relics until the Reformation under Henry VIII.

In the fourteenth and fifteenth centuries Ripon was a regionally important ecclesiastical centre and a relatively large market town. It ranked alongside Pontefract, Doncaster, Whitby and Selby, yet still below the leading Yorkshire towns of York, Beverley, Hull and Scarborough.[1] The minster's economic influence was also considerable and extended well beyond the town itself and into the surrounding area. Specialists such as goldsmiths, glaziers and masons resided in Ripon in part because of the minster's demand for their skills. Carpenters, who were the most important category of medieval craftsmen, also found plenty of opportunities to work at the minster. Two of the carpenters who worked on installing the new bell and making its frame in 1380 were from nearby villages: Lawrence Carpenter was listed in the 1379 poll tax as a resident of Skelton, and Richard Wright as a resident of Thornton.[2] The great quantities of lead needed for roof repairs, and perhaps also the plumbers who worked it, came from nearby Nidderdale, where lead had been mined since

---

[1]   R. B. Dobson, 'Yorkshire towns in the late fourteenth century', *Publications of the Thoresby Society* lix (1986), 1–21 at pp. 4, 6–7.

[2]   *The poll taxes of 1377, 1379 and 1381*, ed. Carolyn C. Fenwick, Oxford 1998–2005, iii. 432–7.

1

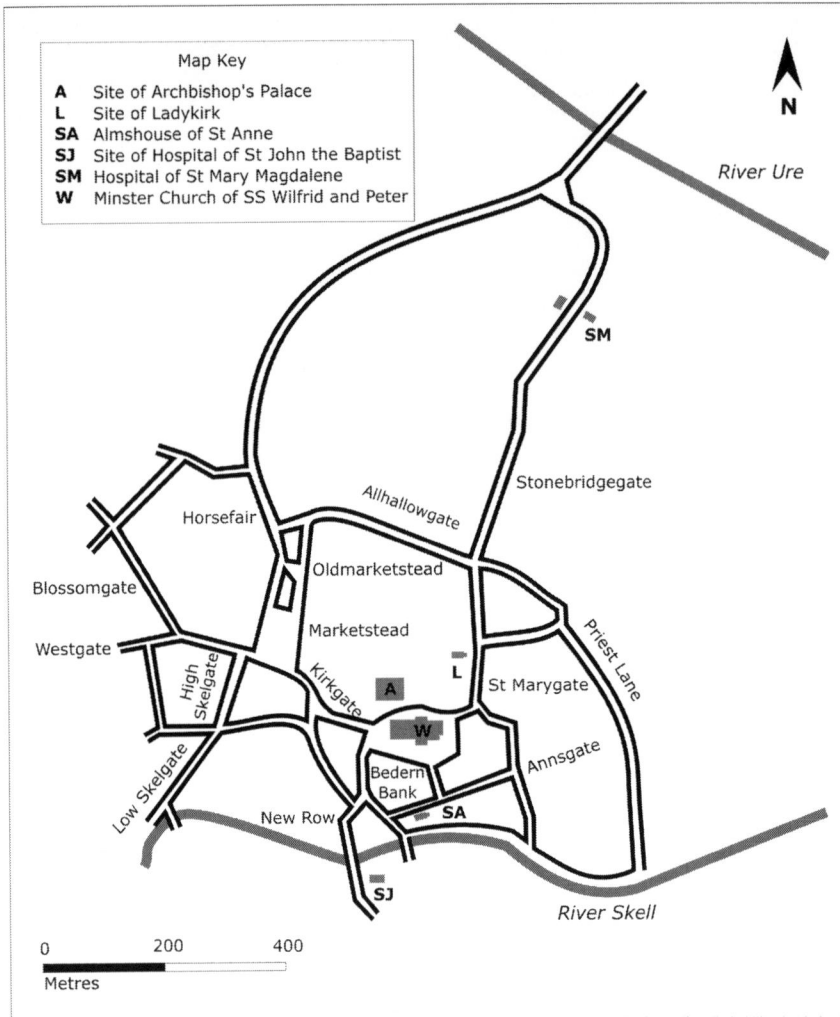

Map Key

A   Site of Archbishop's Palace
L   Site of Ladykirk
SA Almshouse of St Anne
SJ Site of Hospital of St John the Baptist
SM Hospital of St Mary Magdalene
W   Minster Church of SS Wilfrid and Peter

Map 1. Ripon in the later Middle Ages

Roman times.[3] The minster's plumber in 1380 was Richard de Bettys, who lived in Sawley at the edge of Nidderdale.[4] Though they were several miles from the minster, all of these villages were within the parish of Ripon, which was greater than eighty square miles in extent.[5] Though it was not difficult to find

---

[3]   Bernard Jennings (ed.), *A history of Nidderdale*, 2nd edn, Pateley Bridge 1983, 58-9.

[4]   *Poll taxes*, iii. 434.

[5]   Glanville R. J. Jones, 'The Ripon estate: landscape into townscape', *NH* xxxvii (2000), 13-30 at p. 24.

plumbers and carpenters, there was no one in Ripon with the expertise to cast a bell as large as the one that the wardens desired in 1380. They therefore turned to York, a major city and the source for luxury goods throughout the region.[6] Ripon was connected to York by important waterways that could be used to transport goods. From nearby Boroughbridge the River Ure was navigable all the way to the Ouse, which ran through York itself. Having acquired an old bell from nearby Fountains Abbey and a quantity of additional metal, the Ripon fabric wardens shipped these materials down the river to York to be recast as their new bell. They paid William de Stutford 10*d.* just to travel in the boat and keep watch over the shipment.[7]

Ripon was an important commercial centre in its own right, with a weekly market on Thursdays and two annual fairs. The market had been built up by the archbishops of York from around the year 1100 in order to increase the profitability of their portion of the town.[8] In 1379 the area around the market square was home to almost half of the town's population and the majority of its servants.[9] The street names Cornhill and Horsefair show that the market was divided into specialist areas for the selling of both arable and pastoral agricultural produce. The former more commonly came from the lowland parts of the parish around Ripon. The land between the River Ure at the edge of the town and the River Swale a few miles further east, where the villages of Skelton, Givendale, Dishforth, Nunwick, Hutton Conyers and Norton Conyers were located, was especially well suited to growing crops.[10] To the west and north of Ripon were less fertile upland areas, which were better for grazing livestock. Much of this portion of the parish was forest land. Stock rearing, which yielded dairy products and meat, was based on seigneurial control of forests and chases that provided hunting preserves for their lords as well as grazing land for their livestock.[11] The royal forest of Knaresborough at the southern end of Nidderdale, the chase of Nidderdale higher up in the dale, and the archbishop of York's hunting preserve around Thornton were three such areas.[12] Efforts to bring land in Nidderdale under the plough by assarting were halted by the Black Death in the middle of the fourteenth century, and pastoral agriculture continued to predominate there in the fifteenth.[13] The Cistercian monasteries

---

[6]   A. J. Pollard, *North-eastern England during the Wars of the Roses: lay society, war, and politics, 1450–1500*, Oxford 1990, 42.

[7]   *MR* iii. 99, 100.

[8]   Mark Whyman, 'Excavations in Deanery Gardens and Low St Agnesgate, Ripon, North Yorkshire', *YAJ* lxix (1997), 119–63 at p. 160.

[9]   Jones, 'The Ripon estate', 30.

[10]   Pollard, *North-eastern England during the Wars of the Roses*, 31.

[11]   Ibid. 36.

[12]   Jennings, *History of Nidderdale*, 30, 111–14.

[13]   Edward Miller, 'The occupation of the land: Yorkshire and Lancashire', in Joan Thirsk (ed.), *The agrarian history of England and Wales*, III: *1348–1500*, Cambridge 1991, 42–52 at pp. 46–8.

of Fountains, Byland and Jervaulx grazed their enormous flocks of sheep on its upland portion. The nearest of these three venerable monasteries was Fountains, which actually stood within the boundaries of the parish of Ripon.

No doubt large numbers of sheep were bought and sold at Ripon's two annual fairs, one in April and one in October, which were especially important for the marketing of livestock. The fairs were timed to correspond to two of the feasts of St Wilfrid, thereby combining trade and pilgrimage, the two features of Ripon that gave it regional significance. The wool of these sheep was a key component in the region's most important manufacturing industry: cloth production. In the 1390s this was centred on Ripon and the nearby towns of Richmond, Northallerton, Boroughbridge and Bedale.[14] The poll tax of 1379 lists many in the town of Ripon whose professions were related to cloth making, including weavers, dyers and tailors. Over the course of the next century the industrial centre shifted to the West Riding towns of Bradford, Halifax and Leeds so that when the antiquary John Leland visited Ripon in the early sixteenth century, he remarked that 'idelnes is now sore incresid in the toun, and clothe making almost decayed'.[15] He visited the church of Ripon shortly after the completion of its new nave – Ripon's major late medieval building campaign – and just before the institution itself was dissolved. Wilfrid had already been banished from the church, and with the dissolution of the chapter of canons, the abolition of the chantries and the suppression of the guilds the town lost its status as a great ecclesiastical centre not to mention many of its familiar structures and symbols of social hierarchy.

The subject of this book is not the destruction of these things but the things themselves, so little will be said about the Reformation. Instead it aims to analyse the relationship between religion and society in Ripon during the 'long fifteenth century', the nearly 150 years from the casting of the bell in 1380 to the completion of the nave in 1522. The late medieval cult of St Wilfrid is much less studied than his earthly career, yet it is the key to understanding the institutional workings of Ripon Minster as well as those of the enormous parish that surrounded and depended upon it. The historiography of the minster and town is rooted in the antiquarian writers and local historians of the eighteenth and nineteenth centuries. At times this has enabled spurious claims to endure long past the date at which their poor foundations in actual historical evidence should have been uncovered: for example the belief that Scottish raiders caused severe damage to the minster in the tumultuous years after the battle of Bannockburn.[16] However, in lieu of a *Victoria County History* volume covering Ripon's portion of the West Riding, local historians such as John Richard Walbran in the nineteenth century and Tom Gowland in the early twentieth

---

[14]   Pollard, *North-eastern England during the Wars of the Roses*, 39.

[15]   *The itinerary of John Leland in or about the years 1535–1543*, ed. Lucy Toulmin Smith, London 1907–10, i. 82; Pollard, *North-eastern England during the Wars of the Roses*, 71.

[16]   See Stephen Werronen, 'Ripon and the Scottish raids, 1318–1322', NH xlix (2012), 174–84.

century provide many of the important details about local families and the manorial structure of the parish.[17] More recently historians and archaeologists have focused on the development of the medieval town, in particular William McKay, Glanville R. J. Jones, R. A. Hall and Mark Whyman.[18] The most recent works on the archaeology and architectural history of the building were undertaken by M. F. Hearn, Stuart Harrison, Paul Barker and Christopher Wilson, Wilson's entry in the revised edition of the *Buildings of England*'s West Riding volume being an overview of the whole of the minster's architectural history.[19]

The major gaps in scholarship are the cult of St Wilfrid, the religious practices of Ripon's parishioners, the importance of the many chapels of the parish, the remembrance of the dead and the annual liturgical cycle that connected all these elements together. There are a great many written sources for this study, for which the necessary context is the findings of Ripon's archaeologists and architectural historians.[20] The graves, altars, relics and processions that are discussed at length in this book all had a real place in the world, and their relationships to one another in space and time are essential to the arguments advanced: as Roberta Gilchrist has argued it was 'through the spaces and material culture of the parish church' that the religious practices of the church calendar joined the individual to the history of salvation and the vastness of eternity.[21] Nevertheless, because it is based primarily on records

---

[17] John Richard Walbran, *A guide to Ripon, Fountains Abbey, Harrogate, Bolton Priory, and several places of interest in their vicinity*, 12th edn, Ripon 1875; Tom S. Gowland, 'The manors and liberties of Ripon', *YAJ* xxxii (1936), 43–85, and 'Ripon Minster and its precincts', *YAJ* xxxv (1943), 270–87.

[18] William McKay, 'The development of medieval Ripon', *YAJ* liv (1982), 73–82; Jones, 'The Ripon estate'; R. A. Hall and Mark Whyman, 'Settlement and monasticism at Ripon, North Yorkshire, from the 7th to the 11th centuries AD', *Medieval Archaeology* xl (1996), 62–150; Whyman, 'Excavations in Deanery Gardens and Low St Agnesgate'.

[19] M. F. Hearn, 'Ripon Minster: the beginning of the gothic style in northern England', *Transactions of the American Philosophical Society* lxxiii (1983), 1–196; Stuart Harrison, and Paul Barker, 'Ripon Minster: an archaeological analysis and reconstruction of the 12th-century church', *Journal of the British Archaeological Association* clii (1999), 49–78; Christopher Wilson, 'Ripon: the cathedral', in Peter Leach and Nikolaus Pevsner, *The buildings of England: Yorkshire West Riding: Leeds, Bradford, and the North*, New Haven 2014, 637–58.

[20] Many of these were edited for the Surtees Society by J. T. Fowler, and published between 1882 and 1908 as the four-volume *Memorials of Ripon*. Fowler's 1875 edition of the Ripon chapter acts book, also for the Surtees Society, is likewise indispensable. Among the many items not edited by Fowler are a number of manuscripts from the Ripon Dean and Chapter archives (now Brotherton Special Collection, Leeds, MS Dep 1980/1), and naturally the records now held in the National Archives fell outside the scope of his editions. Translations of source material are ordinarily my own, in which case I have provided the original in the footnote. The exceptions are Bede's *Ecclesiastical history* and Stephanus' *Life of Bishop Wilfrid*; in these cases I have used the editors' translations.

[21] Roberta Gilchrist, *Medieval life: archaeology and the life course*, Woodbridge 2012, 14. See also C. Pamela Graves, *The form and fabric of belief: an archaeology of the lay experience of religion in medieval Norfolk and Devon* (British Archaeological Reports, cccxi), Oxford 2000, 7–8, 166–7.

produced by the clergy of Ripon Minster, the analysis proceeds outwards from their church's core component – the cult of St Wilfrid – to the church and clergy surrounding it, then further to the chapels and villages of the wider parish, the structure of the ritual year that bound them to Wilfrid and Ripon, and finally to the dead whose memory often lingered after their spirits had left the world. Its overarching themes are time, memory and society. They are linked by the dynamics of power and authority that underpinned medieval social hierarchy and found expression and support in the great feasts of the calendar and the commemoration of the dead. Not to be confused with mere force, power was a form of influence that shaped society in many subtle ways, a subject which John Arnold has argued deserves greater attention in studies of medieval religious history.[22]

Power and authority

God was the original source of all power in medieval Ripon, but this power descended from heaven through various channels. One of the most direct was Wilfrid, patron saint and founder of the minster. Since late antiquity, when the old taboos about separating the living and the dead had been broken, the bodies of the saints had become sites of tremendous power capable of joining heaven and earth. Wherever there was the body of a saint, or even the fragment of one, there the saint was present and able to aid the living.[23] The shrines of the saints sacralised the space of the world while their feast days sacralised time, turning the calendar into a succession of commemorations that celebrated Christian history.[24] Saintly power was widely valued, and the bodies of saints were divided, translated from one church to another, and even stolen. Centuries after Wilfrid's death his relics became the subject of a dispute between Canterbury and York, the two metropolitan sees of medieval England. The power of the saint to confer authority and prestige on those who possessed his relics was at the heart of this dispute. In the middle of the tenth century the monks of Canterbury began to claim that, after Ripon had been destroyed by recent war, one of their archbishops had removed Wilfrid's relics from the ruins of Ripon Minster and transported them to Canterbury. The archbishops of York responded to Canterbury's claims with their own version of events in which Wilfrid's relics were rescued by an archbishop of York and then restored to Ripon once the church there had been rebuilt. This translation of Wilfrid's relics was later commemorated by an annual feast day, which not only venerated the saint but also celebrated Ripon's possession of his

22 John Arnold, *Belief and unbelief in medieval Europe*, London 2005, 5, 14.
23 Peter Brown, *The cult of saints: its rise and function in Latin Christendom*, Chicago 1981, 88.
24 Jacques le Goff, *À la Recherche du temps sacré: Jacques de Voragine et la Légende dorée*, Paris 2011, 42.

relics. The dispute over the relics continued into the early thirteenth century with the rebuilding of Ripon Minster and a second translation of Wilfrid's relics to a new site by Archbishop Walter de Grey in 1224. These events, together with the establishment of the Ripon fairs corresponding to Wilfrid's feast days, were part of a concerted effort by the archbishops of York to assert their possession of the relics. Powerful though they might have been, relics alone could not transmit the identity and history of the saint. They needed a shrine, a traditional account of the saint's life, images of the saint and feast days.[25] The archbishops of York provided these for Wilfrid, hoping to seal their achievement by attracting pilgrims to Ripon.

Pilgrimage was a central feature of the medieval cult of saints. Pilgrims wished to benefit from the holy power of the saints by approaching their relics and being cured of their afflictions. Saints who could provide cures would continue to attract pilgrims. These pilgrims were essential because the saints, like any other patrons, needed clients to demonstrate their power and to increase their honour.[26] By the end of the twelfth century it became necessary for new cults to be approved by the pope, whose commissioners would investigate the miracles of an alleged saint.[27] By that time Wilfrid's cult was so old and well established that it continued to rest entirely upon the sturdy foundations of his early miracles and his status as supernatural protector of Ripon. As a saint, Wilfrid was typical of his time and place of origin: early medieval saints of northern Europe tended to be powerful men, such as kings or bishops, whose dead bodies performed miracles.[28]

Walter de Grey's translation of Wilfrid's relics to their new shrine at Ripon took place just before the successful canonisation of William of York in 1226. The archbishops of York had long defended Ripon's claim to possess Wilfrid's relics but they never tried to move them to York: in St William, the cathedral church of York at last had the relics of its own saintly archbishop. Together John of Beverley, Wilfrid of Ripon and William of York provided some of the defining features of the York diocese calendar.[29] The annual repetition of the saints' feast days was essential to preserving their memory as well as giving them the honour that they deserved. There was no single universal calendar of saints' feasts at this time, so there was significant variation from place to place. The calendar used at York Minster was used within a relatively small area: the three dioceses of York, Durham and Carlisle which constituted the ecclesiastical province of York. The rest of England was in the southern province where the liturgical use of Sarum was widespread. Before the late fifteenth century, the

[25]   Patrick Geary, *Furta sacra: thefts of relics in the early Middle Ages*, Princeton 1978, 6.

[26]   Kenneth Baxter Wolf, *The life and afterlife of St Elizabeth of Hungary: testimony from her canonization hearings*, Oxford 2011, 38–40.

[27]   André Vauchez, *Sainthood in the later Middle Ages*, trans. Jean Birell, Cambridge 1997, 35–45.

[28]   Arnold, *Belief and unbelief*, 74.

[29]   Richard Pfaff, *The liturgy in medieval England: a history*, Cambridge 2009, 456.

calendar of the Scottish Church was also based on the use of Sarum, which is understandable given the attempts of the archbishops of York to extend their primacy to include southern Scotland.[30] Ripon was a large enough church to generate some of its own very telling variations on the York calendar. Naturally they focused on Wilfrid, who was the crucial source of the minster clergy's local power and authority. Wilfrid had always been a defender of his successors, and some of his earliest posthumous miracles involve his protection of monasteries that he had founded against raiding warriors. As late as the fifteenth century Wilfrid was still instrumental in the preservation of peace in the territory surrounding Ripon. The annual celebration of three feasts honouring the saint reinforced his power and that of the clergy who were his successors while the annual procession with his relics preserved the boundaries of Wilfrid's special sphere of influence.

Great power was concentrated in the hands of the king and exercised by his agents, ordinarily the county sheriffs. Like light passing through a prism, this power was scattered by the franchises and liberties of Ripon. These peculiar combinations of rights and jurisdictions owed their origins to Wilfrid's seventh-century monastery as well as grants allegedly made by King Æthelstan in the tenth century. Wilfrid's monastery had been surrounded by a sacred league within which felons could claim sanctuary. By the time of the Domesday survey in the late eleventh century, this had been divided into two smaller units of lordship, the manors belonging to the archbishop of York and those of the Ripon chapter of canons.[31] With the additional privileges that they inherited from the league of St Wilfrid, these manors formed special jurisdictions or liberties. The rights pertaining to the chapter's liberty were periodically disputed. In 1106 and again in 1229 it was invaded by the sheriff of York, but the chapter's rights were upheld in both instances. The rights and privileges attached to these two liberties, as well as all the other manors in the parish, were enforced in the manorial courts. Those pertaining to the minster were also memorialised at key moments in the liturgical year by the participation of the sanctuary men in rituals honouring St Wilfrid and King Æthelstan.

Beyond the town there were many more manors and lordships within the confines of the parish. Their wealth and power constantly fluctuated, and even the identities of their lords turned upon the accidents of fortune. These lords were knights and esquires whose status had become so closely tied to their manors during the thirteenth century that many took as their surname the name of their chief manor.[32] At one time the Nunwicks were lords of Nunwick and the Clotherholmes were lords of Clotherholme. Both families became extinct in the male line, so that by the fifteenth century Nunwick had been

[30]   Idem, *New liturgical feasts in later medieval England*, Oxford 1970, 8–9.

[31]   Jones, 'The Ripon estate', 17–18.

[32]   Nigel Saul, *For honour and fame: chivalry in England, 1066–1500*, London 2011, 68.

divided between the Norton and Malory families, and the Pigots had become lords of Clotherholme. Other families, like the Markenfields and the Wards of Givendale, endured. New families usually came into the parish through the marriage of a knight to an heiress. He would then inherit the manor with its rights and property, which by the fourteenth century often included two important signs of status: the fortified manor house and the chapel. At the same time the new lords tended to keep their old surnames and heraldry, so their identities remained connected to their own lineage rather than entirely merging with that of their wives.

In addition to managing their estates, knights and esquires could pursue careers as soldiers or lawyers which could bring them into royal service, and might include keeping the peace in their own county as sheriff or justice of the peace. Appointments such as these were desirable as confirmations of status and opportunities to exercise greater authority.[33] Such public powers augmented those that the gentry already exercised through their manorial courts.[34] Equally they could choose to serve one of the regional magnates who could offer protection to their clients, who in turn extended their influence in the lands around Ripon, which had no native magnates of its own. The nearest and most influential noble families were the Scropes of Bolton, their cousins the Scropes of Masham, the Nevilles of Middleham and the Percies of Northumberland. Magnates retained Ripon gentry as soldiers and lawyers alike. In the late fourteenth century the major families of Ripon parish were joined together in John of Gaunt's affinity where their cohesion is best illustrated by an episode in 1386, when the court of chivalry was hearing testimony in York concerning the heraldic dispute between Sir Robert Grosvenor and Sir Richard Scrope, one of John of Gaunt's loyal retainers. Three Ripon knights – Sir Thomas Markenfield II, Sir John Ward and Sir Ralph Pigot – travelled together with their neighbour from Knaresborough, Sir Robert Plumpton, to testify on Scrope's behalf.[35] After the accession of Henry IV these four families were often divided from each other by adherence to either the Nevilles or the Percies. The Nevilles consistently exerted the strongest influence in the parish of Ripon while the Percies were predominant in nearby Knaresborough. The Neville-Percy feud effectively polarised the gentry of the Ripon and Knaresborough area during the Wars of the Roses, as well as earlier in the century when Henry Hotspur Percy rebelled against King Henry IV.[36]

---

[33] Simon Walker, 'Yorkshire justices of the peace, 1389–1413', EHR cviii (1993), 281–313 at p. 299.

[34] Christine Carpenter, 'Gentry and community in medieval England', Journal of British Studies xxxiii (1994), 340–80 at pp. 346–7.

[35] Ralph Hanna, 'Some Yorkshire scribes and their context', in Denis Renevey and Graham D. Caie (eds), Medieval texts in context, Abingdon 2008, 167–91 at p. 175.

[36] Pollard, North-eastern England during the Wars of the Roses, 170; Ruth Wilcock, 'Local disorder in the Honour of Knaresborough, c. 1438–1461 and the national context', NH xli (2004), 39–80 at p. 70.

The other truly great lord in Ripon and the surrounding area was the archbishop of York. With his liberty of Ripon and his manors in Nidderdale, the archbishop had a different standing and different needs from the other northern magnates who exerted influence over the parish. In the fourteenth and fifteenth centuries it was rare for the archbishop to reside in his palace at Ripon, which stood, like his two Ripon hospitals, as a mute symbol of his lordship. His more vocal and active agents were the men who managed his courts and estates. Local knights could act as stewards of the archbishop's liberty of Ripon, and men of slightly lower standing served as his bailiffs and foresters. The Walworth family of Thornton in Nidderdale raised themselves to a status nearly equivalent to that of manorial lords through generations of service to the archbishops. In the last decades of the fifteenth century they leased many of his agricultural estates and even resided in one of his houses, Raventofts Hall.[37] In the troubled era of Archbishop Kemp's term as northern primate, their allegiance drew them into a series of skirmishes with the burgesses of Knaresborough and with Percy retainers.[38] Many of the archbishop's tenants in Ripon and a number of the local gentry also participated in the conflict that Kemp provoked when he tried to impose tolls on the tenants of Knaresborough at the Ripon fairs. The escalating sequence of intimidations and assaults reached a bloody climax after the end of the summer fair in 1441, when the mercenaries hired from the Scottish borders by Kemp to protect the fair fought Sir William Plumpton and his men at Helperby, about seven miles from the Ripon.[39] At times more or less clearly political in motivation, the episodic violence of the decades after 1450, together with the chapter's efforts to keep the peace in the liberty of St Wilfrid, are well documented in the Ripon chapter acts book.

The Ripon chapter lacked the power of the magnates, but did have two mechanisms that it could use to harness the might of other local lords and to curb the sporadic outbreaks of violence within the parish of Ripon. The first of these was a form of secular lordship that bound a number of families to the chapter and to St Wilfrid by oath of fealty. The relationship was based on tenure, and is commonly referred to as Marmion tenure because the Marmion family was, in the thirteenth century, one of the families pledged to the service of Wilfrid and the chapter by such an oath. The term was still in use in the fifteenth century, long after the last Marmion of West Tanfield was killed while serving as a banneret with John of Gaunt in Spain.[40] Marmion tenure is first described in the 1229 inquest into the rights of the chapter. It was recorded that the obligations of the tenant included paying suit of court to the chapter and carrying Wilfrid's relics around the parish

37 Jennings, History of Nidderdale, 114.
38 Wilcock, 'Local disorder in the Honour of Knaresborough', 51–2.
39 Ibid. 52.
40 Hanna, 'Some Yorkshire scribes and their context', 176.

perimeter at the annual beating of the bounds just before the feast of the Ascension.[41]

The second mechanism was the preservation of peace within the liberty of St Wilfrid through the imposition of penance on those who committed violent acts. Though it was not always effective in deterring violence, the threat of excommunication and the shame of public penance was a means by which the chapter could assert its authority within the liberty. The chapter and the local gentry appear to have had a generally harmonious relationship during the fifteenth century, though this probably owed much to the other links between them. The late medieval account rolls show that the minster was farming out its rural properties on a large scale, and that the tenants were often the gentry families whose estates were situated nearby. Moreover, the minster was not an institution composed of men totally foreign to the parish. Many of its members were either from influential local families or their former chaplains.

The chapter court had a wide array of business beyond receiving the Marmion tenants' oaths of fealty and prosecuting all who broke the peace of St Wilfrid. It had all the powers of an archdeacon's court because one of the many privileges of the parish was that it was a peculiar jurisdiction exempt from the authority of the archdeacon of Richmond.[42] It could probate wills, rule on matrimonial disputes, discipline sexual behaviour, enforce contracts and punish deviations from acceptable religious observance. The Ripon chapter acts book preserves an invaluable record of the court's activities in the second half of the fifteenth century, revealing how it regulated the lives and disputes of parishioners. Furthermore, one of the institutional quirks of Ripon Minster was that its chapter had no specified head, so that in practice the senior resident canon presided over the chapter and its court. Rates of residence among the canons were so low that usually there appears to have been only one obvious chapter leader during the fifteenth century. The power of the chapter court was thereby placed in the hands of one man, frequently for a decade or longer. From the 1450s to the 1480s the two men who exercised this authority had extensive local connections. The first was canon William Scrope, from the Scrope of Masham noble family. The second was Christopher Kendale, son of a local heiress and brother of the lord of Markington. Kendale has one of the most intriguing clerical careers of any of the fifteenth-century Ripon clergy, since he was in fact only the appointed commissary, or deputy, of the chapter court and never promoted to the rank of canon. He held this post for over two decades, finally resigning it in 1488 to finish his career as he probably began it, celebrating masses for the dead. Many other chaplains held important administrative offices within the minster and also assisted the vicars with the cure of souls.

The chapter and the archbishop together exerted such great influence over the town of Ripon that there was little room for the development of civic

---

41 MR i. 61.
42 Gowland, 'The manors and liberties of Ripon', 51.

authorities. In the late twelfth century the town was expanding, and from the 1190s at the latest the burgesses paid a fee to farm the town from the king.[43] The town authorities eventually consisted of an unknown number of aldermen and a figurehead, the Wakeman.[44] The identities of these men are known primarily from a list composed around the year 1600,[45] which identifies the professions of some of the Wakemen, showing that they could just as easily be country gentlemen as burgesses. The real power of the urban elites was in fact situated in the religious fraternities that first appear in the records around 1390 and rapidly increase in number in the first decades of the fifteenth century. Religious guilds became increasingly important at this time because they could act as a support network and certify, by regulating the morality of their members, the trustworthiness of the many new immigrants from countryside to town.[46] The most important of Ripon's religious fraternities were the Guild of SS Mary, Wilfrid and All Saints and, later, the Guild of the Holy Cross. Both guilds were, like the office of Wakeman, open to the country gentry. Beyond their social functions, they had the task of remembering their dead members and pooling their resources to employ chaplains who could say masses on their behalf.

Remembering and forgetting

The power to say mass belonged only to the priest. It was the central feature of medieval Christian religious practice, frequently repeated, not just for the benefit of the living, but also for the salvation of the dead. The vast majority of Christians anticipated that they would spend some length of time in purgatory after death. Purgatory was a place where the unspent penance that had accumulated in life could be completed; however terrible the pains of purgatory might have seemed, it was preferable to the alternative that anyone who died without having completed the penances for all his or her sins would be damned. The living could also take comfort from the fact that they were able, through masses, prayers and almsgiving, to shorten the sufferings of the dead in purgatory and that when they were dead others might do the same for them. A chaplain could be hired on a temporary basis with a cash sum, but longer-term arrangements required renewable sources of funding such as rents or properties. This type of endowment was the medieval chantry. First founded in monasteries in the twelfth century, they later spread to churches and chapels of all kinds.[47]

[43] McKay, 'Development of medieval Ripon', 75.

[44] Gowland, 'The manors and liberties of Ripon', 82–3.

[45] Brotherton Special Collections, Leeds, Ripon Cathedral, dean and chapter archives, MS Dep 1980/1 434, fos 21r–22r.

[46] Gervase Rosser, *The art of solidarity in the Middle Ages: guilds in England, 1250–1550*, Oxford 2015, 50, 158–9.

[47] David Crouch, 'The origin of chantries: some further Anglo-Norman evidence', *Journal of Medieval History* xxvii (2001), 159–80 at pp. 172–3.

During the thirteenth century the English parish church increasingly became the focus of gifts and endowments intended to memorialise the dead and help them out of purgatory. The parish church was thus central to the memorial culture of the parish.[48] Beyond the limits of living memory, the dead were recalled through material objects, ritual actions or a combination of the two. The donation of a stained glass window, for example, could earn the donor's name a place on the list of benefactors that was periodically read out to the assembled congregation. The window itself could, through heraldry or an inscription, more frequently remind the living to pray for the donor. The ritual re-enactment of the funeral on the anniversary of a person's death and the more expensive daily chantry masses were means of preserving the memory of the dead through repeated actions. It was difficult to commemorate the dead without, at the same time, affirming their status in society. Depictions on funerary monuments categorise people according to their station in life: knights in their armour, ladies in their fine clothes, bishops with their mitres and croziers, priests in their vestments.[49] The living were dignified by the monuments of their ancestors, and equally so by their chantry foundations and other gifts.[50] When the gentry in particular failed to honour their ancestors, they risked damaging their own reputations. The cost of commemoration reduced their financial resources, but the maintenance of their honour could compensate.[51]

The passage of time had a ravenous appetite for memory. It would inevitably consume the feeble endowments made to commemorate the dead, and only the Last Judgment would arrest its passage, though a belief that the end of time was imminent can help to explain what founders had in mind when they made their endowments perpetual. In any case Ripon provides a number of instructive cases about the limits of memory. Its anniversary endowments were remarkably durable while its earliest chantries had to be revived in the late fourteenth century. The minster had the greatest capacity to remember those who provided it with its privileges and authority, primarily St Wilfrid and King Æthelstan. It was also well equipped to commemorate the parish elite, including the country gentry and the burgesses of the town. The status of medieval English gentry families was dependent in large part on how they were perceived. They seized opportunities of all kinds to display this status to

---

[48] For the most recent overview of this subject see Sally Badham, *Seeking salvation: commemorating the dead in the late medieval English parish*, Donington 2015. For a study with an archaeological emphasis see Mark Douglas, 'The archaeology of memory: an investigation into the links between collective memory and the architecture of the parish church in late medieval Yorkshire', unpubl. PhD diss. Durham 2003, <http://etheses.dur.ac.uk/1260/>

[49] Nigel Saul, *English church monuments in the Middle Ages: history and representation*, Oxford 2009, 370.

[50] Ibid. 136.

[51] Christine Carpenter, 'Religion of the gentry', in Daniel Williams (ed.), *England in the fifteenth century*, Woodbridge 1987, 53–74 at p. 68.

the rest of society. The parish church offered them many opportunities to do so, both in person and through symbols of their identity: heraldry and the tombs of their ancestors. Just as Wilfrid's shrine was appropriate to a saint, so too the many sepulchral monuments installed in the minster by the gentry were appropriate to them. The types and locations of these monuments were significant, and the number of desirable burial places was very limited. The best places were within the walls of the building and near altars and saints' images. Not originally designed as a mausoleum, the church gradually became one and competition over the most desirable burial places ensued.[52] In this competition the most powerful tended to prevail, so that in effect it was the greater gentry families of Ripon that filled these areas with their tombs, while the lesser gentry, burgesses and clergy divided the rest. Monuments combined with liturgical forms of commemoration to alter the meanings of spaces within the church, fusing the memory of families, guilds and individuals to altars, chapels and images of saints. The space of the building was more than a physical structure: it was also the product of these social acts.[53] Time was its counterpart, and though it is less often discussed in these terms, it too was socially produced.

Time and space

Time was more than an invisible force that eroded the memory of the dead while they awaited the resurrection. It also had a perceptible, rhythmic form. The long march to eternity was made up of small, repetitive stages: the years with their natural and liturgical seasons. Religion added meaning to the day and calendar by dividing the former into the hours of the daily office and the latter into seasons of fasting and a multitude of holidays. The religious rituals performed in the minster and elsewhere in the parish manifested the rhythm of the year. Processions joined together altars, feast days and the memory of the dead whose tombs they encountered in their progress around the building. Veiling and unveiling the rood signalled the start and end of the Lenten fast. The annual beating of the bounds with Wilfrid's relics linked the present to the distant past. The rhythm of the liturgical year was inseparable from the symbolic meanings of space within the minster and parish.

Like writing, the power to measure time was in the hands of the clergy and, as Jacques le Goff once wrote, the great majority of laypeople could only obey 'the time imposed on them by bells, trumpets, and horns'.[54] In medieval Ripon time was imposed by the Wakeman's ceremonial horn and the minster's bells

---

[52]   Paul Binski, *Medieval death: ritual and representation*, Ithaca 1996, 74.

[53]   In Henri Lefebvre's terms 'Itself the outcome of past actions, social space is what permits fresh actions to occur, while suggesting others and prohibiting yet others': *The production of space*, trans. Donald Nicholson-Smith, Oxford 1991, 73.

[54]   Jacques le Goff, *Medieval civilization, 400–1500*, trans. Julia Barrow, Oxford 1988, 177.

and clock. Its clock is first mentioned, together with the expenses of the new bell, in the 1379–80 fabric roll. That year the fabric wardens purchased three hundred nails for 'the floor where the clock stands'.[55] The clock was evidently installed with the bells in one of the towers of the west front, and as such it was almost certainly a mechanical clock of the type that begins to appear in cathedral accounts across Europe at the end of the thirteenth century.[56] Work on it probably started the previous year and was completed in 1380, with the twenty-four stone of lead purchased that year being meant for the weights that drove its mechanism.[57] The clock had no clock face, but rather it would have indicated the hour by ringing a bell. The 1453–5 fabric roll records a payment to a man working on 'le Clokbell' as well as a contract of 16s. 8d. with the York clockmaker John Ripley for repairs.[58] Like bell-casting, clock-making expertise was not readily available in Ripon but could be found in York.

Ripon's time-keeping and bell-ringing were entrusted to the same man: the sacristan. His annual fee for keeping the clock was 10s, in addition to his 6s. 8d. salary for cleaning the wall passages and windows of the church.[59] Some sacristans were more conscientious than others. Robert Marshall was cited for neglecting his duties in 1453. He had not rung the bells continuously for half an hour at matins, prime and vespers.[60] These hours, plus the mass and curfew, are described by the capitular statutes of 1504 as the customary times for bell-ringing.[61] Marshall had also improperly maintained the minster's clock and had not followed the custom of ringing the great bell of St Mary daily at the eighth hour.[62] The Virgin Mary bell was one of the four medieval bells commonly mentioned in Ripon's records, and it may have been the bell cast at York in the summer of 1380. Still hanging in Ripon Minster 350 years later, it was over four feet in diameter and inscribed with a prayer: 'Pray for us with a pious mind, O Virgin Mary'.[63] Another of the bells was inscribed with an appeal to the minster's patron for help, reading 'O St Wilfrid, pray for us'.[64] The prayers inscribed on these bells enabled them to protect the surrounding area when they were rung.[65] The tolling of bells was among the loudest of all sounds heard in the Middle Ages. It was rivalled only by thunder, music played in confined

---

[55] 'pro le flore ubi orrologium stat': MR iii. 101.

[56] David S. Landes, *A revolution in time: clocks and the making of the modern world*, Cambridge 1983, 56–7.

[57] MR iii. 103.

[58] MR iii. 161.

[59] MR iii. 133, 139.

[60] AoC, 21.

[61] MR iv. 279.

[62] AoC, 21.

[63] 'Ora mente pia, pro nobis virgo Maria': MR iii. 99–100; Thomas Gent, *The ancient and modern history of the loyal town of Rippon*, York 1733, 120.

[64] 'Sancte Wilfride ora pro nobis': Gent, *Loyal town of Rippon*, 120.

[65] C. M. Woolgar, *The senses in late medieval England*, New Haven 2006, 71.

spaces, certain animal calls and gunpowder explosions.[66] When the sacristan neglected to ring the bells he denied the town and its environs an important form of ritual protection as much as the knowledge of the hour. His earlier lapses notwithstanding, Robert Marshall was still sacristan in 1470, when the treasurer spent 3*d.* on a 2lb. Paris candle so that he would have sufficient light when he rang the curfew in winter.[67] The distinction between day and night was very significant, since the night held dangers both natural and supernatural. A person was most likely to encounter an apparition at night-time, especially during the darkest part of winter, the twelve days of Christmas.[68] Actions undertaken at night were also inherently more suspicious than during the day.[69] Thus the archbishops of York periodically warned the minster's vicars to cease their nocturnal wanderings and keep to their common residence at night for the sake of their reputations.[70] The women whom the vicars hired as their housekeepers were, of course, forbidden from spending the night in the residence.[71] The natural transition between day and night was gradual and therefore needed the recognisable starting point of the curfew rung on the bells of Ripon Minster. Similarly, the blast of the Wakeman's horn signalled the start of the watch.

The seasons, like the hours of the day, pulsed with ritual activity. The liturgical calendar outlined the pattern of saints' feasts and other holidays that gave the ritual year its form. There were two major groups of feast days. The first, the *temporale*, ran from Christmas through Easter and on until the feast of Corpus Christi and midsummer (24 June). The feast days in this period were all concerned with the birth, life, death, resurrection and ascension of Christ, plus the feasts of Pentecost, Holy Trinity and Corpus Christi. The date of Easter was variable, and so all the feasts whose dates depended on Easter also moved around the calendar from year to year. The other set of feasts, the *sanctorale*, comprised the rest of the saints' days. This series ran throughout the year and therefore overlapped with the *temporale* for half of the year. The greatest feast days were marked with the greatest ceremony, and the whole of the parish of Ripon was expected to attend the minster at these times. On less important holidays laypeople of the parish could attend their own local chapels, but were still forbidden from working. Advent and Lent, the two penitential seasons, imposed the obligation of fasting in preparation for the feasts of Christmas and Easter. These, together with the rest of the *temporale* and the major feasts of St Mary and the Apostles were universal throughout Christendom, but many of the holidays celebrated in Ripon were less widely observed.

---

[66]   Ibid. 66.

[67]   MR iii. 217.

[68]   Jean-Claude Schmitt, *Ghosts in the Middle Ages: the living and the dead in medieval society*, trans. Teresa Lavender Fagan, Chicago 1998, 174, 177; le Goff, *Medieval civilization*, 178.

[69]   Woolgar, *The senses in late medieval England*, 153.

[70]   MR ii. 46, 68.

[71]   MR ii. 46.

Ripon Minster's own calendar combined the universal feasts, the significant feasts of the ecclesiastical province of York, and the special holidays of St Wilfrid. The major saints in the York calendar were Wilfrid, John of Beverley and William of York.[72] In Ripon there was greater emphasis on Wilfrid than anywhere else, and the minster celebrated a unique feast commemorating Wilfrid's nativity. This, which took place on the first Sunday after the feast of St Peter *ad vincula* on 1 August, also marked the start of the harvest season.[73] Other feast days denoted equally important moments in the agricultural year, which indeed began with the sowing of crops the Monday after the feast of St William in January.[74] Lambing and the transhumance of the flocks were timed to correspond to the feast of the Annunciation on 25 March.[75] The procession around the boundaries of the parish with Wilfrid's relics at Rogation sought the saint's blessing and protection for the crops and flocks. Wilfrid's summer and winter fairs were opportunities for the marketing of livestock and a visit to the saint's shrine. The division of the day and year was just as important for the merchants, craftsmen and labourers who lived in the town of Ripon as it was for the peasants and lords of the countryside. The minster clock was their clock, and the minster's bells told them the hours. The pay rates of craftsmen varied according to the season, with the shorter winter day accounted for by a lower daily pay rate.[76] By the sixteenth century the fabric wardens of the minster had refined their accounting practices to the point that they paid craftsmen for units of time as small as one quarter of a day.[77]

The very large parish of Ripon was divided into smaller social units that had their own holidays. The various religious fraternities each had its own special patron whose feast day was a time for banqueting with guild colleagues. Guilds were primarily urban in nature, and their rural counterparts were the many villages that had chapels. These chapels had their own patron saints, meaning that the villages with chapels had holidays akin to the patronal feasts of the guilds. In this respect the feast of the Exaltation of Holy Cross had the same social importance for members of the Holy Cross guild as the feast of St Swithun for the villagers of Skelton. During much of the year it was also possible for Ripon's parishioners to use their local chapels for more mundane religious services. Not only the villages but also many of the gentry families of the parish had their own chapels for their religious observances. If they could afford to hire a chaplain, they could hear mass there. Many parishioners were only required to attend the minster on the most important annual feast days,

---

[72] Pfaff, *The liturgy in medieval England*, 456.

[73] Ronald Hutton, *The rise and fall of Merry England: the ritual year, 1400–1700*, Oxford 1994, 44.

[74] Ibid. 16.

[75] Angus J. L. Winchester, *The harvest of the hills: rural life in northern England and the Scottish Borders, 1400–1700*, Edinburgh 2000, 58.

[76] *Building accounts of Henry III*, ed. H. M. Colvin, Oxford 1971, 9.

[77] MR iii. 198–206.

with the result that the crowds of people using the minster ebbed and flowed throughout the year. The major difference between the gentry and their neighbours was that many of the gentry, constantly represented in the minster by their heraldry and the graves of their ancestors, could display their lordship *in absentia* while most others could not. Processions and the use of altars near their graves would constantly remind onlookers of their greatness and benefactions, and of their need for prayers. When gentry families did attend the minster in person the same heraldry and monuments would augment other forms of display such as their clothing and books of hours. The constant presence of their symbols and the impact that they could have on the large crowds of major feast days were both powerful means by which the gentry could shape how they were perceived and remembered within the parish.

The theoretical model for the study of funerary monuments and displays of heraldry in medieval churches is often a spatial one, but the temporal aspects of these forms of commemoration and display are just as important. Indeed, Henri Lefebvre, whose theories about the social production of space have often been adapted for application to medieval churches, wrote that time and space were inseparable and that the rhythm of time depended on repetition in space.[78] Consider the chantry and grave of John Sendale, a fifteenth-century canon of Ripon Minster. Sendale founded his chantry at an altar near the rood screen at the east end of the nave. His new chantry chaplain would say masses for him here, but his grave could also catch the attention of the chaplains of the Holy Cross guild who used altars in this exact part of the building to celebrate their morrow masses. Once a year the Palm Sunday procession halted beside Sendale's grave while the Lenten veil over the great rood was raised and lowered, and a few weeks later the same altar was an important feature in the celebration of the feast of Holy Trinity. As a canon of the minster, Sendale would have had a very clear understanding of the structure of the liturgical year and how its rituals could be linked to his burial place to stamp his memory on the fabric of time and space in Ripon Minster.

Sendale's chantry and funerary monument had important temporal aspects but they could still be described as largely spatial in nature. Their constancy yielded the greatest benefit to Sendale's soul in purgatory. Other commemorative practices, namely anniversaries, were less constant. They were also more easily affordable and generally less well documented than chantries. For Ripon there are unusually detailed records of anniversaries founded by individuals and guilds, so it is possible to analyse their place in the memory of the parish. A predominantly spatial model of commemoration focused primarily on the combination of tombs and chantries cannot easily accommodate the obit or anniversary, so here again it is important to consider the social production of time. Like the funeral which it re-enacted, the anniversary took place at an altar

---

[78] Henri Lefebvre, *Rhythmanalysis: space, time, and everyday life*, trans. Stuart Elden and Gerald Moore, London 2004, 8.

within the minster with the celebration of the office of the dead and a requiem mass. It could involve the attendance of guild members, clerics and poor people just like a funeral. Indeed, the anniversary was really only effective if it succeeded in attracting these types of people and soliciting their prayers for the deceased. Anniversary founders provided for their attendance by offering cash payments, food and drink. Most anniversary foundations at Ripon also paid the bellman, essentially the town crier, to publicise the obit and the sacristan to ring the four big bells of the minster, including those inscribed with prayers to Mary and Wilfrid.

Now we have come full circle, back to the summer of 1380 and the new bell. The casting of this bell and the installation of the minster's clock serve as the starting point for a study of time, memory and society in late medieval Ripon. The chronological focus of the book is essentially the long fifteenth century, beginning around 1380 and ending in the 1520s when the new nave of the church was completed and the high altar was rebuilt. This is a study of local society through the lens of religion. In effect this means that it starts with sources produced by the minster, which are far more numerous than any other form of record, and works out from there. These sources are the financial accounts, chapter acts and wills of medieval Ripon as well as the one manuscript witness to its medieval liturgy, Ripon Cathedral Library, MS 8. York diocesan records and royal records round out the study. While it is an analysis of only one medieval parish, this book offers findings on subjects of wider interest including the cult of saints, parochial chapels and the religion of the gentry; it is also an approach that can be adapted to the study of other large churches as well as parish churches with sufficient surviving liturgical manuscripts and churchwardens' accounts. Time and memory are the focus, not only because of the nature of the Ripon sources but also because it appeared to be the most comprehensive way in which to understand the religious practices of Ripon's parishioners. In considering the social implications of religious practice in late medieval Ripon, it is impossible to start anywhere else than with St Wilfrid. The importance of his cult was inescapable.

1

St Wilfrid, Patron of the Minster and Parish

On 12 September 1453 Matilda Coke appealed to the chapter court on behalf of her husband, Thomas Coke. In a meadow that lay between the towns of Ripon and Bishopton, Robert Poode and John Writhson had attacked and injured him.[1] The meadow was within the bounds of the liberty of Ripon, and thus within the jurisdiction of the chapter court. The court threatened Thomas Coke's assailants with excommunication if they did not appear within fifteen days. On the last day of this grace period, John Writhson's father and one of Robert Poode's relatives persuaded the court to grant an extension of eight days.[2] At the end of this second period, Robert and John finally appeared and submitted to the judgement of the court. Their penance was to lead the Sunday procession in the minster for six weeks, each one carrying his offending weapon in one hand and a lit candle weighing 1lb in the other. At the end of this term they were to leave the wax as an offering 'at the image of St Wilfrid in the nave of the church' and their weapons on the high altar.[3]

Not long afterward, on 7 October of the same year, before the hour of nones, three men attacked the pair of penitents as they approached the minster along Crossgate, the street that leads from Ripon's marketplace to the western portal of the church. The assailants were Milo Pikke, Henry Brancke and another man identified as Thomas Coke's servant. They beat Robert Poode and John Writhson with staffs and other weapons, preventing them from reaching the minster and performing their penance. The court discovered that the three attackers had threatened to kill the two penitents if they could catch them, which may explain why the two men initially fled after assaulting Thomas Coke.[4] The chapter court could not tolerate this vengeful act. It had already passed sentence on Poode and Writhson, and they were under the chapter's protection when performing their penance.[5] Facing excommunication, Pikke, Lowe and Brancke dutifully appeared in court and submitted to the judgement of the chapter. They received the same penance as Poode and Writhson plus two additional Sundays, one at the head of the procession at Beverley Minster and another at York Minster.[6]

---

[1]   AoC, 10.
[2]   Ibid.
[3]   'ymagini Sancti Wilfridi in navi ecclesiæ': AoC, 11.
[4]   Ibid.
[5]   Ibid.
[6]   AoC, 12.

The motive for the assault on Thomas Coke is not recorded in the chapter acts book, nor is revenge the recorded motive for the second attack, though it can be inferred from the circumstances and connections between the parties involved. The words used to describe the defendants in both cases are revealing. Poode and Writhson are called 'usurpers of the liberty of St Wilfrid'.[7] Similarly, their three assailants are termed 'rivals of St Wilfrid'.[8] The violent acts of these five men offended the saint and broke the peace of his special territory, the liberty. As Wilfrid's successors and agents on earth, the chapter of canons needed to defend the liberty by prosecuting its violators in the chapter court. The court's two main weapons were excommunication and penance. Armed invasion of the liberty was but one of the many crimes tried in the chapter court, but the penances for this particular offence were unique in that they included gifts to the image or shrine of the minster's patron saint. No other type of penance required the penitent to make restitution to St Wilfrid.

Wilfrid's power to protect the living and the dead was acknowledged by gifts freely given to the shrine by the faithful and, because the space around his shrine was not available for burial, by requests for interment near his image in the nave. In 1488 the chaplain John Gregson desired to be buried by the saint's image, and so did the cordwainer Geoffrey Sharroke in 1505.[9] Elena Fulford (d. 1453) bequeathed a gold ring to Wilfrid's feretory, and similarly Elizabeth Brown (d. 1458) bequeathed her silver girdle.[10] The feretory, or shrine, which contained Wilfrid's relics was itself made of precious metals. In the fifteenth century it was located behind the high altar, at the opposite end of the building from the image in the nave. The relics housed in the shrine attracted pilgrims to the church, especially on Wilfrid's three annual feast days. Two of these feasts had their own fairs, mixing commerce and piety to swell the numbers of pilgrims and perhaps also increase the minster's income from donations. The feasts of St Wilfrid were important features of the calendar in medieval Ripon and they guaranteed the preservation of the saint's memory together with the authority that was his legacy to the canons of the minster. Once a year the relics were taken out of the church and carried around the perimeter of the parish in a great procession so that the saint himself could secure the boundaries that were, at the same time, imprinted on the minds of everyone following in his wake. Wilfrid exerted a powerful influence on late medieval Ripon; but who was St Wilfrid, and how did he become so important in Ripon?

Saints' *Lives*, a form of holy biography meant to demonstrate the virtues of its subject, provide most of the evidence for Wilfrid's career. They also furnished much of the material for the later medieval liturgy of his feast days.

---

[7] 'libertatis Sancti Wilfridi usurpatores', AoC, 10.

[8] 'Sancti Wilfridi æmulatores', AoC, 12.

[9] AoC, 285, 306.

[10] *Testamenta Eboracensia: a selection of wills from the registry at York*, ed. James Raine (Surtees Society, 1836–1902), ii. 165; AoC, 75.

The fifteenth-century Ripon Psalter preserves this body of texts, which makes it an invaluable record of how Wilfrid was perceived, remembered and represented. One of the primary concerns of the Ripon clergy, not to mention the archbishops of York, was to assert that the relics at Ripon were in fact those of St Wilfrid. For about two hundred years the archbishops of York and Canterbury fought over whether Wilfrid's relics were still in Ripon or had been moved to Canterbury. A great amount of prestige was at stake in this dispute, and it had many lasting implications for Ripon. Wilfrid was above all a mighty patron, and his two main categories of clients were the clergy and the parishioners of Ripon. In exchange for the gifts and veneration that acknowledged his status, Wilfrid could safeguard the rights of the clergy, protect and heal the living, preserve livestock and crops from disease, and beseech Christ's mercy for the dead.

Wilfrid in history and hagiography

Wilfrid was an energetic and combative ecclesiastical figure in seventh-century England. The Augustinian mission of 597 had reintroduced Christianity to Britain, and during the second half of the seventh century there was still plenty of scope for Wilfrid to convert pagans and expand the influence of the Roman Church at the expense of other Christian communities that followed the customs of the Irish, or Celtic, Church. His most famous achievements were his victory at the Synod of Whitby (664), where he replaced the Irish system of calculating the date of Easter with the Roman one, and his creation of a vast network of religious communities, called minsters. These were religious communities that could take a wider range of forms than the modern English term 'monastery' normally implies, and they could also perform pastoral functions and serve as the seat of a bishop.[11] The subking of Deira granted Wilfrid his first minster – Ripon – in about 660, when Wilfrid was still in his twenties.[12] These details and most of the rest of the evidence for his life come from a problematic type of source: hagiography. Saints' *Lives* are a challenging source because their purpose was to demonstrate the sanctity of their subject rather than include biographical detail. One of the best ways to achieve this goal was to link the saint to earlier saints or to the Apostles, sometimes even by lifting passages directly from other texts and simply changing the names.[13] Moreover, it is possible to classify saints by type according to their characteristics, and saints' *Lives* of any given type of saint will often share miracles and episodes with others of the same type. The fundamental distinction is between

---

[11]   John Blair, *The Church in Anglo-Saxon society*, Oxford 2005, 5.

[12]   Ibid. 95.

[13]   Thomas J. Heffernan, *Sacred biography: saints and their biographers in the Middle Ages*, Oxford 1988, 6; Geary, *Furta sacra*, 9.

martyrs and confessors. Wilfrid was a confessor saint because he died peace-
fully at one of his monasteries rather than violently in defence of his beliefs.
Wilfrid's other salient quality was his status as bishop of Northumbria. Not
long after Wilfrid's death, this see was replaced by the province of York, which
is why Wilfrid was regarded as an archbishop of York in later centuries and
why his successors at York were so concerned about the location of his relics.

It is sometimes possible to verify the details of the lives of later medieval
saints using other types of source material, but because he was an early
medieval saint there are few other sources for Wilfrid. Two authors knew
Wilfrid or his associates personally, and the many later versions of his life
are based on one or both of the first two. Wilfrid's original biographer was
Stephanus, who is thought to have been one of the skilled singers whom
Wilfrid brought to Northumbria from Kent around 669. His *Life* of the
saint provides good evidence that he was one of Wilfrid's monks at Ripon,
and he may even have accompanied Wilfrid on his final trip to Rome.[14]
Stephanus probably wrote his account within ten years of Wilfrid's death,
arguably before 714.[15] His aim was to establish that Wilfrid was in fact a saint
in heaven who could protect the faithful, and especially the communities
living in his minsters, on earth. Stephanus therefore lists the various miracles
performed by Wilfrid before and after his death. The posthumous miracles in
particular show how Wilfrid could continue to be a powerful force on earth.
To begin with, the place where Wilfrid's body was washed and the water that
had touched his holy body poured out became the site of many marvels.[16]
Later on Oundle, the monastery where Wilfrid died, witnessed the protective
power of its patron. Invading warriors were unable to set fire to the house in
which Wilfrid died because it was protected by an angel, and the soldiers were
afterward blinded by a bright light and killed by their enemies.[17] Again this
miracle was caused by the residual holiness of the saint, which even lingered there
even after his body was moved elsewhere. Stephanus concluded the account
of his patron's life with the miraculous appearance of an arc of white light on
the first anniversary of Wilfrid's death.[18] From an early date the saint's body
transmitted a power from heaven that could perform miracles and protect
the religious communities of the churches that he had founded. Wilfrid was
typical of male saints of his era, many of whom had been powerful patrons in
life, such as bishops or princes.[19]

[14] *The Life of Bishop Wilfrid by Eddius Stephanus*, ed. and trans. Bertram Colgrave,
Cambridge 1927, p. x.

[15] Ibid.; Clare Stancliffe, 'Dating Wilfrid's death and Stephen's *Life*', in N. J. Higham
(ed.), *Wilfrid: abbot, bishop, saint, papers from the 1300th anniversary conferences*, Donington
2013, 17–26 at p. 24.

[16] *Life of Bishop Wilfrid*, 143.

[17] Ibid. 145–7.

[18] Ibid. 147.

[19] Arnold, *Belief and unbelief*, 72.

Bede borrowed from Stephanus in writing his account of Wilfrid in book v, chapter 19 of his *Ecclesiastical history*, but he depended less on Stephanus for other chapters that mention Wilfrid.[20] Bede was personally acquainted with people who had known Wilfrid, such as Acca, Wilfrid's successor as abbot of Hexham.[21] Bede and Stephanus had different purposes in writing and they do not present every episode of Wilfrid's life in an identical manner. Wilfrid's sojourn in Sussex is a prime example. In 681 Wilfrid's enemies hounded him so effectively, writes Stephanus, that he had to take refuge in pagan territory, 'a certain province of our race which had remained heathen up to this time, and on account of its rocky coast and thick forests could not be conquered by the other kingdoms'.[22] Before long Wilfrid had befriended Aethilwalh, king of pagan Sussex, and evangelised the kingdom so that 'many thousands of pagans of both sexes were baptized in one day, as once they were by the blessed Apostle Peter'.[23] King Aethilwalh then granted Wilfrid enough land for him to found a minster at Selsey.[24] These projects kept Wilfrid busy for about five years. In the next chapter Stephanus recounts the benefits of Wilfrid's friendship with Caedwalla, an exile who had sought his counsel.[25] Bede discusses Caedwalla in chapter 25 of his history, giving some details not found in Stephanus: 'Meanwhile Caedwalla, a young and vigorous prince of the Gewisse, being an exile from his own land, came with an army and slew King Æthelwealh [sic], wasting the kingdom with fierce slaughter and devastation.'[26] The discrepancy prompted one commentator to remark that Stephanus' admiration for Wilfrid led 'him to make Ethelwalch [sic] a heathen in order that he might convert him, and Caedwalla a Christian in order that he may be closely attached to him, and to suppress the fact that one of his patrons was murdered by the other'.[27]

The story of Wilfrid's first pilgrimage to Rome, which is crucial to Stephanus's effort to cast Wilfrid in the role of a holy confessor saint, is similarly problematic. In the course of his journey Wilfrid stays for a while with the bishop of Lyon whom Stephanus names as Dalfinus. Bede, relying on Stephanus for this chapter of his history, reports the same details. While Wilfrid was still in Lyon, the Merovingian queen Balthild dispatched soldiers to kill the bishop. Stephanus tells us that Wilfrid was eager to follow Dalfinus to his death, but that the soldiers thwarted his bid for martyrdom when

---

[20] *Life of Bishop Wilfrid*, p. xii.

[21] Reginald L. Poole, 'St Wilfrid and the see of Ripon', *EHR* cxxxiii (1919), 1–24 at p. 6.

[22] *Life of Bishop Wilfrid*, 83.

[23] Ibid.

[24] Ibid.

[25] Ibid. 85.

[26] *Bede's Ecclesiastical history of the English people*, ed. and trans. Bertram Colgrave and R. A. B. Mynors, Oxford 1969, 381.

[27] Poole, 'St Wilfrid and the see of Ripon', 7.

they discovered that he was a foreigner and therefore refused to kill him.[28] Stephanus makes the best of the situation, arguing that Wilfrid's willingness to suffer martyrdom made him 'a confessor like John the Apostle and Evangelist, who sat uninjured in a cauldron of boiling oil and drank deadly poison unharmed'.[29] Confessor status was a respectable alternative conferred on more and more men and women who lived holy lives in the increasingly Christianised Europe of Wilfrid's own day, when martyrdom was harder to achieve than it had been in the era of pagan Rome. Stephanus' version of events, however, is not substantiated by other sources. While a bishop of Lyon called Dalphinus, or Aunemundus as he is known in French sources, was killed, the biography of this bishop does not implicate Balthild in his death and does not even mention Wilfrid.[30]

The eighth-century sources, contradictory as they are, pose thorny problems for historians of the early medieval period and the actual, historical life of Wilfrid. None the less, when perceptions of a saint many centuries after his death are at issue, there are different concerns. Saints' *Lives*, produced to enshrine the memory of the saint in writing and liturgy, are an important source, but the key is to establish what the clergy and parishioners thought of St Wilfrid in the fourteenth and fifteenth centuries. Wilfrid's eighth-century hagiography alone cannot answer these questions, though it did supply the source material for later revisions of his life and liturgy. Instead, it is necessary to consider the new *Lives* of St Wilfrid that were written in the tenth, eleventh and twelfth centuries as various authors tried to make use of Wilfrid's legacy for their own purposes and even to make rival claims about the location of his relics. The contest for possession of Wilfrid's body only took place because Wilfrid was indeed regarded as a saint, and as a predecessor of the archbishops of York; the dispute over his relics ultimately gave shape not only to the texts that preserved his memory in late medieval Ripon, but also to Ripon's liturgical calendar, the minster church and the geography of the parish.

The location of Wilfrid's relics

Frithegod's *Breviloqium*, written in the middle of the tenth century, was the first *Life* of St Wilfrid to assert Canterbury's claim to Wilfrid's relics. In the prologue to his work, Frithegod alleged that Odo, archbishop of Canterbury, discovered Wilfrid's relics in the ruins of Ripon Minster, which had been destroyed by King Eadred around the year 950.[31] According to Frithegod, Odo

---

[28]   *Life of Bishop Wilfrid*, 14–15.

[29]   Ibid.

[30]   Janet T. Nelson, 'Queens as Jezebels: the careers of Brunhild and Balthild in Merovingian history', in Derek Baker (ed.), *Medieval women* (Studies in Church History, subsidia, 1978), 31–77 at pp. 64–6.

[31]   *The historians of the Church of York*, ed. James Raine, London 1879-94, i. 105-7.

then translated the relics to Canterbury. This claim became part of the institutional memory of Canterbury Cathedral priory and was later elaborated by Eadmer, a Canterbury monk writing in the early years of the twelfth century. He reasserted Canterbury's claim to Wilfrid's relics and tried to promote Wilfrid's veneration there in opposition to the rival tradition that Wilfrid was still at Ripon.[32] In Eadmer's version, Odo generously left a small portion of Wilfrid in Ripon when he returned to Canterbury, where the whole city rejoiced at the acquisition of the relics:[33] in the centuries before Thomas Becket became one of the most famous saints in Europe, Canterbury enhanced its prestige by collecting the relics of a number of English saints. Eadmer's treatment of Wilfrid and Odo also reflects his concern with the contest between York and Canterbury for primacy in Britain.[34] During his lifetime, Wilfrid had been an opponent of Theodore, archbishop of Canterbury. Hence the translation of his relics to Canterbury implied his eventual submission to its primacy over the whole of Britain.[35] Wilfrid was thus a great addition to the Canterbury ranks, but York was naturally unwilling to let him go. Eadmer wrote in order to promote the cult of St Wilfrid at Canterbury, but his project was threatened by a different version of events in which Oswald, archbishop of York, had translated the real Wilfrid to a new shrine in Ripon.[36] The rival tradition was supported by Byrhtferth of Ramsey's c. 1000 *Life* of St Oswald, which claimed that Oswald had discovered the real relics of St Wilfrid when touring his diocese around the year 980.[37] This act of translation was commemorated in northern England by the creation of an annual feast day, so that by Eadmer's time the northern church province had two feasts commemorating Wilfrid.[38] By contrast, there is no evidence that Wilfrid's feast days were celebrated at this time in Canterbury.[39]

A series of twelfth- and thirteenth-century archbishops of York built on the foundations provided by their own tradition of Wilfrid's translation and the feast days of the York calendar. Their strategy was to validate the relics at Ripon by promoting pilgrimage to Wilfrid's shrine on his feast days. In the twelfth century, these were 24 April and 12 October. The April feast was the older of the two, and originally commemorated Wilfrid's death. The second feast, in October, commemorated the translation of Wilfrid's relics by Archbishop Oswald. At some point the identities of the feast days were switched because

[32] Paul A. Hayward, 'St Wilfrid of Ripon and the northern Church in Anglo-Norman historiography', *NH* xlix (2012), 11–35 at pp. 13, 15.

[33] *The historians of the Church of York*, i. 224.

[34] Hayward, 'St Wilfrid of Ripon', 17.

[35] Ibid. 18.

[36] Ibid. 20.

[37] Ibid. 13.

[38] Alan Thacker, 'Wilfrid, his cult, and his biographer', in Higham, *Wilfrid: abbot, bishop, saint*, 1–16 at p. 2.

[39] Hayward, 'St Wilfrid of Ripon', 19.

the feast of Wilfrid's death was the more important of the two and its April date sometimes clashed with Easter and associated feast days.[40] The April feast became the occasion for commerce and pilgrimage in the early twelfth century when King Henry I granted Archbishop Thomas II (1109–14) a four-day fair.[41] Medieval pilgrimage and fairs had a complex relationship. Pilgrims increased the revenues of churches by donating money, wax and other valuables to their saints. Churches that drew crowds of pilgrims could capitalise on this traffic by establishing markets and fairs and channelling the fees and tolls into their coffers. The relationship could be inverted so that fairs were established to attract crowds to churches that hoped to promote their saints. By aligning the fair with this feast, Archbishop Thomas publicised the translation of St Wilfrid and celebrated the retention of Wilfrid's relics in Ripon. With the foundation of the hospital of St John the Baptist in Ripon, he was providing accommodation for the pilgrims that he hoped would come to Ripon. An inquest in 1341 discovered that Thomas had founded the hospital of St John the Baptist at Ripon to give hospitality to pilgrims 'when the lands around Ripon were forest'.[42] The hospital's dedication to St John the Baptist was common among hospitals for the poor and travellers founded at this time.[43] By the fourteenth century it had become a school for poor scholars whom it also housed and fed.[44] The combination of a fair and a pilgrim hospital is a strong indication of an archiepiscopal strategy to augment Wilfrid's cult in the early twelfth century. Efforts accelerated in the twelfth century and culminated in the rebuilding of the minster (c. 1175–1207), the writing of a new *Life* for Wilfrid (c. 1189–1207), and the translation of his relics to a new shrine at Christmas 1224.

The rivalry between Canterbury and York had a personal dimension in the late twelfth century when the promotion of Roger Pont l'Evêque (r. 1154–81) to the see of York was followed by the elevation of his nemesis, Thomas Becket, to Canterbury. Even in death Becket troubled Pont l'Evêque, by becoming a saint. In response, the archbishop of York turned to Wilfrid as a rival to Becket's cult.[45] Early in his tenure Pont l'Evêque had expanded the York Minster choir in an effort to rival that at Canterbury.[46] Once that was largely completed he

---

[40]   Thacker, 'Wilfrid, his cult, and his biographer', 2.

[41]   *MR* i. 94.

[42]   'quando patriæ propinquæ juxta Ripon' fuerant forestæ': *MR* i. 218.

[43]   Sethina Watson, 'City as charter: charity and the lordship of English towns, 1170–1250', in Caroline Goodson, Anne E. Lester and Carol Symes (eds), *Cities, texts, and social networks, 400–1500: experiences and perceptions of medieval urban space*, Farnham–Burlington, VT 2010, 235–62 at p. 239.

[44]   *MR* i. 218.

[45]   See Hearn, 'The beginning of the gothic style in northern England', 93–4.

[46]   Peter Draper, *The formation of English gothic: architecture and identity*, New Haven 2006, 110.

initiated new work at Ripon around 1175.[47] Pont l'Evêque did not live long enough to see the new church at Ripon: his successor, Geoffrey Plantagenet, probably oversaw its completion and certainly commissioned Peter of Blois (c. 1135–1212) to write a new life of Wilfrid.[48] Peter's *Life* of St Wilfrid fits into a wider trope of renovating a saint's cult through the twin enterprises of rebuilding the church that housed his shrine and commissioning an updated *Life* for the clergy of that church. One contemporary example is the new *Life* of St Kentigern written by Jocelin of Furness, sometime between 1175 and 1190 when Glasgow Cathedral was being rebuilt.[49] In a similar way a new life was written for St Erkenwald when, following the fire of 1087, his cult became the central liturgical focus at St Paul's, London.[50]

The Wilfrid of late medieval Ripon was in most of his essentials the Wilfrid of Bede and Stephanus transmitted through later versions of Peter of Blois, among others. It has long been thought that the Peter of Blois *Life* of St Wilfrid was entirely lost save for a few lines copied by John Leland. In fact, portions of it have been preserved in a liturgical manuscript from late medieval Ripon. The lengthiest sections can be found in the lessons for the feast of Wilfrid's nativity, a third feast that was added to the Ripon calendar sometime between the early thirteenth century and the middle of the fourteenth.[51] Peter clearly relied very heavily on earlier *Lives* of St Wilfrid when composing his own. The readings for Wilfrid's nativity include episodes that can be found in the original Stephanus life of Wilfrid, but with a somewhat greater emphasis on Wilfrid's apostolic qualities. Stephanus demonstrated these characteristics by emphasising Wilfrid's special connection to Andrew and comparing him to Peter, Paul and John the Evangelist.[52] Peter of Blois developed this theme and he is sometimes more explicit about Wilfrid's apostolic credentials. His handling of Wilfrid's miraculous birth, which also features in Stephanus, is one example. At the moment of his birth, the house in which Wilfrid was being born appeared to be burning, but the miraculous fire did not consume the house. Stephanus used the words 'magnalia Dei', also found in Acts ii.11, to describe the crowd's reaction to Wilfrid's birth and thereby link it to the coming of the Holy Spirit.[53] Commenting on this same miracle, Peter wrote that 'He who therefore poured out the Holy Spirit in a form of fire to the

[47]   Harrison and Barker, 'Ripon Minster', 74–5; Draper, *Formation of English gothic*, 110.

[48]   Harrison and Barker, 'Ripon Minster', 75.

[49]   Helen Birkett, *The saints' Lives of Jocelin of Furness: hagiography, patronage, and ecclesiastical politics*, York 2010, 9.

[50]   Alan Thacker, 'The cult of saints and the liturgy', in Derek Keene, Arthur Burns and Andrew Saint (eds), *St Paul's: the cathedral church of London, 604–2004*, New Haven 2004, 113–22 at p. 116.

[51]   Ripon Cathedral Library, Brotherton Special Collections, MS 8, fos 162v–166v.

[52]   Thacker, 'Wilfrid, his cult, and his biographer', 5.

[53]   Sandra Duncan, 'Prophets shining in dark places: biblical themes and theological motifs in the Vita Sancti Wilfridi', in Higham, *Wilfrid: abbot, bishop, saint*, 80–92 at p. 88.

Apostles already perfected with age, by wondrous grace of dispensation kindled the fire of the same spirit in Wilfrid from the first light of infancy.'[54]

The category of 'apostle' had already been widened by the twelfth century to include important missionaries like St Martial of Limoges, St Denis and St Remi.[55] Wilfrid's missionary activities were extensively documented by Stephanus and Bede, and his close connections to St Peter, the pope and Rome in the works of both these authors identified Wilfrid as a true successor to the biblical Apostles. Around the year 1200 this apostolic status was intended to give Wilfrid and the province of York an edge over Becket and Canterbury. As M. F. Hearn observed in his chapter on the patronage and iconography of Ripon Minster, the use of the new gothic style, which had been employed in rebuilding numerous apostolic saints' shrines in the decades before Ripon was rebuilt, may have been intended to signal Wilfrid's own status as an apostle and thereby give his cult a quality that Becket's lacked.[56] The same strategy is evident in the battle for primacy waged in the competing lives of St Wilfrid. Eadmer used the common formula 'primate of all Britain' to describe Archbishop Odo and thereby assert Canterbury's dominance over York.[57] In one of the more telling adaptations of the life of St Wilfrid, Peter transforms Stephanus' description of Wilfrid as a holy bishop who will light up the Church of Britain into a special title: 'the light of all Britain'.[58] With this reformulation of the words used to denote the primacy of Canterbury over York, Peter of Blois deployed the apostolic Wilfrid against the southern metropolitan see.[59]

The church completed at Ripon in the early thirteenth century was a pilgrimage church intended to showcase the shrine of northern England's apostle, Wilfrid. Much of that building is still standing today, with the exception of half the central tower and the south transept arcade (repaired after the partial collapse of the tower in 1450) and the nave (replaced 1503–22). There is some debate over the design and date of the west front, and the eastern arm of the church was altered around 1300 and again after 1450.[60] The original design of the east end is unclear, but it may have had

---

[54] 'Qui ergo apostolis iam etate perfectis spiritum sanctum sub specie ignis infudit, a primo lumine infancie in Wilfrido eiusdem spiritus ignem mirabili gratia dispensacionis accendit': Ripon Cathedral Library, MS 8, fo. 163v.

[55] Robert Bartlett, *Why can the dead do such great things? Saints and worshippers from the martyrs to the Reformation*, Princeton 2013, 172–3.

[56] Hearn, 'The beginning of the gothic style in northern England', 101. See also Stephan Wander, 'Westminster Abbey and the apostolic churches of northern France', *Studies in Iconography* iv (1978), 3–22.

[57] 'totius Britanniae primas': Hayward, 'St Wilfrid of Ripon', 17.

[58] 'tocius britannie lumen': Ripon Cathedral Library, MS 8, fo. 163r.

[59] The present discussion of Peter of Blois's life of St Wilfrid is necessarily brief, but I am preparing a lengthier analysis of it for publication as an article.

[60] Harrison and Barker, 'Ripon Minster', 51.

a projecting eastern aisle that served as an ambulatory.[61] If not before, then after the remodelling of the choir in the late thirteenth century the final bay acted as an ambulatory behind the high altar, which was one bay to the west.[62] Wilfrid's shrine was ultimately located behind the high altar where pilgrims could access it through the choir aisles and ambulatory without entering the choir itself. Leland confirms that this was its location, writing that the relics of St Wilfrid had until recently been 'under an arch near the high altar'.[63] Exactly how long they had been there is debatable. Hearn has argued that Wilfrid's body still lay in its grave in the crypt, undisturbed since Oswald's time, when Archbishop Grey had it exhumed in 1224.[64] It may have been at that date that the new shrine was established in the choir, or it may have been at the end of the same century. In the former case Hearn suggests the precedent of Thomas Becket's translation from the Canterbury Cathedral crypt to his shrine in the Trinity Chapel behind the high altar (1220), and in the latter case St William's translation to a new shrine in the east end of York Minster (1283).[65] Either way Wilfrid's body was in a shrine in the choir by the beginning of the fourteenth century. The location of his head, which Archbishop Grey separated from his body, remains a mystery.

At Christmas in 1224 Archbishop Walter de Grey translated Wilfrid's relics to a new shrine. He inspected the relics, and included his appraisal in an indulgence that he offered as a reward for pilgrims. 'The body was whole, with – as we believe for certain – no major or minor bone or article missing', he declared, continuing, 'But we took the head of this saint away to be preserved apart and placed honourably, in order both that the faith of the faithful may be strengthened and their devotion may be advanced by sight of it.'[66] He thus rejected Canterbury's claims to possess any of Wilfrid. He chose a major feast day to maximise the impact of the translation. Had he wanted to create a new feast day, it would have been better to pick a date that was not an important holiday. Wilfrid already had a feast commemorating his trans-lation, so there was no need for a second one. In fact, the liturgy for the feast of St Wilfrid's translation was re-written after 1224 to memorialise the second translation, enshrining the indulgence in the institutional memory of the minster. The third lesson for the feast of St Wilfrid's translation begins with a summary of Archbishop Oswald's tenth-century translation, before describing

---

[61] Ibid. 52–3.

[62] Ibid. 53.

[63] 'sub arcu prope mag. altare': *Itinerary of Leland*, v. 143.

[64] Hearn, 'The beginning of the gothic style in northern England', 96.

[65] Ibid. 96–7.

[66] 'corpus ipsum totum, nullo majore vel minore osse vel articulo, ut pro certo credamus, deficiente. Caput autem ipsius Sancti duximus exterius servandum et honorifice collo-candum, ut ex ejus visione et fides fidelium roboretur et devotio augeatur', *The registers, or rolls, of Walter Grey, lord archbishop of York*, ed. James Raine (Surtees Society, 1872), 149.

Grey's second translation in 1224.[67] The feast, fair, indulgence and pilgrims all affirmed Wilfrid's presence in Ripon.

Wilfrid as patron of the minster

The links between Wilfrid and the archbishops of York are clear, but Wilfrid was also very important to the clergy of Ripon Minster. In local matters they were the visible representatives of St Wilfrid, and part of a Christian tradition that originated with the bishops who wrested control of the patronage of the saints from the noble families of late antiquity.[68] The archbishops of York often wished to be identified as Wilfrid's earthly representatives, especially in their conflict with Canterbury. A century of diligent cultivation appears to have borne fruit, though some of it proved to be bitter. Having made great efforts to complete the work of his predecessors, Archbishop Walter de Grey found himself locked in a dispute with the very institution that he had empowered by validating the relics of its patron saint. At issue was the lordship of the town of Ripon, together with a number of rights and privileges that the chapter of Ripon claimed to possess. Some of these could be traced back to Wilfrid and his monastery, while others were attributed to the tenth-century king, Æthelstan. The details of the subsequent royal inquest reveal the overlapping set of territories – the parish, the liberty of St Wilfrid and the sanctuary zone – which had developed between 710 and 1229, and would continue to be crucial to the wealth and status of the minster in later centuries. Within these areas the chapter had special forms of jurisdiction and exemption from the usual hierarchy of royal and ecclesiastical authority. The fifteenth-century chapter defended its territories by regularly invoking its patron saint. In exchange for his blessings they venerated Wilfrid with a number of annual feast days, including the unique and relatively new feast of St Wilfrid's nativity.

In order to comprehend Wilfrid's status as patron of the minster and parish, it is first necessary to consider the transformation of Wilfrid's monastery into the minster and town of Ripon. These developments ultimately led to the divided lordship of the town and the conflict between archbishop and chapter in the late 1220s. The monks of Wilfrid's minster had followed the Benedictine rule which, according to Stephanus, Wilfrid had introduced during his first exclusion from the see of Northumbria in the 660s.[69] For a long time afterwards developments in Ripon are obscure. Like so many other minsters its history can be compared to a 'subterranean river ... vanishing around 700 only to reappear changed out of all recognition several centuries later'.[70] One known

---

[67] Ripon Cathedral Library, MS 8, fo. 168r-v.

[68] Brown, *Cult of saints*, 38–9.

[69] *Life of Bishop Wilfrid*, 31.

[70] Richard Morris, *Churches in the landscape*, London 1989, 131.

feature of this period is the dispute over Wilfrid's relics that began in the tenth century. A second key development was that by the time of the Conquest the monks of earlier centuries had been replaced by secular canons.[71] The canons of eleventh-century Ripon and later were clergy who served the church as a group but did not live together like monks. Settlement patterns and privileged jurisdictions around Ripon also changed during these same centuries. Ripon, like many other important churches, gained a sanctuary zone that stretched a mile in any direction. Criminals could seek refuge within this zone, and would then be under the protection of the minster. Anyone who violated this protection was liable to pay compensation, and the penalty increased with proximity to the church. This zone eventually developed jurisdictional privileges, probably during the tenth century.[72] The Ripon sanctuary zone is called 'St Wilfrid's league' in Domesday Book, and like many other sanctuary zones in the north of England its privileges were later attributed to King Æthelstan (924-39).[73] The Bishopton Cross near the meadow where Robert Poode and John Writhson beat Thomas Coke was one of the eight roadside crosses that marked the outer boundary of St Wilfrid's league. The sanctuary privileges of the minster were still in force in the fifteenth century. While any late medieval parish church could offer temporary sanctuary, the perpetual immunity that Ripon could extend to felons was a privilege shared with only a few other major churches.[74] Permanent sanctuary seekers were obliged to participate in the Rogation procession and in King Æthelstan's obit in exchange for their protected status, and by so doing enabled the minster clergy to assert their right to offer sanctuary.

The old monastic enclosure at Ripon changed significantly between the seventh and twelfth centuries as the archbishops of York developed Ripon into an important market town and regional pilgrimage centre. The site of Wilfrid's monastery was surrounded on all sides by natural barriers. It was bounded on the north by the River Ure and on the south by the River Skell. The two rivers meet to the east of Ripon, while to the west a ridge, long since levelled, completed the enclosure.[75] The Anglo-Saxon monastic site had a number of churches, one of which was Wilfrid's basilica built over the crypt which was later incorporated into the present building. Archaeological excavations have uncovered evidence for two or three other chapels within the monastic enclosure as well as numerous graves. One notable site is Ailcy Hill, which was used as a cemetery from the early seventh century until sometime in the ninth or tenth century.[76] Another cluster of graves surrounds the chapel dedicated to

---

[71] Gowland, 'The manors and liberties of Ripon', 45.

[72] Blair, *The Church in Anglo-Saxon society*, 225.

[73] Ibid. 223.

[74] R. N. Swanson, *Church and society in late medieval England*, Oxford 1989, 153-4.

[75] Hall and Whyman, 'Settlement and monasticism at Ripon', 137.

[76] Ibid. 99.

St Mary (the Ladykirk). The religious fraternity dedicated to SS Mary, Wilfrid and All Saints used this chapel for masses and meetings in the late fourteenth century. To the north of the Ladykirk, the street of Allhallowgate took its name from a chapel dedicated to All Saints. Presumably this chapel was demolished before 1229, when its former site is referred to simply as 'the hill of All Saints', without any mention of the chapel.[77] The street of Annsgate, which runs along the bank of the Skell just to the south of the minster churchyard, must likewise have been named for the chapel of St Anne that was later used as an almshouse.

The decision to preserve the minster as a collegiate church suitable to guard Wilfrid's shrine and memory was part of the same archiepiscopal strategy of promoting Wilfrid's cult that culminated in the rebuilding of the minster at the end of the twelfth century and the translation of Wilfrid's relics in 1224. In the new minster building all the functions of the chapels in the old minster complex were combined, and the tithes of the whole parish remained in the hands of the canons (or prebendaries). These two decisions were the reason why, although the town of Ripon increased in size, it never had more than one parish church. The growth of the town was also largely due to the work of the archbishops of York. Although it is not mentioned in Domesday, Ripon probably had a marketing function before the end of the eleventh century.[78] Glanville Jones has demonstrated how the town developed under the post-Conquest archbishops of York, and identified broad differences between the occupants of different parts of the town. Thus, the south-east of the town – namely the minster with its churchyard, the archbishop's palace and the street of Annsgate was the ecclesiastical part of the town, while the rest was largely secular.[79] He concluded that the separation of the town into ecclesiastical and secular areas 'stemmed from the dual organisation of the ancient Ripon estate, a dichotomy already evident c. 1020 and probably much earlier'.[80] At the end of the twelfth century, when the minster church was rebuilt, the precinct around the church was shrinking as the town itself grew.[81]

Economic developments created tensions between the archbishop and chapter, and in the 1220s these erupted into a legal dispute over the lordship and the privileges of the canons. Already in the eleventh century Ripon was divided into two separate lordships or manors, which were distinct legal and economic units. Both manors were immune from the interference of royal agents thanks to the privileges granted, according to tradition, by King Æthelstan to the monastery in the tenth century.[82] In 1229 a royal inquest was held to settle

[77] 'monte Omnium Sanctorum': MR i. 60.

[78] McKay, 'The development of medieval Ripon', 73. See also Jones, 'The Ripon estate', 25.

[79] Jones, 'The Ripon estate', 30.

[80] Ibid. 15, 30.

[81] Whyman, 'Excavations in Deanery Gardens and Low St Agnesgate', 160.

[82] Æthelstan's visits to Ripon and Beverley were both legendary rather than historical: Blair, The Church in Anglo-Saxon society, 314.

a dispute provoked when Philip de Ascelles, sheriff of York, and William de Wychcombe, the archbishop's bailiff, had invaded the chapter's liberty five years earlier.[83] When the case was heard in the Ripon Minster chapter house by royal justices during the summer of 1229, the sheriff and bailiff both argued that the chapter did not have the separate jurisdiction that it claimed. Archbishop Grey also alleged that the chapter had begun usurping the rights of the archbishops because his bailiffs had been too lenient.[84] The chapter's spokesman, a canon named Geoffrey de Larder, supported the chapter's claims by producing royal charters from Æthelstan, Henry I and Stephen.[85] The royal justices summoned twenty-four jurors who found in favour of the chapter, upholding their rights and awarding them £10 in damages.[86] Within Ripon, the chapter's liberty included the streets of Stonebridgegate, Allhallowgate, Priest Lane, Annsgate, most of Westgate and Blossomgate and half of Skellgate.[87] A number of other places, only some of which are named in the records from the 1229 court case, were also within the liberty of St Wilfrid.[88] The chapter was the lord of this liberty, and none of the canons had any separate lordship either in the town or in the wider parish.[89] The liberty, also called the canon fee manor, was a patchwork of privileged areas under the jurisdiction of the chapter. Assaults committed within these areas, such as that suffered by Thomas Coke, were considered invasions of the liberty of St Wilfrid, and the chapter preserved the peace of St Wilfrid in these areas by prosecuting the invaders in the chapter court and sentencing them to public penance.

The third territory was the parish as a whole, which was more than eighty square miles in size.[90] Wilfrid's church at Ripon was supported by the tithes of this enormous parish, and without the need to maintain his church and shrine at Ripon it seems likely that the parish would have been divided into many smaller parishes over the centuries. As things stood, the boundaries of the parish needed to be preserved in order to prevent the loss of the minster's tithe income and spiritual jurisdiction. The parish as a whole enjoyed an unusual status in the church hierarchy. Ordinarily it would have been subject to the authority of the archdeacon of Richmond but it enjoyed exemption

---

[83]   MR i. 54.

[84]   MR i. 55.

[85]   The Æthelstan charters were actually forgeries: Gowland, 'The manors and liberties of Ripon', 46, 75; MR i. 54-6.

[86]   MR i. 63. For more detail on this case and its economic as well as political importance for the chapter see Gowland, 'The manors and liberties of Ripon', 43-85, and T. B. Lambert, 'Spiritual protection and secular power: the evolution of sanctuary and legal privileges in Ripon and Beverley, 900-1300', in T. B. Lambert and David Rollason (eds), *Peace and protection in the Middle Ages*, Durham 2009, 121-40.

[87]   MR i. 60.

[88]   MR i. 62.

[89]   MR i. 63.

[90]   Jones, 'The Ripon estate', 24.

as a peculiar jurisdiction, meaning that the chapter court had all the powers normally possessed by an archdeacon.[91] It could hear matrimonial and testamentary cases, punish parishioners for failing in their religious duties, resolve breach of contract disputes, and regulate the morality of all its parishioners. The chapter court's spiritual jurisdiction only extended to the border of the parish, so as with tithe income, any loss of territory was detrimental to its rights. The memory of this boundary was safeguarded by ritual. Every year on the three days before Ascension Thursday, the clergy and parishioners of Ripon carried the relics of St Wilfrid around the boundary of the parish in a ceremony called Rogation or the beating of the bounds. During the Rogation procession, as on Wilfrid's three feasts, the chapter and clergy of the minster mediated between the saint and the wider world.

The close relationship between clergy and saint was forcefully demonstrated by their control over his relics. The Rogation procession is a dramatic example, but access to the relics of the saint appears to have fluctuated through the year. On his three feast days Wilfrid's shrine was probably more accessible than under ordinary circumstances. Whether the relics were in the crypt or behind the high altar (as they were by the fourteenth century), the minster clergy was able to limit access to them. In the event that they did so, laypeople could still approach the saint *via* his image in the nave. By keeping the saint's shrine and relics separate from the daily concerns of Ripon's parishioners, the chapter could preserve the special status of the shrine and also maintain their special connection with the saint. Extant accounts show that there were a range of sites where people could venerate the saint on occasions when the minster clergy permitted wider access to his relics. These were Wilfrid's three feast days, plus the feast of the Ascension and the three days leading up to it. Throughout the fourteenth and fifteenth centuries the fabric wardens collected money at the choir door at the feast of Wilfrid's nativity in August as well as during the summer and winter fairs. They also collected money during the Rogation procession. Ripon's chamberlains raised money during the two fairs, the feast of Wilfrid's nativity and the feast of the Ascension. They collected these donations at Wilfrid's head, tomb and in the Anglo-Saxon crypt. The locations and circumstances of donations increase somewhat in the chamberlains' accounts after 1450. The head and feretory are then itemised separately, and the St William altar features in the extant accounts after 1472. The high mass on the feast of Wilfrid's nativity had also become an occasion to collect donations by this point. On all of these holidays the minster clergy venerated Wilfrid by celebrating special versions of the mass and office written for these feasts. Laypeople descended on the minster from all corners of the parish to pay honour to Wilfrid in their own ways on his great feasts, and sought his help by other means throughout the year.

---

[91]   Gowland, 'The manors and liberties of Ripon', 51.

Wilfrid as patron of the parish

St Wilfrid was the patron of ordinary parishioners as much as the clergy of the minster, though what he offered them and what he received from them in exchange was somewhat different. For the most part Wilfrid did not confer prestige or authority on the laypeople of the parish. Instead, he exercised his powers to heal injury and illness, fend off plague, protect crops and livestock from disease, preserve the parish from diabolical forces, and lead the dead out of the wilderness of purgatory and into paradise. In return for Wilfrid's help, laypeople observed his feast days and made donations of wax, money and valuable belongings to his shrine, thereby attesting his powers. Wilfrid's status as a patron saint rested on his ability to act the part, and like any other saint he needed clients whom he could help.[92] The chapter court represented Wilfrid as keeper of the peace within his liberty, so an appeal to the court to redress injuries like those suffered by Thomas Coke was effectively an appeal to the saint. Another sign of Wilfrid's lordship was the tenurial relationship between Wilfrid and his tenants, which came complete with obligatory oaths of fealty and feudal service.

This form of landholding was Marmion tenure, in reference to Lord Marmion, one of a number of men who owed this service in 1229.[93] Other Marmion tenants at that date included the lord of Aldfield, Simon Ward, Roger de Nunwick and the master of the hospital of St Mary Magdalene.[94] The typical procedure for admission of a Marmion tenant was for the heir, following the death of the former tenant, to appear before the two resident canons in the chapter house, often on the Monday before the feast of the Ascension, and to swear 'fealty to God and to St Wilfrid and to the chapter in the customary form expressed in the book of St Wilfrid'.[95] J. T. Fowler thought that the *textus Sancti Wilfridi* was the set of Gospels given to the minster by Wilfrid, and that the oath was written on a blank leaf in this manuscript.[96] More recently, James Carley has traced the provenance of the Morgan Golden Gospels (Pierpont Morgan Library, New York, MS M.23) to Ripon, where John Leland acquired them in 1541.[97] Carley has argued that the Morgan Golden Gospels were made to replace the originals donated by Wilfrid following their destruction when the minster was burned by Eadred in the mid-tenth century.[98] In any case it is likely that in

[92]   Wolf, *The life and afterlife of St Elizabeth*, 38–40.

[93]   Gowland, 'The manors and liberties of Ripon', 48.

[94]   Ibid.

[95]   'fidelitatem Deo et Beato Wilfrido et capitulo in forma consueta in textu Sancti Wilfridi expressata': AoC, 245 and n.

[96]   AoC, 245n.

[97]   James Carley, 'The provenance of the Morgan Golden Gospels (Pierpont Morgan Library, MS M.23): a new hypothesis', in Kathleen Doyle and Scot McKendrick (eds), *1000 years of royal books and manuscripts*, London 2013, 53–67 at pp. 62–3.

[98]   Ibid. 64–6.

the fifteenth century the book was believed to be the original given by Wilfrid to the church that he founded in Ripon because the replacement's leaves were dyed purple and the writing was gold so that it fitted Stephanus' description of the Gospels given to Ripon by Wilfrid.[99] Marmion tenants therefore swore their oath of fealty on a book that they believed Wilfrid himself had touched. The terms of their tenure included the duty of carrying Wilfrid's relics in the single most important procession of the year, the Rogation procession on the three days before the feast of the Ascension. Marmion tenure was still a term in the late fifteenth century when the names of Marmion tenants were recorded in the chapter acts book. The list contained therein covers the period between 1466 and 1490, naming some of the most prominent local families, such as the Pigots (Clotherholme), Wards (Givendale), Malories (Studley), Markenfields (Markenfield) and Kendales (Markington).[100] No women are named in the list, so although widows could inherit their husband's lands, only their husbands and sons could fulfil the other requirements of Marmion tenure. Many of these families were armigerous, and fittingly so was Wilfrid. His blazon was *azure, three estoiles or*, and it is displayed alongside the heraldry of the minster's benefactors in various parts of the church.

Although there are no late medieval lists of Wilfrid's miracles, his power to heal and protect is attested by various financial records from the minster. It was customary for medieval pilgrims to leave gifts at the shrines of saints in thanksgiving for a successful cure. Often the gift was wax, either measured according to the dimensions of the person who had obtained a cure or shaped to resemble the afflicted body part that the saint had healed.[101] The treasurer's roll of 1470-1 records 10*d.* worth of profit from 'diverse wax images' sold that year, and these were most likely gifts at Wilfrid's shrine.[102] Wilfrid's power was present not only in his relics but also diffused through other objects. Two examples from the fabric rolls are St Wilfrid's burning iron and pox stone. The burning iron first appears in the accounts from the 1390s, and is later described as being made available 'to all the faithful of Christ using it to sign their cattle for the welcome salvation of the same cattle from the murrain and illness befalling them'.[103] Presumably the burning iron was sought out by those who wanted supernatural protection for cattle that they had just purchased at one of the two annual fairs. The use of the pox stone is never described, but must have had similar powers to protect against disease. Over the years Wilfrid acquired new objects to help him transmit his holy power, such as the ring and chalice mentioned in the later chamberlain's rolls.

---

[99] Ibid. 63.

[100] AoC, 244-8.

[101] Eamon Duffy, *The stripping of the altars: traditional religion in England, 1400–1580*, 2nd edn, New Haven 2005, 196–200; Bartlett, *Why can the dead do such great things?*, 356.

[102] 'diversarum ymaginum ceræ': MR iii. 214.

[103] 'universis Christi fidelibus illud exigentibus ad signand. averia sua pro graciori salvacione eorundem averiorum a morina ac morbis eis contingentibus': MR iii. 167.

Wilfrid's patronage extended to the dead whom he could help complete their purgation by interceding on their behalf with Christ in heaven. One way to appeal to the saint for his help was to be buried near his image. In his 1488 will John Gregson requested burial 'in the nave of the church before the image of St Wilfrid'.[104] In 1505 Geoffrey Scharroke requested burial before the same image. He paid 6s. 8d. for the privilege and left a further £3 to the Fabric, no doubt intending to help fund the rebuilding of the nave.[105] Gregson and Scharroke meant their tombs to win for them the benefit of the saint's help. They were also well-positioned to catch the attention and prayers of living people who approached the saint's image for assistance with their own concerns. It may not have been possible to be buried by Wilfrid's relics, but parishioners could bequeath personal items to the shrine. William Stow (d. 1431), a retainer of the earl of Northumberland whose will also connects him to the Wards and Markenfields, bequeathed his livery collar to the feretory.[106] John Turret donated 4d. in cash to the tomb of St Wilfrid in his will.[107] A far greater number of parishioners sought the saint's help through the tolling of the Wilfrid bell – which was inscribed with a prayer to the saint and was commonly rung at funerals and obits – than by placing their graves near his image or making lavish bequests to his shrine.

St Wilfrid's bell, like his three feast days and the Rogation procession, sacralised time in late medieval Ripon by marking its passage with a combination of appeals to Wilfrid for his help and thanksgiving for his blessings. The bell was also just one of a bewildering number of objects, groups and privileged spaces named for the saint. Nothing quite so succinctly outlines his influence in the parish of Ripon as a list of these things, including pieces of the saint and objects that he had touched: the collegiate church of St Wilfrid, Wilfrid's head, Wilfrid's shrine, Wilfrid's tomb, Wilfrid's Golden Gospels, Wilfrid's image in the nave, Wilfrid's burning iron, Wilfrid's pox stone, Wilfrid's ring, Wilfrid's chalice, the Guild of St Wilfrid, the Guild of SS Mary, Wilfrid and All Saints, the Wilfrid chantry, the altar of St Wilfrid, the sacred league of St Wilfrid, the liberty of St Wilfrid – even something as banal as a pasture owned by the fabric wardens eventually came to be known as 'Seinte Wilfride reyn'.[108] The roots of the cult of St Wilfrid ran wide and deep.

---

[104] 'in navi ecclesiæ coram ymagine Sancti Wilfridi': AoC, 285. His devotion to St Wilfrid is manifest in additional bequests to the saint's shrine and chantry: AoC, 286.

[105] AoC, 306.

[106] TE ii. 13.

[107] AoC, 143.

[108] MR iii. 165.

2

The Minster Clergy

Carved during the last decades of the fifteenth century, the choir stalls of Ripon Minster replaced the earlier set that had been damaged by the fall of the lantern tower in 1450. The tower collapse strained the minster's resources for many years, but essential masonry repairs to the tower itself, the south transept and the choir had been completed by about 1480, permitting the minster clergy to beautify the choir with new woodwork.[1] The stalls have folding seats with misericords: adorned with fantastic images of dragons, birds, griffins, flowers, green men, pigs playing bagpipes, mermaids and much else, they provided ledges for the clergy to lean against during the portions of the liturgy when they were expected to stand rather than sit. One of the bench-ends on the south side of the choir displays a shield with three wavy-armed stars crowned by a mitre: the arms of St Wilfrid. The richness of the carving exemplifies the grandeur of the medieval minster, while the number of stalls conveys its institutional scale. There are thirty-four stalls in total, arranged just as they would have been in a cathedral or monastic choir. There were places for the minster canons and also the vicars and chantry priests, all of whom were expected to gather in the choir for the daily round of services. Together with their deacons, subdeacons and others in minor orders, the minster clergy performed a grand and elaborate liturgy not to be found in most medieval parish churches.

The minster clergy, like St Wilfrid, strongly influenced religion and society in the parish of Ripon. They struck a balance between their own liturgical requirements and those of their parishioners, but the cure of souls within the parish was not always their primary concern. At one and the same time their institution was similar in many ways to a monastery or cathedral while also resembling six parish churches fused into one. A significant development in its long history was the formal establishment in the early fourteenth century of vicars for each of the six prebends. Their task was to guarantee that the cure of souls was performed within each of the parish's six territorial divisions. The canons, who were supposed to provide for this, often did not reside in Ripon personally and did not always hire a vicar to act in their stead. Even so, the size of the parish caused logistical problems for the vicars. Between 1200 and about 1350 many chapels were established in the villages and at the manors of the lords. These chapels were supported at the cost of their founders, but the chapter of canons always ensured that the minster's parochial rights were preserved. After 1350 there were many new perpetual chantry foundations at

---

[1] John Harvey, *The perpendicular style, 1330–1485*, London 1978, 204.

altars in the minster. Their main purpose was to generate masses that would help their founders escape from purgatory. Many founders desired that their chantries should also augment the corporate liturgy of the minster by increasing the number of priests in the choir during the mass and the daily office, and in 1504 perpetual chantry chaplains were finally assigned their own stalls in acknowledgement of their status. The new chantries significantly increased the number of beneficed clergy in the minster and supplied the majority of its administrators. The chief leadership role was still that of the resident canon. His subordinates – often chantry chaplains – held the offices of fabric warden, chamberlain and sub-treasurer. The administration of the minster became increasingly complex during the fifteenth century, and could not have been managed without the chaplains. Significantly, the office of lay churchwarden, a standard feature of most parish churches, never existed in medieval Ripon because the laity were not responsible for the fabric of the minster. Instead, the townspeople who would have been Ripon's churchwardens must have been its guild wardens instead. In the villages, the resources of the chapels were most likely managed by officers whose responsibilities were similar to those of parish churchwardens.

As well as dealing with the challenges posed by its broad geographical extent, the parish's unusual status as a peculiar, exempt from the authority of the archdeacon of Richmond, meant that the chapter court of Ripon Minster exercised archidiaconal powers within the parish; it was this court which

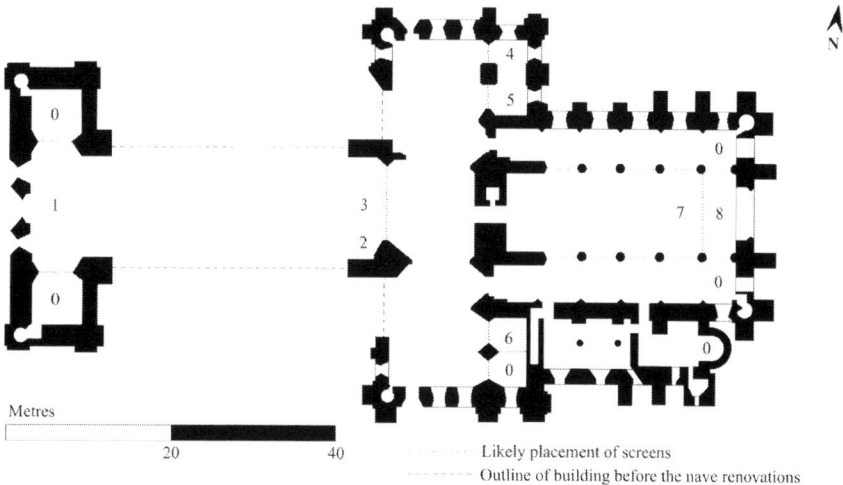

Likely placement of screens
Outline of building before the nave renovations

Map 2. Plan of Ripon Minster showing the location of the font, St Wilfrid's shrine and altars

1 = font; 2 = Sendale's Holy Trinity altar; 3 = Holy Cross altar; 4 = St Andrew/Monkton altar
5 = SS John the Baptist and John the Evangelist/Thorpe altar; 6 = Assumption of the Virgin Mary/
Givendale altar; 7 = high altar; 8 = shrine of St Wilfrid; 0 = other altar sites whose precise dedications
are uncertain

was responsible for enforcing proper religious observance, regulating sexual conduct, settling matrimonial disputes, probating wills and even deciding small debt cases. The court also had a role in keeping the peace, and it imposed penances on those who violated the peace of St Wilfrid within the chapter's liberty. The rights, privileges and powers of the minster clergy rested on the shoulders of their patron saint. Their institution was first and foremost a religious community which preserved the saint's relics and his memory. Because its function as a parish church was always only an adaptation of this earlier purpose, the history of the church and clergy of Ripon from the late twelfth century to the end of the fourteenth century is the necessary context for any analysis of the institution in the fifteenth century.

The clergy and their church, c. 1175–1380

Around the year 1200, when Ripon Minster was being rebuilt, many parish churches had a very simple plan, generally a rectangular nave with a small chancel at the east end. The sacred space around the altar was separated from the nave by the chancel arch, and later by the rood screen. From the early thirteenth century the rector was responsible for maintaining the chancel and the parishioners of the church were charged with the upkeep of the nave. The office of churchwarden developed from this lay responsibility, and in that sense the ordinary parish church belonged partly to its parishioners.[2] In scale and plan Ripon was vastly different. It was a large cruciform church with a full choir, rather than just a chancel, at its east end. It had a chapter house where its clergy met to judge the behaviour of laity and clergy alike. It possessed a gold and silver saint's shrine and the holy bones of its patron. It had three towers with tall lead spires: one over the central crossing and two at the west front. Ripon Minster looked like a small cathedral or monastery and in many ways it operated like one.

Ripon Minster was designed to resemble York Minster in form and function. York and Ripon both had a chapter of canons that used the choir for their religious services. The Ripon choir, like the choir at York, was probably never intended for use by the laity.[3] Before 1224 Wilfrid's shrine was most likely in the crypt under the central crossing of the building where it could be reached by pilgrims who would enter and leave the church *via* its transepts.[4] Sometime after this date, and probably before the year 1300, the shrine was moved to its late medieval position behind the high altar.[5] The choir aisles and ambulatory

---

[2] Beat Kümin, *The shaping of a community: the rise and reformation of the English parish, c. 1400–1560*, Aldershot 1996, 17–18. Duffy, *Stripping the Altars*, 132–4.

[3] Hearn, 'The beginning of the gothic style in northern England', 99–100.

[4] Ibid. 100.

[5] Ibid. 96–7.

provided the pilgrimage route in this arrangement. As before, pilgrims were kept out of the choir itself, and would not disturb the services taking place within it. The eastern part of Ripon Minster was the seat of the clergy's power. In addition to the choir and the shrine of St Wilfrid, the chapter house was there too. It was exceptional for laypeople to enter this part of the building. Pilgrims were admitted to the shrine, and so were penitents, who could also enter the choir, either to fulfil the penance assigned to them for a crime or in order for them to partake in the special liturgy of Holy Friday and Easter morning. During most high masses only elite men were allowed in the choir. Laypeople had greater access to the transepts and nave of the minster, but they still had less control over the fabric of the building than the average parishioners in their parish churches because the minster clergy appointed their own clerical fabric wardens to oversee building maintenance.

Wilfrid's original foundation at Ripon had been a monastery, but at some point before the early eleventh century it was converted into a college of secular canons.[6] Canons led a religious life with a common liturgy, but they had separate residences and were not bound by a monastic rule. Ripon's canons were prebendaries, each one deriving his income from an estate, a prebend. Prebendaries needed no provost since each took the tithes – in corn, hay, wool and lambs – directly from his own prebend rather than drawing them from a common fund.[7] These were parochial dues and, as with all such tithes, were the price that the laity paid for the spiritual care that the canons should have provided personally or through a delegate such as a vicar. In 1301 Archbishop Greenfield decided that the canons should be identified by their prebends instead of their altars in the minster, as had previously been the custom.[8] Each of the six prebends was named for its most important village: Monkton, Nunwick, Sharrow, Skelton (or Givendale), Studley and Thorpe. These six were situated around Ripon itself, and none of them had ever been an independent parish. Archbishop Grey created a seventh prebend in 1230, endowing it with the income from Stanwick parish church in Richmondshire.[9] Stanwick remained a separate parish and was served by a perpetual vicar, appointed and paid by the Ripon chapter, but the new canon of Stanwick was to be perpetually resident in Ripon. At the time the Ripon chapter had no formal leader, and the creation of the new prebend gave the archbishop a means to appoint a leader for an institution that had asserted its independence and defeated him in an important court case the previous year.

At the very moment that the minster was being rebuilt, the religious responsibilities of the laity throughout Christendom were being extended and more

---

[6]   Gowland, 'The manors and liberties of Ripon', 45.

[7]   A. Hamilton Thompson, 'Collegiate Church of St Peter and St Wilfrid, Ripon', in William Page (ed.), *VCH, York*, iii, London 1913, 367–72 at p. 369.

[8]   *MR* ii. 32.

[9]   *MR* ii. 2.

clearly codified by the Church. After the Fourth Lateran Council in 1215, all Christians were expected to make confession and receive communion once a year. These two sacraments required a priest, and there needed to be some framework of oversight to verify that laypeople really fulfilled their annual obligations. Ordinarily this system was the parish, but the huge parish of Ripon created a number of logistical problems that were compounded by the frequent absence of many of its canons. The residents of Ripon's six prebends paid tithes like ordinary parishioners, but many lived far from the minster and often seem to have lacked regular contact with the essential clergy. Moreover, some parishioners desired much more than the minimum amount of access to a priest and the sacraments. The inadequacies of the situation in Ripon are highlighted by the wave of chapel foundations that took place throughout the parish during the thirteenth century. The licensing of new chapels was no doubt encouraged by Archbishop Grey and the canons appointed at Ripon from around 1230 onwards, and around a dozen or so had been established by 1255.[10] The archbishops of York also took other steps to improve clerical provision in the parish. During the final two decades of the thirteenth century, they made repeated efforts to force the canons to reside in Ripon, saying that they feared that the spiritual care of the parish was being neglected and that the canons were not earning their stipends.[11] Finally, in 1303, Archbishop Corbridge made vicars mandatory for all canons.[12] He regularised their salaries, ordering each canon to pay his vicar six marks (£4) every year, in four instalments.[13]

Corbridge's system maintained the prebend as the essential subdivision of the parish, simply substituting the vicar for the canon as the party responsible for the pastoral care of the laity. Parishioners understood the connection between where they lived and which vicar was their own. If their tithes went to the canon of Nunwick, then the vicar of Nunwick was their vicar. The connection extended further to include the altar used by the vicar. Because Ripon's vicars were not merely vicars choral who stood in for absent canons in the choir, they needed altars that were more accessible to the laity than the high altar, especially so that they could give communion to the laity at Easter. They probably had about a dozen or so to choose from at the start of the fourteenth century.[14] The twelfth-century minster had been designed to provide enough altars for the canons to say their own daily masses, with two in each of the transepts and probably another three behind the high altar.[15] The most obvious solution would have been to assign to each vicar the altar originally intended

[10]   Jeffrey A. K. Miller, 'The building program of Archbishop Walter de Gray: architectural production and reform in the archdiocese of York, 1215–1255', unpubl. PhD diss. Columbia 2012, 148.

[11]   MR ii. 15, 32.

[12]   R. Gilyard-Beer, 'Bedern Bank and the Bedern Ripon', YAJ lviii (1986), 141–5 at p. 141.

[13]   MR ii. 14, 44–6.

[14]   Hearn, 'The beginning of the gothic style in northern England', 99.

[15]   Ibid. 100; Miller, 'The building program of Archbishop Walter de Gray', 140.

for his canon. The altars in the space behind the high altar were less suitable for this purpose than those in the transepts, and so it seems very likely that two other altars somewhere in the nave were used instead. The decision to assign a vicar to each prebend and an altar to each vicar effectively mapped the geography of the parish onto the minster building. When the vicars used their altars to serve their parishioners, the altars became firmly associated with their prebends as distinct units within the wider parish. This link is expressed in many wills in which the testator refers to 'my parochial altar'. The dedications of the parochial altars were to St Andrew (Monkton), St John the Baptist (Thorpe), St Stephen (Sharow), St Lawrence (Nunwick), St Wilfrid (Studley) and St Mary (Givendale). The altar of St Andrew was in the outer chapel of the north transept and the altar of St John was in the adjacent inner chapel. The locations of the other four altars are less certain. Wall paintings depicting scenes from the life of St Mary adorn the inner chapel of the south transept, making it the most likely site of the prebendal altar of Givendale. It is unclear which of the other three parochial altars was in the second chapel in the south transept, or where exactly the remaining two altars were located. Their most likely locatation was at the western end of the building under the towers, where there is evidence that there were once altars.[16] The space beneath each of the western towers could have been adapted for a similar type of chapel as was found in the transepts, and altars located there would have been as accessible to laypeople as those known to have been used as parochial altars. Later references to parochial altars mention their doors, so they were probably enclosed by screens.

At Easter the parishioners came to their vicars, but on other occasions the vicars had to travel to them. In 1338 the vicars appealed to Archbishop Melton (r. 1317–40), claiming that their stipends of 6 marks were insufficient to pay for the horses and servants that they needed to minister to their scattered parishioners.[17] They argued that they deserved higher pay because they often had to travel as far as nine miles in order to visit the sick and perform other tasks related to their cure of souls.[18] Their petition was successful and their salaries were raised to £6 annually.[19] Visiting the sick and transporting the viaticum to dying parishioners was probably the extent of the vicars' regular work in the villages. There were many chapels in the parish but it is unlikely that the vicars said mass in any of them except on rare occasions. Instead, these chapels were raised and supported, sometimes on an *ad hoc* basis, by gentry families and local villagers. Many of the resources that could have been used to endow chantries in the minster were applied to these local chapels, and it was only at the end of the fourteenth century, once most of the chapels had been established, that

---

[16] Hearn, 'The beginning of the gothic style in northern England', 99.

[17] MR iv. 11.

[18] Ibid.

[19] MR iv. 15.

families and groups of parishioners with the necessary resources to endow a chantry began to locate their new chantries in the minster.

By and large the history of Ripon's chantries is concentrated in the fourteenth and fifteenth centuries. Its oldest chantry was founded in the thirteenth century, but needed to be re-endowed in 1370 in order to keep it viable.[20] This followed the establishment of two or three new perpetual chantries. The Plumpton family created a chantry at the altar of Holy Trinity behind the high altar in 1345.[21] There was a chantry at the altar of SS John the Baptist and John the Evangelist from 1325, which was re-endowed in 1364.[22] The clerical taxation of 1381 lists four chantry chaplains, so the fourth chantry in 1381 must have been the chantry of St Mary in the Ladyloft.[23] All the other chantries have known foundation dates later than 1406. From that point onward the number of perpetual chantries based in Ripon steadily increased, driven largely by the new religious guilds that were forming in the parish around the year 1400. The absenteeism of the canons continued, but the creation of so many new chantries supplied chaplains who would hold many of the administrative offices, such as sub-treasurer, chamberlain and fabric warden at Ripon in the fifteenth century.

The minster during the long fifteenth century

Ripon Minster continued to change during the years between 1380 and 1520, as institutional developments as well as continuities affected its place in society. The non-residence of earlier centuries continued, so that there were ordinarily no more than two canons in Ripon at one time: a resident canon was effectively the president of the chapter court, and as such possessed a great deal of power and authority within the parish. The late fifteenth-century chapter acts book illuminates the workings of this court and its impact. The number of vicars did not change during this period, but their privileges were increased when they were incorporated in 1414. The cure of souls in the parish continued to be their primary responsibility, and they were aided no doubt by the growing number of chaplains at the minster and elsewhere. In the decades around 1400, when a number of new perpetual chantries were founded in Ripon, their chaplains began to play an increasingly important role in the day-to-day administration of the minster by holding the offices of chamberlain, sub-treasurer and fabric warden. These offices augmented their salaries and also gave them responsibility for fundraising, maintaining rental properties, purchasing building materials and hiring craftsmen.

---

[20]   MR iv. 131–6.
[21]   *CPR Edward III*, London 1891–1916, vi. 455.
[22]   *CPR Edward II*, London 1894–1904, v. 190–1; *CPR Edward III*, xiii. 45–6.
[23]   TNA, Kew, E 179/63/12 m 1.

The canons and the chapter court

Most of Ripon's canons held multiple benefices simultaneously and hence were usually non-resident during the fifteenth century. Ripon's prebends were not very rich by comparison to those of York Minster and the other English cathedrals, but they were a welcome addition to the incomes of those who already had livings. A pluralist canon could not reside everywhere at the same time, and some with prebends at Ripon chose not to live there at all. Many of the non-resident pluralists were appointed not by the archbishop, to whom that right ordinarily belonged, but either by the pope or the king. The pope's appointments were often Italians who never visited Ripon and were admitted by proxy. Royal ordinances of the mid-fourteenth century curbed the papacy's ability to provide candidates for ecclesiastical offices, and afterwards it was more common for the king to appoint his own candidates when the see of York was vacant.[24] The kings of England usually appointed their royal clerks so that they could then enjoy their services in the royal bureaucracy without paying them.[25]

A number of former canons of Ripon later became bishops. One was Nicholas Bubwith (d. 1424), who rose to the upper ranks of royal administration to become master of the rolls and then treasurer of England.[26] He was also elected bishop of London, later translated to Salisbury, and ended his career as bishop of Bath and Wells.[27] Another example is George Neville, who became canon of Thorpe in 1454 and two years later was elected bishop of Exeter.[28] By 1465 he had become archbishop of York and was able to issue a dispensation for non-residence to John Southwell, canon of Monkton. Southwell was a pluralist, and needed the dispensation so he could serve as dean of a collegiate chapel founded by George Neville's older brother Richard, earl of Warwick and Salisbury.[29] Pluralists who would later become bishops mainly came from magnate families like the Nevilles. As non-resident canons they had their greatest impact on the minster simply by not being there and leaving its governance to the resident canons and chaplains.

One resident canon who might have dreamed of wearing a bishop's mitre was William Scrope. One of the sons of Stephen Scrope, second Baron Masham, and a kinsman of Archbishop Richard Scrope (d. 1405),[30] he had begun his ecclesiastical career in 1410 with a papal dispensation to be

---

[24]   Swanson, *Church and society in late medieval England*, 70, 73.
[25]   Ibid. 105. For a full list of Ripon's canons, see *MR* ii. 184–258.
[26]   *MR* ii. 202.
[27]   Ibid.
[28]   *MR* ii. 216.
[29]   *AoC*, 156–7.
[30]   *TE* iii. 35n.

beneficed, notwithstanding that he was only sixteen years old.[31] He held the prebend of Nunwick from 1411 until his death in 1463, and never advanced to any higher ecclesiastical office, probably due to his family's repeated implication in treasonous plots.[32] He was a pluralist, holding a number of other benefices scattered across the north of England, but he was a resident canon at Ripon during the last decade of his life. He frequently appears in the chapter acts as president of the chapter court, a role conferred on him by his status as senior resident canon.

The seven canons together constituted the minster's governing body, the chapter. Chapters were common in secular cathedrals like York as well as in other collegiate churches such as Beverley and Southwell. Ordinarily a chapter was headed by a dean, but Ripon's chapter had neither dean nor other formal head so that in practice the senior residentiary canon was its leader. As, in the fourteenth and fifteenth centuries, it was common for there to be only one or two canons residing in Ripon at any given time, any canon who chose to reside there for any length of time effectively became its head. The other reward for residence was a stipend from the minster's common fund to qualify for which the canon needed to reside at Ripon for twelve weeks during the year.[33] The prebendary of Stanwick did not qualify because he was already obliged to reside at Ripon to act as rector of the choir.[34] He had oversight of liturgical matters in the choir while the resident canon had authority over the moral conduct of the vicars, chaplains, deacons, sub-deacons and acolytes, not to mention an archdeacon's spiritual authority over the whole parish, and St Wilfrid's rights of lordship over the liberty. The canon of Stanwick appears to have headed the chapter only when no other canons were resident. The chapter could also choose a commissary from among the minster's chaplains and delegate its spiritual powers to him. In the late fifteenth century it selected chaplains from parish gentry families like John Frankish and Christopher Kendale.

The chief residentiary canon or his deputy presided over the chapter court, the most powerful instrument of its authority. Cases could begin either at the instance of a plaintiff (*ad instanciam*) or at the court's own instance (*ex officio*), perhaps in response to rumours of bad conduct. Parishioners used the court to settle various types of disputes, thus demonstrating that they acknowledged its authority and felt confident that it could provide the remedy that they wanted. The majority of the cases begun at the instance of parishioners were brought by creditors attempting to recover small sums of money from their debtors in the parish. Ripon was not unusual in this respect: debt cases, treated as a form of broken oath and therefore within the jurisdiction of ecclesiastical courts, were

---

[31]   Ibid.
[32]   MR ii. 194–6.
[33]   MR ii. 110.
[34]   MR ii. 2.

the main source of business for many of the church courts in England.[35] Since the court was very effective at settling such cases it was frequently used. The butcher John Rande (d. 1476) cited four debtors in the court between 1457 and 1464, and won all his cases. The sums of money owed to him ranged from 5s. to £2 10s.[36] Ripon's clergy likewise used the court to recover sums of money from their debtors. In most cases the creditors appear to have been chaplains rather than canons or vicars.

Matrimonial cases were also brought at the instance of a plaintiff. Valid marriages could be formed by consent of the two parties alone, on the condition that they were free to marry at the time of the exchange of vows. Vows given in the present tense and vows in the future tense followed by consummation both formed valid marriages. The Church preferred to be involved, but priests and even witnesses were not necessary provided that the parties exchanged their consent.[37] When they were involved, priests were not permitted to solemnise weddings without first publishing the banns and thereby verifying that the couple were free to marry.[38] Clandestine marriages were those performed in a church without the proper publicity, rather than those contracted privately between the couple without a priest or witnesses.[39] Though valid, marriages contracted outside the church could be disputed if one of the partners subsequently denied the contract or if a third party later alleged a pre-existing contract. None of the cases in the Ripon chapter acts involved marriages that had already been solemnised in church. Instead, they were actions to enforce an alleged marriage or to refute claims of a pre-contract that prevented a proposed marriage from taking place. There are only a few of these, but they produced the greatest number of witnesses and the most detailed testimony.

The marital status of Ripon's parishioners would have been well known provided that the marriages had been solemnised by the Ripon clergy. There is little evidence for how wedding ceremonies were actually performed at Ripon, but when one of the dependent chapels was used, the vicar of the relevant prebend was licensed to perform the wedding. The same system probably applied to the rest of Ripon's parishioners, so that a vicar would always know whether the parishioners in his prebend were free to marry or not. Without this knowledge it would have been difficult to punish fornication and adultery.[40] The clergy's desire to solemnise the marriages of Ripon's parishioners is evident in the licence for John Pigot and Katherine Heton to be married in the chapel of one of Ripon's hospitals in 1486. The licence notes

---

[35]   Swanson, *Church and society in late medieval England*, 167–8.

[36]   *AoC*, 63, 66, 81, 117.

[37]   Charles Donahue, *Law, marriage, and society in the later Middle Ages: arguments about marriage in five courts*, Cambridge 2007, 2.

[38]   Ibid. 32.

[39]   Shannon McSheffrey, 'Place, space, and situation: public and private in the making of marriage in late-medieval London', *Speculum* lxxix (2004), 960–90 at pp. 961, 970.

[40]   Donahue, *Law, marriage, and society*, 4.

that the two had already lived together for a long time as man and wife, yet this was clearly deemed insufficient.[41] Cases of adultery and fornication are the most numerous type brought by the chapter at its own instance, showing that the court was as interested in curtailing illicit sexual relationships as it was in regularising and publicising marriages. Like other *ex officio* cases, they regulated the moral conduct of the parishioners and clergy of Ripon alike, and imposed public penance on those found guilty of the charges.

Unable to impose the harsher sentences of the secular courts, Ripon's chapter court used penance and excommunication as its two most powerful means of correction and coercion. While debt and marriage cases were ordinarily settled by the enforcement of a contract, convictions in cases of fornication, adultery, neglect of religious duties and invasion of the liberty bore penitential sentences. Public penance was, as John Arnold has argued, emblematic of the Church's power: it could turn transgression into a moral lesson while displaying its willingness to forgive.[42] He contends that in this context hegemony, defined as a means by which a more powerful group can persuade others to accept a particular view of the world and limit the conceivable alternatives, is a useful interpretive concept.[43] Arnold cites the example of a Lollard sentenced for heresy, but the same model applies equally well to the penances assigned by the Ripon chapter for other crimes. The Ripon chapter court's penances usually involved floggings in the church or marketplace plus other forms of humiliation, submission and restitution appropriate to the particular offence. The common element of many of these penances was participation in the Sunday procession in penitential attire and carrying a lit candle, often for a number of weeks in a row.

When Agnes Legg admitted to a long-standing but irregular relationship with Robert Cutler (they lived together and had a child but were evidently unmarried), she was sentenced to lead three Sunday processions 'with bare feet and lower legs, wearing a veil on her head, with one burning candle in her hand worth 1d, which she should offer at the high altar at the offertory of the mass, on the last day of her penance'.[44] The procession preceded the high mass on Sundays, and would be witnessed by all those who attended mass in the minster. The exact path of the procession is unknown, but its purpose was to sprinkle the altars of the minster with holy water, so it would have travelled around the whole church, including the length of the nave and the transepts where most of the laypeople attending the mass would have stood watching. The onlookers who witnessed Agnes Legg's humiliation and that of other penitents on other occasions represented the community into which

---

[41]   *TE* iii. 350.

[42]   Arnold, *Belief and unbelief*, 15.

[43]   Ibid. 14. See also Graves, *Form and fabric of belief*, 13.

[44]   'nudis pedibus et tibiis, capite flameolo cooperto, cum j cereo ardente precii j d in manu sua, quem offerre debet summo altari tempore offerendæ missæ, ultimo die dictæ pœnitenciæ', AoC, 91.

such penitents would be reincorporated following the completion of their penances. On Sundays this group of parishioners would likely have included only the people who lived close to the minster, whereas on feast days a far wider segment of the parish was expected to attend and the humiliation would have been proportionally greater. Penances that mention beatings 'before the cross' probably refer to the processional cross rather than, as Fowler thought, the market cross.[45] References to the market cross are rare, and the number of floggings assigned usually appears to be identical with the number of weeks a penitent was expected to head the procession.

Penitential attire varied according to gender and whether or not the penitent was a cleric, so that penitents essentially appeared as humbled women, laymen or clergy. In all cases the penance was intended to strip away the usual signs of status represented by clothing and made the temporary exclusion of the penitent obvious to all.[46] The covered head was a regular requirement for female penitents. Margaret Bron of Skelton was assigned a penance for adultery in 1466, and like Agnes Legg she was to have her head covered by a veil.[47] The veil of the penitent woman could never be confused with the more honourable veil of the chaste widow because the female penitent was required to process with bare feet and lower legs. Thomas Hawton, clerk, was sentenced to six floggings before the procession in 1454 after he admitted to adultery with Margaret Heryngton of Annsgate. Hawton was to complete his penance wearing his surplice, with a bare head, and holding a lit candle that weighed 1lb in his hand.[48] The surplice was replaced by a shirt if the penitent were a layman, but the bare head was a general feature of male penitential attire in contrast to that of female penitents. Bare feet and lower legs were common to all penitents. Thus Ralph Simson, who broke the peace of St Wilfrid in 1462, was to lead the procession 'with bare feet and lower legs, an uncovered head, dressed only in his shirt and breeches'.[49] Simson's offence had been to interfere with William Scrope's bailiff when he was sent to seize a cow and three bullocks from Christopher Hogson and William Fynchden, who had not paid all their parish dues.[50] Since this seizure had nothing to do with him directly, Simson must have been motivated by another grievance that is absent from the records. This same record describes the customary flogging in unusual detail, revealing that its force was mainly symbolic and that the real weapon was public shame. A deacon would lead the procession with Simson and beat him with a rod

---

[45] 'ante crucem', AoC, 36n.

[46] Charles Phythian-Adams, 'Ritual constructions of society', in Rosemary Horrox and W. Mark Ormrod (eds), *A social history of England, 1200–1500*, Cambridge 2006, 369–82 at p. 374.

[47] AoC, 123.

[48] AoC, 36.

[49] 'nudis pedibus et tibiis, capite discooperto, suis camisia et braccis tantummodo indutus': AoC, 191.

[50] AoC, 190.

'three times publicly, yet lightly'.[51] Ralph had to endure these blows 'patiently, as a humble penitent'.[52]

The donation of the candle carried by penitents prolonged the penance. Penitents had to remain in the church, exposed to the gaze of their neighbours, during the mass and then enter the choir to leave their candles on the high altar. In these instances admission to the choir, which was normally restricted to the clergy, was a sign of shame and submission rather than privilege. Those convicted of invading the liberty of St Wilfrid had to carry their weapons, which were symbols of their offence, as well as lit candles. After the procession they surrendered these weapons on the high altar. In this way the penance blunted the power of the weapons and reasserted the authority of the chapter and St Wilfrid. Ordinarily the penance for breaking Wilfrid's peace included gifts of restitution to Wilfrid, either to his shrine or to his image in the nave. In 1453 the men who assaulted Thomas Coke and the men who later attacked them when they tried to perform their penance were all ordered to make gifts of wax before the image of St Wilfrid in the nave and to leave their weapons on the high altar.[53] The previous year each man convicted of breaking into the home of Ralph Pigot was sentenced to lead the procession carrying a candle in one hand and in the other his bare sword held aloft 'like a cross', and then give the candle and the sword 'to the relics of St Wilfrid'.[54] The men who broke into the house of John Thomson the day after the feast of the Exaltation of Holy Cross in 1467 had to hang silver groats on the shrine of St Wilfrid.[55] Like many other invaders of the liberty, these men only submitted to judgement after first being excommunicated.

Excommunication operated first and foremost as an ecclesiastical form of outlawry, compelling people to attend the chapter court.[56] It was very often used to bring violators of the liberty of St Wilfrid to the court because many of them actually resided outside the parish and had fled the court's jurisdiction after committing their crimes. The assault on John Thomson and his servant in 1467 is a good example of how the sentence of lesser excommunication was used. Only one of the three assailants, William Howe, was actually from Ripon. John Loweswater and Thomas Bank were both from the diocese of Durham.[57] They were excommunicated until they attended the court, and their status was to be publicised on Sundays and feast days at Ripon.[58] To begin with they were placed under a ban of lesser excommunication, but if they did not

---

[51] 'trina vice publice, leviter tamen': AoC, 191.

[52] 'ut humilis pœnitens, pacienter': ibid.

[53] AoC, 11–12.

[54] 'in modum crucis' and 'reliquis Sancti Wilfridi': AoC, 2.

[55] AoC, 195.

[56] Swanson, *Church and society in late medieval England*, 179.

[57] AoC, 192.

[58] AoC, 193.

appear in Ripon within thirty days to answer the charges, they would incur the more extreme sentence of greater excommunication.[59] Their excommunication and the warning to attend the court were announced each week by the vicar who officiated at the high mass. On Sunday 11 October John Tone, vicar of Nunwick, was the vicar on duty, and six days later William Howe submitted to the judgement of the chapter court.[60] The next Sunday (18 October), Robert Sherop, vicar of Studley, publicised the same warning, and on 23 October Thomas Bank surrendered to the court's judgment.[61] William Sawley, vicar of Givendale, issued the third and final warning on the feast of St John of Beverley (25 October), and in late November John Loweswater finally appeared.[62] None of the three would have learned of his excommunication directly from the vicar at mass, not least because his excommunication would have barred him from attending. Instead, the warning would have reached them by word of mouth, and thus it took longer for the two more distant assailants to respond. John Loweswater was probably also deterred as much by fear of prosecution for other crimes as anything else. Before he could complete his penance he was arrested by the archbishop of York's bailiff, William Walworth.[63]

The scribe records the chapter's indignation at this 'injury to the said liberty and franchise of the chapter and detestable harm to the church'.[64] Ordinarily it would not accept any form of interference with its penitents. When Thomas Coke's friends tried to avenge him in 1453, they were given an even harsher penitence than his assailants.[65] In the case of John Loweswater there was much less that the chapter could do to respond. It is a revealing case because William Walworth, though he was a parishioner of Ripon, was also the archbishop of York's agent. Backed by an even more powerful ecclesiastical authority than the minster, he was in an unusual position to contradict the wishes of the chapter. In doing so he evidently feared the displeasure of the archbishop more than the wrath of St Wilfrid. At the time of this incident in 1467, George Neville was archbishop of York, and some of the leading families of the parish were his kinsmen's retainers. The chapter court had no real scope for action beyond recording its disgust in writing, and Walworth had little to fear from earthly powers.

In March 1461 John Bayne, Richard Bayne and John Wardrop were cited for violating the liberty of St Wilfrid and stealing livestock. Unlike most people accused of invading the liberty, they proposed to prove their innocence

---

[59]   AoC, 193-4.

[60]   AoC, 194.

[61]   Ibid.

[62]   Ibid.

[63]   AoC, 195.

[64]   'gravamen libertatum quoque franchizarium dictorum capituli et ecclesiæ detestabile detrimentum': ibid.

[65]   AoC, 12.

through purgation.[66] According to this judicial procedure, the accused would swear to his or her innocence, and if he or she could find an adequate number of reputable people to testify that they believed the oath, then the charges would be dropped.[67] The number of supporting witnesses, or compurgators, in the Ripon records is usually six or twelve. John, Richard and John needed twelve, whom they found, and therefore succeeded in purging themselves of the alleged invasion of the liberty.[68] This was the manner of resolution for a large number of the cases in the Ripon chapter acts book, and especially those dealing with adultery, fornication and clerical incontinence. Other defendants attempted and failed to find enough compurgators. Cited because 'she is said to be a common whore' in 1461, Joan Claton needed the oaths of twelve 'honest neighbour women, who have personal knowledge of her way of life'.[69] Whether because the number was too high or the reputation of her friends and neighbours too low, Joan was unable to defend herself from the charges. Nevertheless she refused to accept her conviction and penance, together with the reputational damage and humiliation that they entailed.[70] Another strategy to resolve cases with a minimum of public humiliation was to admit to the charges but to pay a fine in lieu of the penance. The fine was no doubt higher than the monetary cost of the penitential candle, but many feared the public shame so much that they were willing to pay.

Some parishioners tried to defend their reputations actively through the court rather than wait to be summoned in response to rumours. Depending on the situation, there were various means available. John Grange, a chantry chaplain, was cited by the court in 1454 at his own instance so that he could answer the charge that he had committed fornication with Alice Walker. He purged himself of the allegation with six witnesses, and the court set a date after which it would no longer hear testimony contradicting his oath of innocence.[71] On more than one occasion Margaret Sadler defended her reputation by having the court cite her detractors for defamation. In 1465, for example, she alleged that William Sporeer had called her an 'old whore', and though the outcome of the cases is not recorded, she had witnesses ready to testify on her behalf.[72] In certain circumstances another possibility was to petition the court to recognise a marriage. Alice Thomson attempted this in the spring of 1454, and as the testimony in this case shows her reputation had already been badly damaged by then. She claimed that around the time of midsummer

---

[66] AoC, 3.

[67] Swanson, *Church and society in late medieval England*, 152–3.

[68] AoC, 3–4.

[69] 'dicitur communis meretrix' and 'honestarum mulierum et vicinarum, ipsius vitæ noticiam habencium', AoC, 122.

[70] Ibid.

[71] AoC, 33.

[72] 'senem meretricem', AoC, 120.

the previous year, she and John Walker exchanged vows in the future tense and afterwards had intercourse.[73] At that time they were both servants in the house of John Dogson, and she said that Dogson and his wife expelled her in the middle of her term of service after they found out about her affair.[74] John Walker never admitted an exchange of vows, though he did confirm that they had had intercourse and that he talked with Alice after she had been expelled from Dogson's household. He claimed this was because he had heard that she was pregnant.[75] Alice ultimately lost her case, and was immediately cited for fornication, which due to her testimony in the matrimonial case she was forced to admit. The chapter court took pity on Alice, commuting her penance of six weeks leading the procession to a cash payment of 8d. 'by way of mercy, to avoid a scandal'.[76] Her reputation continued to be a liability, and her new master was cited for committing adultery with her shortly after the failure of her matrimonial case.[77]

As demonstrated in this brief survey of the chapter court's activities, it was an important mechanism for resolving disputes and keeping the peace. Ripon's parishioners understood the court's potential, which is why so many of them used it to enforce payments from their debtors or to defend their reputations from defamation. Because it had the powers of an archdeacon's court, the Ripon chapter court could also probate wills and serve as the court of first instance in local matrimonial disputes. For the same reason it was responsible for enforcing proper religious observance and curbing immorality. The court could, however, only be effective at prosecuting parishioners when it was well informed. Its best source of information about religious observance and marital status was the group of clergy who actually undertook the cure of souls in the parish: the vicars.

The incorporation of the vicars

In 1414 the vicars of Ripon Minster were formally incorporated. As previously, they remained responsible for the cure of souls and their duties were parcelled out in the same way, but from this point onwards they could elect a provost as their representative and use a common seal. At the same time they were provided with a new common residence and a mortmain licence enabling them to alienate rents and properties to an annual value of £5.[78] The licence was the most significant aspect of the incorporation as it regularised an existing

---

73   AoC, 32, 39.

74   AoC, 39.

75   Ibid.

76   'per viam misericordiæ propter scandalum vitandum': AoC, 34–5.

77   AoC, 33.

78   MR i. 123–8.

practice of donating rents and properties to the vicars in exchange for anniversaries. Following their incorporation the vicars could more easily distribute the burden of performing these services among themselves or hire stipendiary chaplains to handle them instead. At the same time they could legally hold the related rents and properties as opposed to shifting them around through a system of trusts as they had been doing in the decades leading up to their incorporation. The grant of a new common residence, where they were expected to live together in good order, preserving their reputations from all reproach, gave the corporation of vicars its own space outside the minster.

Reputation, status and common residences are recurring and entangled themes in the history of the Ripon vicars as well as the vicars of many other English collegiate churches and cathedrals. It is possible to glean an impression of the Ripon vicars' status in society from the objects and people named in their wills. Robert Brompton (d. 1471) bequeathed his best silver collar to the high altar and pairs of silver spoons to a number of his associates.[79] His mortuary gift to the minster was a white horse with a saddle and harness, and he could also afford a funerary monument.[80] Among the bequests of John Exilby (d. 1471) were his golden ring and his gilded drinking horn.[81] Robert Atkinson (d. 1506) mentioned his own gilded horn and silver spoon.[82] John Ely (d. 1427) bequeathed a silver collar to the shrine of St Wilfrid and gave a wide range of valuable clothing items, bedding, and accessories to his sister Margery.[83] Richard de Wakefield (d. 1399) had a servant, to whom he gave his psalter and a robe.[84] The highlights from Thomas Braithwaite's will are the featherbed, beaver hat and four beehives that he owned.[85] He was the same Thomas Braithwaite who testified in John Owlthwaite's matrimonial case in 1471. At that time he was a twenty-four-year-old deacon, so he was around fifty-seven at the time of his death in 1504 and had been a cleric in Ripon for over thirty years.[86] His decades of service in Ripon had certainly not impoverished him, and his origins were probably typical of many of the vicars and chaplains of late medieval Ripon. In contrast to the canons, who often came from magnate families and went on to become bishops, the vicars and chaplains of Ripon came from gentry or burgess families if not even humbler backgrounds. Obtaining a benefice at Ripon was their ultimate success. Regardless of their origins, the bequests listed here (a mere a fraction of those contained in each of the wills) illustrate the kind of objects that the vicars possessed which many

---

[79]   AoC, 153–4.
[80]   AoC, 153.
[81]   AoC, 169.
[82]   AoC, 326.
[83]   MR i. 329–30.
[84]   MR iv. 167.
[85]   AoC, 294.
[86]   AoC, 164–5.

other people did not. The fine clothes, silver rings and collars mentioned in these wills were symbols of their social standing that the vicars would have worn in public, while the silver spoons and gilded drinking horns would have been on display when they entertained guests. Whether or not their self-image impinged on their ability to properly fulfil their religious duties was a different matter, sometimes mentioned following visits by the archbishop of York. In 1439, for example, Archbishop Kemp reminded the minster clergy that priests with a cure of souls ought not to be distracted by secular activities such as hunting, hawking or fishing, least of all when these pursuits violated his own seigneurial fishing rights in the River Ure or constituted poaching on his hunting preserves near Ripon.[87]

Living quarters were another important symbol of the vicars' status. As David Stocker has shown, the changing social standing of the vicars in English secular cathedrals was closely connected to the architectural layout of their living quarters. He found that over time their residences developed from shared dormitories to dormitories divided into rooms, and finally into separate houses.[88] It is possible to trace a similar pattern in the history of the Ripon vicars. When he instituted them in 1303, Archbishop Corbridge desired that 'as quickly as they will comfortably be able, they should provide for themselves a house as close to the church as it can be made, in which all should at the same time abide, eat, and spend the night'.[89] Nicholas de Bondgate responded by offering a common residence, provided that the vicars perform chantry masses at the minster's altar of St John the Evangelist as well as two annual obits for him in exchange.[90] The vicars seem to have preferred not to live in their common residence, and Archbishop Greenfield (r. 1306–16) ordered them to take up residence there in a letter dated 1308.[91] This first residence no longer exists, but it was presumably one of the common dormitory types. It was located in a street to the west of the minster, originally Walkmiln Bank, its name later changed to Bedern Bank, acknowledging the presence of the common residence, the Bedern.[92] The name implies that the residence would be a house of prayer.

Common residences were intended to preserve discipline among the vicars and to guarantee that they did not spend their nights in the wrong kind of company. Ideally the vicars' dwelling would have been located in a walled quarter near the church so that the vicars would not have laypeople – especially women – as neighbours. The Ripon close was generally more

---

[87]   *MR* ii. 151.

[88]   David Stocker, 'The quest for one's own front door: housing the vicars choral at English cathedrals', *Vernacular Architecture* xxxvi (2005), 15–31.

[89]   'quam cito commode potuerint, provideant sibi de domo quantum prope ecclesiam fieri potest, in qua omnes simul maneant, comedant, et pernoctent': *MR* ii. 46.

[90]   His endowment also names the six vicars serving at Ripon in 1304: *MR* i. 119–21.

[91]   *MR* ii. 60.

[92]   Gilyard-Beer, 'Bedern Bank and the Bedern Ripon', 141.

permeable than at most English cathedrals. Rather than an inner court with the churchyard and an outer court with essential workshops and living quarters, Ripon had only an inner court with a churchyard, some workshops and a house of rented rooms, the *astelaria*. There was a wall around the churchyard but no outer court or second boundary wall. Many canons' and chaplains' residences were located in the surrounding streets, especially in Annsgate. They also lived within the churchyard itself, in the *astelaria* and above the churchyard gates. This arrangement probably made clerical behaviour more difficult to control. In cases of alleged clerical fornication, more often than not the woman involved was a resident of Annsgate or one of the other streets near the minster churchyard. The case of Thomas Hawton and Margaret Heryngton is just one example.[93] Substantial or not, rumours circulated about liaisons between these women and the clergy who lived nearby. Even when the archbishops of York could persuade the vicars to reside together, they were still concerned that they should not seek out the company of disreputable women elsewhere in the town. Another of Archbishop Kemp's commands in 1439 was that the ministers of the church, including the vicars, 'should abstain from common taverns and consorting with suspect women, and from standing, sitting, or conversing with the same altogether in suspect places and times'.[94] The most suspicious time was at night, when all activities were inherently more suspect and clergy should not be abroad unless they were visiting the sick.[95]

Ripon's vicars abandoned their first common residence sometime during the fourteenth century, perhaps to escape supervision or because they considered communal living was beneath them. Their dispersal concerned the chapter of canons just as much as it did the archbishop of York. In the early fifteenth century the two cooperated to place the vicars in a new common residence, when in the summer of 1408 the vicars had once again ceased living together, and the canons ordered them to return to their common residence at once.[96] In September the chapter threatened three rebellious vicars, John Ely, Richard Morton and John Quinton, with excommunication unless they returned to their residence.[97] The grant issued by Henry V in 1414 and confirmed by Archbishop Bowet the following year provided for a new residence for the vicars, describing its dimensions as 140 feet long and 67 feet wide.[98] It was located to the north of the minster, not far from the archbishop's palace. John Leland saw the second residence in the sixteenth century, and wrote that the

---

[93]   AoC, 36.

[94]   'a tabernis communibus et consorcio mulierum suspectarum, ac locis et temporibus suspectis stando, sedendo, vel confabulando cum eisdem omnino ... se abstineant': MR ii. 148.

[95]   Woolgar, *The senses in late medieval England*, 153.

[96]   MR iv. 149–51.

[97]   MR iv. 151–2.

[98]   MR i. 124–5.

vicars had houses 'in a fair quadrant of square stone buildid by Henry Bouet Archebisshop of York'.[99] The quadrangle described by Leland sounds very much like Stocker's most desirable category of accommodation, which gave the vicars separate rooms with their own front doors.[100] The Ripon vicars finally had such houses, and with them they received a hall and chapel too.

In 1471 the vicar John Exilby bequeathed the chapel of St Nicholas in the New Bedern a small breviary (*portiferium*) if his fellow vicars would spend 6 marks on a chaplain to say mass for him immediately after his death.[101] Exilby wanted to be remembered in the hall as well as the chapel, and therefore gave the vicars his mazer, a maplewood drinking vessel decorated with gold and silver.[102] Archbishop Bowet was well ahead of him, stipulating in 1415 that in exchange for the grant of land for their new residence, the vicars' provost should perform a daily mass for him while he was alive, an anniversary for him when he was dead, and that the vicars should say a Psalm and a prayer for him every day after dinner in their common hall.[103] At the time of Bowet's grant, the formerly rebellious John Ely was the provost of the corporation of Ripon vicars.[104] Naturally the vicars had their own cook, and Ely bequeathed him a worsted doublet and a russet tunic in his 1427 will.[105] The chantry chaplain John Birtby may have had the vicars' hall in mind when he bequeathed his 'great chair' to the New Bedern in 1477.[106] Such bequests were strands that connected the vicars to the much wider web of memory in medieval Ripon. Another strand was the perpetual anniversary: even before their incorporation in 1414 they had already become specialists in this form of commemoration.

The obit or anniversary re-enacted the funeral of a dead person in order to aid that person's soul in purgatory. The liturgical aspects of the obit were the office of the dead and the requiem mass, more or less the same as in an actual funeral. The requiem mass was beneficial to the spirit of the deceased, and so were the prayers of the people who attended the anniversary. Bells were the usual means by which obits were publicised, and those who attended might well be rewarded with food, ale, cash or clothing depending on the arrangements made by the deceased. It was customary to hold anniversaries a week, month and year after the person commemorated had died. Some people endowed perpetual obits, which required a perpetual endowment. In the parish context it was common for such endowments to be entrusted to the churchwardens,

---

[99]   *Itinerary of Leland*, i. 81.

[100]   Stocker, 'Quest for one's own front door', 29.

[101]   *AoC*, 169.

[102]   Ibid.

[103]   *MR* i. 127.

[104]   *MR* i. 126-7.

[105]   *MR* i. 330.

[106]   'magnam cathedram': *AoC*, 180-1.

who would find a chaplain to perform the necessary mass and office.[107] At Ripon there were no churchwardens; the vicars were responsible for managing the endowments of perpetual chantries and either performing the liturgy themselves or hiring a chaplain. They had begun celebrating anniversaries in the early fourteenth century and by the time that they were incorporated a century or so later they were responsible for most of Ripon's obits.

Anniversaries are usually poorly documented, but Ripon is fortunate to have a partial cartulary from about 1459 which details some of the yearly cycle of obits.[108] This fragment is now bound together with material produced by the chapter to form Ripon Cathedral, dean and chapter archives, MS Dep 1980/1 40.[109] The fragment is ten leaves in length and covers, in chronological order, that portion of the year starting at the end of June or beginning of July and running until the end of October. Each entry begins with the name or names of the founders underlined in red, followed by instructions for the obit, and finally copies of the charters used to convey the obit's endowments to the vicars. The latest date mentioned in the fragment is 8 November 1459.[110] The vicars' provost took the lead role in organising the grants of property for the new anniversaries founded after 1414, while before that date the grants were sometimes attached to some other type of foundation. In other cases they appear to have been entrusted to one or more of the contemporary vicars, who would later transfer the same rents to their successors. In 1386, for instance, Thomas Pakhardy and his wife Alice granted a rent to John Clynt, Jr, and two other vicars. Then, in 1411, Clynt granted the same rent to three other, presumably younger, vicars. Copies of all these charters are included in the cartulary.[111] Many of the older obits came into the hands of the vicars complete with complex arrangements to pay for the anniversaries because their fourteenth-century founders had combined their endowments with all kinds of other bequests to the fabric and various chantries. The vicars' provost needed the cartulary to keep track of all these different payments, both from the old foundations and their own new properties. Once he had obtained the money, the provost then had to pay it out according to the wishes of the founder. He needed to find a vicar or chaplain to perform the office of the dead and the requiem mass, and he frequently had to pay the sacrist to ring the minster bells and the town bellman to announce the obit. A few anniversaries never became the responsibility of the vicars. The new guilds of the fifteenth century founded their own obits, making them the responsibility of the guild's chantry

---

[107] Clive Burgess, '"A fond thing vainly invented": an essay on purgatory and pious motivation in late medieval England', in S. J. Wright (ed.), Parish, church, and people: local studies in lay religion, 1350–1750, London 1988, 56–84 at pp. 77–8.

[108] Idem, '"By quick and by dead": wills and pious provision in late medieval Bristol', EHR cii (1987), 837–58 at p. 840.

[109] The obit roll is fos 103a–103j. It was published in MR i. 130–50.

[110] Ripon Cathedral, dean and chapter archives, MS Dep 1980/1 40, fo. 103bv.

[111] Ibid. fo. 103cr–v.

chaplain instead. These may have multiplied afterwards, but none of the guilds' records survive so there is no way to know for certain.

The commemoration of the dead through anniversaries did not excuse the vicars from their primary duties, which were the cure of souls in the parish of Ripon and the performance of the liturgy in the minster. Vicars were required to attend matins, mass and vespers in the choir of the minster and they took turns in officiating at these services on a weekly basis. Any vicar who missed the services without permission from the precentor (the prebendary of Stanwick) was subject to a monetary fine.[112] Each vicar gave communion to the parishioners of his own prebend at their parochial altar at Easter, and he probably heard the confessions of these same parishioners in the days just beforehand. Prior to a wedding ceremony, vicars were responsible for publishing the banns for their own parishioners. If the wedding took place outside of the minster, the vicar of the relevant prebend performed the ceremony. It may be supposed that the same division of labour applied, for the most part, to baptisms and funerals. Vicars would occasionally have had to travel significant distances to visit sick and dying parishioners. By the beginning of the fifteenth century their workload had been reduced by the foundation of a large number of chapels all throughout the parish. Likewise, after 1350, the number of perpetual chantries within the minster itself began to increase, so there were ever more chaplains available to assist with the cure of souls in the town of Ripon itself.

New perpetual chantries

With the foundation of the St George chantry in 1521, Ripon Minster attained its highest total of perpetual chantries. The *Valor Ecclesiasticus* of 1536 and chantry certificates for Ripon for 1546 recorded nine and eight chantries respectively, but their figures are inaccurate because the St George chantry was hidden from the surveyors.[113] Therefore in 1521 there were ten perpetual chantry chaplains in the minster. The Holy Cross guild employed another two stipendiary chaplains, using enfeoffment as a mechanism to avoid the statute of mortmain.[114] There were no doubt a great number of other unbeneficed chaplains performing the many obits and temporary chantries established in the minster. In 1381 there were already four perpetual chantries and twelve stipendiary chaplains.[115] The clerical taxation list that provides these totals is a rare piece of evidence, so for the fifteenth century it is only possible to discuss the perpetual chantries in any detail. Their number increased sharply between 1381 and 1419, rising by three in the just twelve years from 1407 to 1419.

---

[112]   MR ii. 149-50.
[113]   MR iii. 5-7; *Chantry certificates*, ii. 354-60; TNA, E 178/2609 m 6.
[114]   TNA, E 178/2609 m 6.
[115]   TNA, E 179/63/12 m 1.

The foundation or re-foundation dates of Ripon's chantries are Plumpton Holy Trinity (1345), SS John and John (1325, re-endowed 1364), St Andrew (1230s, re-endowed 1369), St James (1407), Assumption (1416), St Thomas (1419), Sendale Holy Trinity (1466) and St George (1521). The dates of the Ladyloft and St Wilfrid chantries are unknown, but they were most likely established in the late fourteenth and late fifteenth centuries respectively. The main occupation of chantry chaplains was to perform masses for the salvation of their patrons' souls, but chantry founders also intended their chaplains to augment the liturgy of the minster and to assist the vicars in the cure of souls. This much is clear from the foundation documents of these chantries, which tend to be more explicit about the liturgical contributions of the chaplains (choir attendance and participation in processions) than about the ways in which the chaplains would aid in the cure of souls. They could have assisted the vicars in the latter by hearing confessions and by visiting the sick and the dying. Many of the chantry chaplains also held crucial administrative offices in the minster, thereby relieving the administrative burden that might otherwise have fallen on the vicars.

Chantries posed a number of logistical problems for their founders and for the minster. First, the founders had to endow the chantry with adequate income. Large sums of cash were only sufficient to endow temporary chantries, so perpetual chantries required properties or annual rents. A perpetual chantry also needed a royal licence under the statute of mortmain, and that licence cost money. The endowment of the chantry had to be maintained by its chaplain, and so did its vestments, liturgical books and plate. When the chaplain died or resigned, someone had to choose his replacement. The majority of Ripon's chantry founders designated the chapter as the patron of the chantry. They were confident that this deathless institution was the most dependable patron. A few chantries had instead gentry patrons, who were able thus to advance the careers of their clerks. The Markenfields, for example, were patrons of the St Andrew chantry. In 1410 Sir Thomas Markenfield II nominated Robert Litster, *alias* Aismunderby, to the chantry.[116] Aismunderby was a village located between Ripon and Markenfield, so Robert was presumably well known to Thomas Markenfield. John Radcliff and Ralph Batty, the two esquires who founded the St George chantry, agreed to take turns nominating their new chaplains.[117] The last chaplain of this chantry was, unsurprisingly, one Nicholas Batty.[118] Sometimes the chapter actually granted its own right of patronage temporarily to one of the gentry families. In 1487 Lady Elizabeth Malory nominated the chaplain of her chantry at Hutton Conyers to be the new chaplain of the St John chantry in the minster.[119] The right to appoint chantry

---

[116]   *MR* iv. 159–60.
[117]   *MR* i. 182–3.
[118]   TNA, E 178/2609 m 6.
[119]   *AoC*, 282.

priests was as useful to the chapter as to the gentry, and not just because the right itself could be granted to other patrons with whom the chapter wanted to preserve a good relationship. When they exercised the right of nomination themselves, it allowed the canons to provide a living for a reliable chaplain who had previously served in another, perhaps more precarious role performing anniversaries and temporary chantries for cash.

Every new perpetual chantry permanently increased the number of priests who celebrated mass in the minster. Each chantry had its assigned altar, some of which were also parochial altars used by the vicars. When the chaplains performed their chantry masses, it was primarily for the benefit of the chantry founders. However, because many of the chantries were located at altars in the transepts and nave of the minster, their masses were more accessible to the laity than the high mass performed in the choir. It was easier therefore for laypeople to attend these masses and to witness the elevation of the host. For the majority of laypeople, who only received communion once a year, seeing the elevation was an important substitute, a kind of communion by sight, and the greater the number of chantries the greater number of opportunities to behold the miracle of transubstantiation.[120] When guilds founded chantries in the minster they may have envisioned the benefit to living members as much as the dead. Chantries were flexible institutions that could be established wherever there was an available altar, making them ideal for staffing dependent chapels.[121] In fact, this was their preferred application in medieval Ripon, and it was only after a wide array of domestic and village chapels had been established that any great number of chantries was founded within the minster itself.

Religious fraternities founded many of Ripon's fifteenth-century chantries, stipulating a number of duties beyond the routine requiem mass and the office of the dead. The chaplain of the chantry of St Thomas was charged with maintaining the 23 July obit of the brethren and sisters of the fraternity of St Wilfrid, who were co-founders of the chantry.[122] He needed to provide torches and lights on various occasions, including at the feasts of Ascension, Corpus Christi and the October feast of St Wilfrid as well as for the funerals of guild members.[123] The chaplain of the Guild of the Assumption was to observe the obit of the de Lynton and Feriby families on 18 November each year.[124] As for the living, he was obliged to visit fraternity members when they were stricken with illness.[125] Like most pious people, the members of the

---

[120] Duffy, *Stripping of the altars*, 95–6; Clive Burgess, '"For increase of divine service": chantries in the parish in late medieval Bristol', *Journal of Ecclesiastical History* xxxvi (1985), 46–65 at pp. 51, 59–60; Simon Roffey, *The medieval chantry chapel: an archaeology*, Woodbridge 2007, 86–113.

[121] Alan Kreider, *English chantries: the road to dissolution*, Cambridge, MA 1979, 54–5.

[122] *MR* iv. 201.

[123] Ibid.

[124] *MR* iv. 246.

[125] *MR* iv. 245.

Assumption guild were afraid that they might die unshriven, and they hoped that their guild chaplain would spare them from this fate. They chose not to rely on their vicars, who were bound to visit the sick and dying as part of his cure of souls, but might be less reliable because of other duties. Some chantry founders expected their chaplains to take part in the communal liturgy of the minster by attending high mass and the daily office in the choir, and participating in the processions on Sundays and important feast days. These services and processions were of course already attended by the resident canons and vicars. The chaplain of the St James chantry was to attend the canonical hours on every Sunday, feast day and every day in Lent as well as to take part in all processions whenever they took place.[126] The founders of the St Thomas chantry similarly ordered their chaplain to be present in all processions, but only required attendance in the choir on Sundays and feast days.[127] As early as 1369 the chaplain of the re-founded St Andrew chantry was expected to be in the choir for matins, vespers and high mass, and also to take part in processions.[128]

When the chantries were dissolved in the 1540s, the surveyors noted that every chaplain was obliged 'to be present in the saide quyer in his habyt at matins, masse, evensonge, and processions, and in principall and double feastes and to execute and do service at the high alter as he shalbe appoynted by th'officers of the same quere'.[129] At some point, probably in the middle of the fifteenth century, these requirements had been extended to chaplains whose chantries had not originally bound them so strictly to choir attendance. Statutes from the early sixteenth century show how the chaplains had become integrated into the main body of minster clergy. In 1504 each chantry chaplain was assigned a stall in the choir by a convocation of the chapter, formalising an arrangement that had probably existed at least since the new choir stalls were completed in the 1490s.[130] To this end they were required to be proficient at plainsong, whereas their counterparts the vicars needed to be accomplished in the more difficult art of polyphonic singing.[131] The necessary musical accompaniment for polyphonic singing was provided by the minster's organist, who was frequently also the chaplain of the chantry known as the Ladyloft. In 1505 the organist was John Walker who was paid a salary of 3s. 4d.[132] At the same 1504 convocation it was decided that in processions the chaplains should be ranked

---

[126]   MR i. 164.

[127]   MR iv. 199.

[128]   MR iv. 133. For comparable examples see Burgess, '"For increase of divine service"', 52–4.

[129]   *Chantry certificates*, ii. 354–60.

[130]   MR iv. 276.

[131]   MR iv. 275.

[132]   TNA, SC 6/HENVII/1031.

by seniority in accordance with the current practice.[133] Chantry chaplains were accustomed to wear almuces of *calayber*, or squirrel fur, like cantarists at Beverley Minster, and this right was confirmed to them in perpetuity.[134] The almuce was a type of hooded cape, similar to the copes worn for special occasions, but furred and ordinarily only worn by canons in cathedrals and collegiate churches. To judge from their vestments, choir stalls and places in the procession, chantry chaplains were at least equal to the vicars in status. Together these two groups of clergy far outnumbered the canons of the minster.

The wills of Ripon's chantry chaplains are as revealing as those of the vicars and show that they were similarly wealthy and well connected. Thomas Hawk (d. 1469) made a large number of bequests to members of the Markenfield family, including a helmet, sword and battle-axe to Robert Markenfield.[135] To Margaret Markenfield, mother of Sir Thomas Markenfield III, he bequeathed 'a green coverlet that she had pawned to me'.[136] William Forster (d. 1459) bequeathed his sword, bow and arrows to his servant, William Webster.[137] His bequests call to mind some of the injunctions that Archbishop Kemp made when he visited the minster twenty years earlier and ordered the minster clergy to cease fishing in the River Ure and hunting and hawking in his park within the lordship of Ripon.[138] Kemp had also forbidden the Ripon clergy from attending services in the choir wearing swords or ornamental daggers under their habits.[139] One significant difference between the vicars and the chantry chaplains of Ripon is that the chaplains never had a common residence. They lived in rented rooms or houses provided for them as part of their benefice. Their wills often list the contents of their houses, giving a sense of what their kitchens and bedrooms contained. Robert Laton's will describes his rich bedding, which he bequeathed to Alice Croser. He owned a featherbed with a bolster, a bedspread, two linen sheets, two covers and a curtain to hang over the bed.[140] He also gave Alice a cow, and her servant Margaret was to receive a red and silver ornamental girdle.[141] Many of Laton's kitchen items were already in the possession of Elizabeth Carlisle, who was to keep them after his death. These included a number of pots, pans, basins, ewers, a candelabrum and a table.[142]

Chaplains had many potential sources of income. On top of their salaries, they could make money by attending funerals and obits. These services were

---

[133] *MR* iv. 278.
[134] *MR* iv. 279–80.
[135] *AoC*, 137.
[136] 'unum coverlet veridis coloris quod mihi fuit impignoratum': *AoC*, 136.
[137] *AoC*, 86.
[138] *MR* ii. 151.
[139] *MR* ii. 149.
[140] *AoC*, 178.
[141] *AoC*, 178–9.
[142] *AoC*, 179.

numerous enough in Ripon to be profitable to those who regularly attended.[143] Like Thomas Hawk, some chaplains apparently lent money, and even used the chapter court to enforce payments from their debtors. In 1454 Thomas Sherburne of Bondgate was cited at the instance of the chaplain John Birtby for failing to repay the 15s. 4d. that he owed.[144] John Grange had Richard Spencer cited in December 1453 over a debt of 3s., which Spencer denied that he owed.[145] Grange was not a very popular chaplain at the time, perhaps because he was such a litigious creditor. The previous month the chapter court cited Walter Rede for assault at Grange's instance, after Grange alleged that Rede violently laid hands on him near the east door of the church.[146] Rede confessed and was given three weeks leading the procession as penance.[147] The other obvious way for chantry chaplains to augment their income was to take on additional administrative tasks in the minster, each of which brought with it a significant salary.

Administration

The minster had three main departments: the treasury, the chamber and the fabric. Each of these had at least one paid overseer, and the fabric ordinarily had two wardens. The term of office was one year, at the end of which the official or wardens produced a parchment account roll. Many of these still exist, providing a crucial source of evidence about how these departments functioned as well as many other aspects of the minster's history. From the period between 1370 and 1530 there are twenty-four extant fabric rolls, twelve chamberlain's accounts and four treasurer's rolls. When a number of rolls from the same period survive, they show that the office-holders remained fairly stable from year to year. They also show that the same man could hold more than one office at the same time. The office-holders are usually identified as chaplains, and although a few of them appear to have been canons or vicars at the time that they held office, the majority were probably chaplains of perpetual chantries or stipendiary chaplains.

The fabric wardens hired building craftsmen to maintain the minster church and the many properties owned by the fabric fund. The modest income of the fabric, drawn mainly from gifts and rental properties, was enough to cover these expenses but woefully inadequate to support a major building campaign. The fall of the central tower in 1450 forced the wardens to find additional income, as did the better documented campaign to replace the nave between

---

[143]   Kathleen Wood-Legh, *Perpetual chantries in Britain*, Cambridge 1965, 203.
[144]   AoC, 34.
[145]   AoC, 26.
[146]   Ibid.
[147]   Ibid.

1503 and 1522. The fabric actually created a second, special account for the first phase of the tower repairs between 1453 and 1457, but no evidence survives for how they handled the later phases of construction. Among its many unusual features, this roll describes how the residue of the special fund was paid into the ordinary fabric account at midsummer in 1457. The transaction took place publicly, with many important benefactors of the works as witnesses. These included Roger Ward, William Malory, Ralph Radcliff and William Wrampayn.[148] These men therefore had some influence over the works even if they did not manage the accounts. The nave campaign in the early sixteenth-century was heavily subsidised by the canons and the chamberlain, and the resident canon Andrew Newman supervised the campaign with the two ordinary wardens as his deputies. The major works of the fifteenth and sixteenth centuries required careful oversight and detailed records, and it was the many chaplains of the minster who provided this necessary clerical expertise. As the volume and detail of record keeping increased, the look of the final account rolls changed.

The length, appearance and content of the fabric rolls transform dramatically between the end of the fourteenth century and the beginning of the sixteenth. The earliest rolls are longer and more detailed, but much plainer in appearance. The headings are no more ostentatious than the rest of the entries. By the middle of the fifteenth century the headings feature elaborate capital letters ornamented by pen flourishes, the marginal headings are more distinct and the capital 'S' in 'Summa' for the total of all receipts and expenses is much larger and more decorative than in the many sub-sections. In the sixteenth-century rolls the capital 'C' of 'Compotus', the first word of the heading, becomes a vast sprawl of pen flourishes filling much of the top corner of the roll. Yet while the appearance of the later accounts is much more sumptuous than the earlier ones, their content is far less detailed. The names of building craftsmen, so frequently found in the late fourteenth-century rolls, are largely absent. The proliferation of supplementary account books explains the difference in content. The later rolls often refer the auditor to paper notebooks and schedules (*quaternus, cedula*) where the details were recorded. The only surviving example is a paper account book from the latter stages of the building campaign of the 1520s. It is fourteen folios long and shows that wage rates were calculated down to fractions as small as one quarter of a day.[149]

The names of twenty different wardens are known from the period between 1370 and 1530. The wardens are usually identified vaguely as chaplains in their account rolls, and for the most part it is impossible to identify their benefices or even to be certain that they had one. Presumably the perpetual chantry chaplains, of whom there were an increasing number during the fifteenth century, were in a position to take on these roles. Other wardens may in fact

---

[148] MR iii. 164.

[149] Ripon Cathedral, dean and chapter archives, MS Dep 1980/1 78; MR iii. 198–206.

have been stipendiary chaplains, for whom the additional 20s. per year salary was essential to augment what they could make saying masses for the dead. Only John Ely appears to have been a vicar at the same time that he was a fabric warden (1424–6). John de Walkingham in the 1390s and John Preston in the early sixteenth century were both chaplains of the Plumpton Holy Trinity chantry when they were fabric wardens. John Rednes was probably chaplain of the Ladyloft chantry in the minster when he was fabric warden in the first decades of the fifteenth century. He combined these two posts with the office of sub-treasurer. John de Dene is the last identifiable canon to act as fabric warden, and he held that office in the first decades of the fifteenth century before most of the new chantries were established.

The prebendary of Monkton was customarily the minster's treasurer, but in practice an appointed sub-treasurer actually kept the accounts.[150] The sub-treasurer handled the purchase of all material required for the sacraments and religious services in Ripon Minster. He needed to acquire huge numbers of communion wafers and many gallons of wine just for the regular round of masses. In 1401 John Rednes purchased 13,000 wafers, which would have been sufficient for more than thirty-five priests to say mass once every day all year.[151] The next year he bought 14,000.[152] Apparently these were all intended for use by the clergy, since he bought three bushels of flour to make wafers for the communion of parishioners at Easter. In 1470 Christopher Kendale bought two bushels of flour to make the wafers for Easter communion and still purchased more than 11,000 other wafers 'for the celebration of divine services'.[153] These figures are the best indication that there was still a large number of stipendiary chaplains in the fifteenth century, and probably an even greater number than there had been in 1381. The sub-treasurer's other regular expenses were chrism, incense, charcoal and wax, not to mention the ale, spices and sweetmeats that were distributed to parishioners on Holy Thursday. The sub-treasurer paid the clerks to fill the font, clean the bells and relics, bake the Easter communion wafers, and burn the old Palm Sunday palms. His income was mainly customary fees related to the sacraments or other rituals performed by the clergy, namely weddings, baptisms and the churching of women, the plough money collected at the start of the agricultural year in January, and the wax left in the church at the feast of the Purification, before the images of the saints, and at funerals or anniversaries. In the few extant account rolls the sub-treasurer overspent his income and the shortfall was made up from other sources.

Ripon's chamberlain paid the minster clergy their regular salaries and other sums for particular services. The resident canons also received their stipends

---

[150] MR ii. 110.
[151] MR iii. 211.
[152] MR iii. 213.
[153] 'pro celebracione divinorum': MR, iii. 216.

from the chamberlain, who in addition paid the lectors at Christmas, the lesser clergy for processing in their copes on the three most important feast days, and so on. The chamberlain hired all manner of other personnel for special tasks on feast days. Among them were minstrels, players and the man who carried the dragon in the Rogation procession. The chamberlain's income came from a range of sources, including rental properties, annual fees from dependent chapels and the Lenten fines of the parishioners, as well as gifts at particular services, in chests, and before many saints' images in the minster. He also received the gifts given at weddings, baptisms and churchings. These gifts were sums of money in excess of the customary fee paid to the treasurer on these occasions. The income of the chamberlain far exceeded that of the treasurer and fabric. In 1478-9, for example, this sum was nearly £150.[154] It was for this reason that when the nave of the minster was completely rebuilt, the chamberlain regularly paid the residue of his account to the fabric wardens at the end of the year. At £3 6s. 8d. the salary of the chamberlain was also higher than the salaries of the fabric wardens (£1) and sub-treasurers (£2). The chamberlain also paid the salary (£1) of another official, the shrine keeper or warden of St Wilfrid's head. Some accounts name two wardens of Wilfrid's head, in which case they appear to have split the salary.

By the late fifteenth century the chamberlains were farming their incomes on a large scale. In particular the minute tithes – in this case flax, hemp and poultry – were being leased to collectors who, in exchange for an agreed sum, could keep whatever else they gathered. Many of the farmers were local lords. In 1478 Christopher Ward farmed the minute tithes of Skelton and Newby, Lady Margaret Pigot farmed the tithes of Clotherholme, and Sir Thomas Markenfield farmed the tithes of Aismunderby, Ingerthorpe, Wallerthwaite, Markington and Markenfield.[155] Margaret Pigot also farmed the chamberlain's forest tithes in the wood of Clotherholme.[156] These leases gave the local gentry additional sources of wealth, converting some of what would have been church profits into their own profits and helping them to build up their power locally.[157] Many of these same families farmed the gifts given by other parishioners who used their domestic chapels, meaning that they had significant financial interests in the spiritualities of their own domains. The Walworths, who were not manorial lords but were nevertheless a parish gentry family, farmed the great tithes, altarage, and minute tithes of the important chapel of Pateley Bridge in Nidderdale. The fee for these was £6 13s. 4d. in 1478.[158] Even more than the knights and esquires of Ripon parish, the Walworths depended on leasing tithes and agricultural estates and holding office for the archbishop

[154] MR iii. 256.
[155] MR iii. 254.
[156] MR iii. 255.
[157] Swanson, *Church and society in late medieval England*, 239.
[158] MR iii. 255.

of York to sustain their wealth and influence. Their unflinching devotion to the archbishops was on display when William Walworth arrested one of the chapter's penitents in 1467.[159] He must have learned this quality from his father John Walworth, whose loyalty to Archbishop Kemp embroiled him in a conflict with the tenants of Knaresborough in the early 1440s.[160]

The late fifteenth-century chapter acts show that there were occasional conflicts between one family and another, but that the gentry and the chapter were rarely if ever at odds with one another. Farming the small tithes evidently suited both parties equally well, not to mention the many reductions in rent that were made to encourage the gentry as well as townspeople to lease the chamberlain's properties. The expense sections of the chamberlain's accounts record these reductions, showing that properties and land in and around the town were being let to the Malories, Nortons, Wards and others at lower rates than the chamberlain thought that they were worth.[161] The fabric wardens had to use similar strategies to keep their properties occupied from the second half of the fourteenth century onwards. Both they and the chamberlains spent an appreciable portion of their income every year on maintaining their rental properties. Another common method of making properties more attractive to potential tenants was to improve the quality of roofs by replacing thatch with slate.[162] In the 1390s the fabric wardens went one step further and entirely replaced one of their houses in Annsgate. The project cost more than £20 in total, and it would have taken thirty years of rent payments at the full 13s. 4d. rate to recover the costs.[163] Few if any of the fabric wardens held office for that length of time, so it was a strategy intended to benefit the minster in the long term rather than to balance the books of any given warden. The beneficiaries of the fabric's rental practices included not only the gentry but also the craftsmen and other burgesses who lived in Ripon.

The fabric wardens most frequently needed the services of carpenters to repair woodwork in the minster and plumbers to work on the roof. They also periodically hired glaziers and masons. These craftsmen and the many unskilled labourers could be found in and around the town of Ripon. Specialist work required expertise from elsewhere, such as the bell-founders and clockmakers of York, and major construction projects necessitated the hiring of a greater number of masons together with a master mason to draw up the designs. For master carpenters they did not need to look further afield than the parish itself. In 1520, when Christopher Scune was employed as the consulting master mason, the carpenters working at Ripon were overseen by William

---

[159]   AoC, 195.

[160]   Wilcock, 'Local disorder in the Honour of Knaresborough', 50–2.

[161]   MR iii. 257–8.

[162]   Christopher Dyer, *An age of transition? Economy and society in England in the later Middle Ages*, Oxford 2005, 154.

[163]   MR iii. 116, 120.

Carver, alias Bromfleet.[164] A few years earlier, in 1518, he had been contracted by John Radcliff to build a loft and carve an image for his new St George chantry.[165] Again in 1523 William Bromfleet was in charge of the carpenters rebuilding the high altar and St Wilfrid's shrine.[166] His fourteenth-century predecessor, William Wright, was a Ripon carpenter and timber merchant who built the new roodloft in 1399 and sold timber to the fabric in 1391.[167] Ripon's plumbers could also double as its lead suppliers. In the last decades of the fourteenth century the minster's chief lead suppliers and plumbers were the Bettys family from Sawley.[168] Only the more detailed fabric rolls of the late fourteenth and early fifteenth century actually list the names of suppliers, but they indicate that the wealthier craftsmen, merchants of the town and even the clergy supplied building materials. In all these matters the fabric wardens controlled the purse strings of their account, sometimes even paying themselves for supplies as John de Dene did when he sold a tree to the fabric in 1396.[169] It is unfortunate that the nature and survival rate of the records allows for no more than a general impression of the impact that the minster and its office-holders had on the local economy and urban landscape.

The career of Christopher Kendale

One of the many chaplains who at one time or another controlled the minster's finances and presided over its court was Christopher Kendale. He is also one of the better documented chaplains of late medieval Ripon, and because there are so few examples of clerics whose social origins are known, it is worth considering his career in detail.[170] He is already a chaplain the first time that he is mentioned in any of the extant records: a canon fee court roll dated February 1449.[171] Since he must have been at least twenty-four years old when he was ordained, Christopher Kendale had to have been born sometime before 1425.[172] At that time his family's fortunes had recovered from their low point during the rebellious years at the start of Henry IV's reign. In June 1405 the king had made John Norton warrener of Ripon for life after expelling Hugh Kendale from the same office in a settling of scores after Archbishop Scrope's

---

[164] MR iii. 181.
[165] MR iv. 294.
[166] MR iii. 198–206.
[167] MR iii. 133; John Harvey, *English mediaeval architects: a biographical dictionary down to 1550*, Gloucester 1984, 350.
[168] MR iii. 102, 110, 124; *Poll taxes*, iii. 434.
[169] MR iii. 124.
[170] Swanson, *Church and society in late medieval England*, 36.
[171] Ripon Cathedral, dean and chapter archives, MS Dep 1980/1 288.3
[172] Swanson, *Church and society in late medieval England*, 24.

rebellion. Hugh had been supported by John Scrope and William Plumpton, whereas Norton had been a loyal adherent of the earl of Westmoreland.[173] By the time of Hugh Kendale's expulsion, Sir William Plumpton had already been executed for his role in the rebellion.[174] Hugh Kendale was almost certainly Christopher Kendale's father. Christopher's grandfather, Robert Kendale, died in 1426. His will refers to his son, Hugh, and his daughter-in-law, Alice.[175] When Alice died in 1451 her heirs were John and Christopher the chaplain.[176] Alice (née Gyliot) was one of the co-heiresses of Markington, and her son John would later become lord of Markington after the death of her sister in 1457. The manor was in the south of the parish of Ripon, not far from the archbishop of York's hunting preserves in Thornton and Nidderdale. It had been held by Alice's ancestors, the Gyliot family, for a very long time: William Gyliot was one of the Marmion tenants named in the 1229 inquest.[177] The Kendale family's most substantial neighbours were the Markenfields and the Walworths. In wealth and status the Kendales were much more similar to the Walworths than the Markenfields, who were one of the truly elite families of knights in Yorkshire.

Christopher Kendale's clerical career at Ripon is documented primarily by court records, and his great talent appears to have been in administration. While he is commonly referred to as 'chaplain', it is not clear from any surviving records whose chaplain he was before 1488 when he became chaplain of the St Thomas chantry. After his first appearance in the court roll of 1449, he is named as an executor of wills throughout the 1450s and 1460s. He was at this time occasionally called by the court to answer for his alleged misconduct. In September 1454 he was cited to answer the charge that he had committed adultery with a woman named Katherine Barber, who lived in Crossgate by the western edge of the churchyard.[178] At the same time he was charged with failing to attend the processions on Sundays and feast days, which he was obliged to do by his oath.[179] A decade later he began to acquire the powers of spiritual jurisdiction that had been directed against him on this occasion. In 1464 he was part of the delegation that visited Stanwick parish church, and in July 1467 he was made commissary of the chapter court.[180] As such he was empowered to act in its stead in spiritual matters. In effect this meant that all the archidiaconal powers that were already concentrated in the hands of the senior resident canon passed to Kendale, who never rose higher in the ecclesiastical

---

173   CPR Henry IV, London 1903-9, iii. 19.
174   Keith Dockray, 'Plumpton Family (per. c.1165-c.1550)', ODNB.
175   Borthwick Institute, York, probate register 2, fo. 501v.
176   AoC, 208.
177   MR i. 62.
178   AoC, 33.
179   Ibid.
180   AoC, 215-16, 218-23.

hierarchy than chantry chaplain. One of the more intriguing episodes in his career as commissary took place in 1468, when the court heard a matrimonial case between John Wardell of Aldborough and Margaret, the daughter of John Kendale.

Wardell initiated the case in person before the chapter court in the chapter house on 20 September, alleging that he and Margaret Kendale had exchanged vows in the present tense.[181] Margaret was not in court at this time and so the chapter's bailiff was to summon her to answer the charge on 8 October, when the court would meet in the chapel of St Mary, Stonebridgegate, instead.[182] This ancient chapel had been the focus of the Guild of SS Mary, Wilfrid and All Saints at the end of the fourteenth century. More recently, it was probably the 'small nearby chapel' where the minster clergy were forced to hold their services for a time after the fall of the minster's main tower in 1450.[183] No reason is given for changing the location to the Ladykirk, which incidentally had become the preferred burial place of the Kendale family. When John Kendale died the following year he asked to be buried 'by the bodies of my parents', and his mother Alice had specified the churchyard of this chapel as her burial place in her own will nearly twenty years before.[184] The Ladykirk had clearly become central to the family's memory and hence its honour. This same honour was at stake in the matrimonial dispute between Margaret Kendale and John Wardell. John Kendale needed no reminding, but perhaps the intention was to impress Sir Richard Aldborough. He was a knight and Marmion tenant who resided outside the parish but held lands from the chapter. Sir Richard had sworn his oath of fealty to St Wilfrid and the chapter on the feast of the Ascension in 1466.[185] He may have been present at the time this case was heard because he owed suit of court to the chapter, but at Wardell's instance he also tried to mediate the dispute. Margaret Kendale vehemently denied that any exchange of vows had been made and Christopher Kendale ruled there should be a continuance, and subsequently also decided that a separate commission should be created to investigate the case.[186] As much as he might have liked to try to guarantee a favourable outcome for his niece, he was aware of the legal issues that could arise.

Kendale appointed John Levesham, rector of Easington, to head the commission.[187] On 23 November the commission was prepared to present its findings to the chapter court, now meeting in the chapter house again. On this occasion Margaret swore that they had not exchanged vows, and John Wardell

---

[181] AoC, 199–200.

[182] AoC, 200.

[183] 'modica vicina capella': MR ii. 152.

[184] 'juxta sepulcra parentum meorum': AoC, 208, 227.

[185] AoC, 244.

[186] AoC, 200.

[187] AoC, 200-1.

withdrew his claim and agreed never to pursue it again.[188] Levesham accordingly ruled in Margaret's favour and issued her with letters testimonial to that effect.[189] This was the best possible result for Margaret Kendale, especially as the court of appeal would have been York, which tended to favour the plaintiff and presume the existence of a marriage.[190] The matter was clearly decided outside the court, which only met at the end of November when Wardell had decided to abandon his claim. Richard Aldborough did not attend on this final occasion because his support was no longer necessary. Christopher Kendale may have given his official powers in the matter to John Levesham, but the Kendales and their friends must have been actively working to convince Wardell to abandon his claim in the meantime.

In the spring of 1472 Kendale was made sub-treasurer of the minster, having already served as warden of the special fabric fund in the 1450s.[191] Afterwards he was chamberlain at times, while simultaneously retaining the office of sub-treasurer until 1488 when he resigned it to become chaplain of the St Thomas chantry.[192] Three years later he was dead. The chapter acts book records that Emma and John Kendale appeared before the court on 17 June 1491, renounced the will, and left Christopher's goods to be committed to administration.[193] As such there is no record of his intended bequests. It was an unfortunate and ironic outcome for a chaplain who had faithfully undertaken the burden of executing the wills of at least half a dozen people during his career; indeed his activity as an executor of wills is almost as well documented as his role in the chapter court. A number of these wills were those of his fellow clergy. Kendale's attitude towards processions had improved by 1466 when he and his fellow executors of the will of William Rodez agreed to buy a lavish processional cross in his honour. Made by a goldsmith in York, the gilded and enamelled silver cross had images of Mary and John flanking the crucified Christ and cost £23.[194] Even this huge expenditure did not exhaust the residue of the deceased's finances, so they spent the rest on distributions to Ripon's hospitals, the production of two new missals and the wages of two of the masons working at Ripon for two years.[195] Kendale himself was sometimes one of the beneficiaries of a will, as in 1459 when the chaplain William Forster bequeathed him a small dinner table with trestles.[196] It is hardly surprising that he was executor of his mother's will, or that his brother John charged him

---

188 AoC, 201-2.

189 AoC, 202-3.

190 Donahue, *Law, marriage, and society*, 76, 84.

191 MR iv. 4-6.

192 AoC, 284; MR iv. 179.

193 AoC, 267.

194 AoC, 205-6.

195 AoC, 206.

196 AoC, 87.

with the education of his children.[197] He was even executor to John Walworth (d. 1459), the head of a prominent family from Thornton near Markington.[198]

Christopher Kendale and the other chaplains supplied the minster with the majority of its administrators in the fifteenth century. Together with the resident canons and the vicars, they were the institution that preserved the rights, honour and income of St Wilfrid's church. In so doing they stood as the visible representatives of Ripon's patron saint. They also honoured Wilfrid, the other saints and above all Christ, when they celebrated the liturgy in the minster. The sacramental roles of the minster's clergy shaped the religious character of the parish of Ripon, and they were at least as important as their administrative ones. The sacraments and other closely related ceremonies are the focus of the following chapter, which examines the religious practices of Ripon's parishioners.

---

[197] AoC, 207-9, 227-9.
[198] Borthwick Institute, probate register 2, fo. 394r.

3

The Minster and its Parishioners: The Living

Medieval religion was structured around the seven sacraments: baptism, confirmation, ordination, marriage, extreme unction, penance and the eucharist. Penance and the eucharist were the most regularly repeated of the two. On Sundays and feast days laypeople encountered the eucharist as a component of the mass, though for the most part they only consumed the consecrated host once a year, at Easter. They prepared themselves for this act by making their annual confessions and undertaking the penance assigned to them by their confessors. The other five sacraments marked changes of status and are therefore often interpreted as rites of passage.[1] Through baptism in the parish font an infant became a member of the parish as well as of the wider Church. Membership brought certain obligations, including the payment of tithes, church attendance on Sundays and feast days, and annual confession and communion. Marriages were solemnised in parish churches after the priest had ascertained that the couple were in fact free to wed. Similarly, when a person died after properly receiving extreme unction, the parish churchyard was the most likely place of burial. Most laypeople would look to receive the sacraments from the hands of their parish clergy at their parish churches, so that in theory the 'model of the Christian extended life course – from conception to afterlife – was fully realised in the materiality of the parish church and cemetery'.[2] The parish church was also a conduit of saintly help. It would normally have an image of its patron saint and any number of other saints' images. The images of the saints helped laypeople to seek their patronage and honour them. Groups such as guilds formed for fellowship, mutual support, moral development and the veneration of their own particular patron saints.

In practice the workings of the parish of Ripon were more complex, but the principle still applies: to understand how the parishioners of Ripon practised their religion, it is necessary to determine where they ordinarily heard mass and where they received the other sacraments. When focusing on sacraments and saints, it is immediately apparent that religious practices varied significantly depending on an individual's status, proximity to the minster and membership of a guild. Above all, these factors affected when and where a parishioner heard mass. It was very rare for the majority of parishioners to be in the minster together at the same time. Chapels divided the vast parish into smaller, more manageable units under the oversight of the minster and its clergy. Chapels

---

[1]   Gilchrist, *Medieval life*, 182.
[2]   Ibid. 169.

76

were central features of the many smaller units of parishioners – gentry house-holds and villages – that made up the larger parish. The town of Ripon had its own chapels, and the establishment of a number of guilds around the year 1400 endowed many more accessible masses within the minster. In the course of the fifteenth century guilds and their masses, in particular those of the Holy Cross guild, transformed the minster building into a more recognisably parochial church. A similar pattern of development is evident in the proliferation of saints' images to be found there. Guild members and townspeople alike were beneficiaries of these developments. For parishioners who lived further afield, the village chapels were in most respects their parish churches. Both the guilds and the chapels served as the focus of many communal identities without ever fully supplanting the minster's control over the sacraments or the idea of a unified parish with Wilfrid and the chapter of canons at its head. Aside from one exceptionally distant chapel, the minster largely retained control over baptism, feast day church attendance and burial within the parish. Only the wealthiest knights and esquires could, if they wished, escape the minster's oversight.

Liturgy and laity in the minster

The late twelfth-century architect of Ripon Minster designed it as a collegiate church and architectural setting for the shrine of St Wilfrid. The church was modelled after York Minster, which had recently been renovated by Archbishop Roger Pont l'Evêque.[3] The building was intended primarily to meet the needs of its clerical community and only secondarily to serve the laypeople of the parish. Like the size and structure of the parish of Ripon, the minster building was out of step with developments in the English parish system. The old form of parish organisation, in which a minster church with a community of clergy served a large territory, had been retained as the official structure during the reign of William the Conqueror, but was rapidly eroded by the creation of many smaller parishes, each with its own parish church, in the decades between about 1070 and 1120.[4] Ripon was never divided in this way, and although it was not unique, it was an anachronism. Adaptation – by its clergy and its parishioners – characterises its later history. The reasons for this were manifold: changing ideas about pastoral care, new forms of piety and devotion, the desire for posthumous commemoration, and the need to display social status. Ripon's laypeople participated in the liturgy of the minster, but how and when depended to a large degree on the status and identity of the individual, not to mention where he or she lived. By the end of the thirteenth century, the parish of Ripon was filled with chapels that could be used by local people to pray and,

---

[3]   Harrison and Barker, 'Ripon Minster', 49–51.
[4]   Blair, The Church in Anglo-Saxon society, 368–9.

if they could afford to hire a chaplain, hear mass. The chapter licensed these chapels for regular use, provided that the obligation to attend the minster on certain major feast days was observed. Thus, while attendance swelled on feast days, the parishioners who used the minster more regularly were probably those who lived closest to the church. Whether in church or chapel, the central and regularly repeated feature of medieval religion was the mass, its significance as a social phenomenon well established.[5]

The priests of Ripon Minster celebrated thousands of masses every year. Some of these were the high masses performed in the choir on Sundays and feast days, but the majority were less elaborate low masses said at the many subsidiary altars in the building. The feast day and Sunday high masses were similar in most respects, though the holiday processions were sometimes grander than on Sundays and the crowds of people in the minster during high mass were largest on the major feast days. The crucial moment in every mass was the consecration, which turned the wafer into the body of Christ. Laypeople, who spent most of the mass reciting their own prayers, were supposed to look up at the moment of consecration and see Christ in the form of the consecrated host, so it was primarily at this point in the liturgy that the laity and the clergy intersected.[6] Most of the time laypeople took communion in this way – by sight alone – rather than by actually consuming the host. Only the elites took communion more often than the prescribed once a year.[7] Seeing the host was therefore their chief form of interaction with it most of the time. Moreover, since it was believed that the sense of sight operated like a form of touching, the act of gazing at the host was a powerful form of interaction in its own right.[8] Various blessings could be obtained by attending the mass and witnessing the consecration. These included protection for travellers, safe delivery for mothers in labour and a guarantee against sudden death.[9] Individual experience of the mass, including the likelihood of seeing the elevation, depended on the circumstances and the condition of the individual, especially his or her social status and gender. It also depended on the type of church and altar used for the mass. In Ripon the high masses in the choir were grander but more remote than the many less elaborate masses at its other altars, and there were rules about who could be present when it took place.

High mass in the choir of Ripon Minster was very different from high mass in the average parish church. One notable difference was the richness of the liturgy, which developed over the course of the fifteenth century as the number of chantry chaplains increased and the chapter raised the required

---

[5] See John Bossy, 'The mass as a social institution, 1200–1700', *P&P* c (Aug. 1983), 29–61; Duffy, *Stripping of the altars*, 91–130; Miri Rubin, *Corpus Christi: the eucharist in late medieval culture*, Cambridge 1991, 12–82.

[6] Duffy, *Stripping of the altars*, 117–18.

[7] Ibid. 93.

[8] Woolgar, *The senses in late medieval England*, 148; Rubin, *Corpus Christi*, 290.

[9] Duffy, *Stripping of the altars*, 100.

level of singing ability. When they met in March 1504, the canons decided that potential vicars and deacons should be able 'to sing plainsong and pricksong', and new chantry chaplains should be capable of singing plainsong at least.[10] In May of the same year, they decided that the clergy should sing the Psalms with suitable pauses 'for the praise of God and the devotion of those listening'.[11] The minster had an organ from at least the late fourteenth century. In the enclosed space of the church, with the acoustics found only in large gothic churches, the music of Ripon's liturgy would have been louder and more overawing than most other sounds that people were likely to hear.[12] Although there was more to hear, there was less to see once the procession entered the choir. The standard arrangement in a late medieval parish church was to have a nave and a chancel, separated from each other by the rood screen. The nave was where laypeople stood or sat, depending on whether or not they had installed seating in their churches. The rood screens that separated the chancel from the nave generally had a solid lower portion, called the dado, and an open upper half so that the actions of the priest in the chancel were visible to the laity in the nave. Even the dado could be pierced by slits so that people kneeling before it during the mass could observe the moment of consecration.[13] Architectural arrangements were very different at Ripon. It had a full choir with two ranks of stalls on either side, the choir itself being so much larger than the chancel of an ordinary parish church that many of the smaller parish churches of England could actually have been able to fit inside it. Moreover, a solid stone screen called a pulpitum separated the choir from the main body of the minster. Unless the door to this screen remained open during the mass it was not possible for anyone outside the choir to see what was happening within. Few if any laypeople were able to see the moment of elevation during the Ripon high mass unless they had special access to the choir.

The most substantial evidence for laypeople in the choir during the mass comes from the early fourteenth century. In October 1312 Archbishop Greenfield (r. 1304–15) wrote to the chapter detailing his concerns about allowing laypeople in the choir during services. He thought that they were a distraction and commanded that 'no women, religious or secular, nor laypeople except for great and noble persons' be present there during mass.[14] Greenfield does not name any individuals, but presumably the local knights fit his definition of *magnas et nobiles personas*. These knights were also the most likely to establish their own domestic chapels, which were representative of

---

[10] 'cantare cantum planum et eciam fractum': MR iv. 275–6.

[11] 'ad laudem Dei et deuocionem audiencium': MR iv. 279.

[12] Woolgar, The senses in late medieval England, 66.

[13] Duffy, Stripping of the altars, 97.

[14] 'nullas ... mulieres, religiosas vel sæculares, nec laicos nisi magnas et nobiles personas': MR ii. 71.

their status, not to mention more convenient for them.[15] As a counterpart to their possession of private chapels, permission to attend the high mass in the choir affirmed the status of these men when they did appear in the minster in person. No later archbishop ever mentioned the issue, most likely because during the course of the fourteenth century most of Ripon's leading families established perpetual chantries in their domestic chapels and heard mass there, rather than in the minster, during much of the year.

Aside from the elevation, four features of the high mass involved the laity directly: the procession before the mass, the bidding of the bedes before the offertory, the kissing of the pax after the consecration and the distribution of blessed bread at the end of the mass. These four are essential to any discussion of the social significance of the mass.[16] The Ripon high mass procession, with its capacity to express social hierarchy, discipline parishioners and incorporate the memory of the dead in the mass, is the most remarkable of the four. The main participants in the procession, which made a circuit of the whole minster in order to bless all the altars with holy water, were the clergy, including the chantry chaplains. Their presence was intended by many of the fifteenth-century chantry founders to represent their contributions to the liturgy of the minster. The chaplains were probably well known to those who regularly attended divine services in the minster, and they may also have worn insignia to identify their benefactors. Indeed, the chaplain of the St George chantry was 'to have oon abbit after suche fourme as the roode priests within the saide Churche hath, with Saynt George on horsbake upon the breast of the said abbit inbrowderid'.[17]

Heraldry was displayed along the path of the procession and possibly also on some of its participants. In 1503 Ralph Pigot bequeathed new almuces of *calayber* to all the ministers of the choir.[18] His will does not mention whether or not his heraldry appeared on these vestments, but the bequest would have given him that opportunity. In any case the Pigot arms (*sable, three mill picks argent*) were carved within the choir and on the screen which separated the choir from the crossing. The same screen displays the heraldry of the Wards of Givendale and a merchant's mark, to name just two further symbols of benefaction. The tombs of the great families of the parish, also adorned with heraldry, likewise sat along the route of the procession. Together with the tombs of other parishioners and the minster clergy, they clustered around the altars in the transepts and at the east end of the nave, and were therefore impossible for the procession to avoid as it moved from one altar to the next and then into the choir. The high mass processions were clearly charged with the kind of social significance normally ascribed by scholars to feast day processions,

[15]   Nigel Saul, 'The gentry and the parish', in Clive Burgess and Eamon Duffy (eds), *The parish in late medieval England*, Donington 2006, 243–60 at p. 246.

[16]   For an overview of the social implications of the mass see Bossy, 'The mass as a social institution', 29–61.

[17]   *MR* i. 183.

[18]   *TE* iv. 214.

especially those of Corpus Christi. In contrast to annual feast day processions, the regularity of the Sunday processions at Ripon gave them a subtler power to reinforce social hierarchy, and one that was less open to challenge than the ranking of guilds in Corpus Christi processions or play cycles. At the pinnacle of society in Ripon were the clergy, the great families of the parish and the guilds that founded chantries in the minster. The route and the participants in the procession incorporated all three in a regularly repeated ritual representation of society that was all the more hegemonic for being so commonplace.[19]

The bidding of the bedes and the gifts of penitents belong to the same ritual articulation of hierarchy and power. The bidding of the bedes was a call to prayer, made by the priest before the offertory of the mass, in which he exhorted the laity to pray for the most important leaders of the Church and rulers of the kingdom, and afterward the important benefactors of the church and recently deceased parishioners.[20] In this way the bidding prayers situated the local social order within the universal order of Christendom. After these prayers the same priest would announce upcoming fast and feast days.[21] Improper observance of fasts and holidays were two of the many spiritual offences punished with public penance by the chapter court. At the offertory of the mass, the congregation was often reminded of the consequences of sin by the penitents who had led the procession carrying lit candles. Once a penitent had completed the assigned number of weeks leading the procession, he or she went into the choir and left the penitential candle on the high altar. Invaders of the liberty were also made to leave their weapons there, though sometimes they placed them on Wilfrid's shrine instead.[22] The audience to all of these actions was the parish, though the number of parishioners in attendance varied according to whether or not it was a major feast day. The public humiliation of penitents on feast days was more severe, and this made it more appropriate for certain offences. The sanctuary men who failed in their obligation to march in the Rogation procession of 1453 were sentenced to be flogged before the procession not on the next four Sundays, but rather on the next four major feast days: Pentecost, Holy Trinity, Corpus Christi and the nativity of St Wilfrid.[23] In 1498 two priests, Nicholas Burnet and Robert Smith, were assigned public penance for fighting in the church. After skipping the first Sunday, they were obliged to stand in penitential garb holding their weapons and candles outside the western portal of the church while the entire Palm Sunday procession filed past.[24]

---

[19]   Arnold, *Belief and unbelief*, 14; Graves, 'Form and fabric of belief', 36, 166–7.

[20]   Duffy, *Stripping of the altars*, 124–5.

[21]   Ibid. 125.

[22]   These two might in fact have amounted to the same thing, since the shrine was evidently directly behind the altar and therefore attached directly to it.

[23]   AoC, 72–3.

[24]   AoC, 287–8.

The procession, prayers and offertory all took place before the pivotal moment of the mass, the consecration of the host. The kissing of the pax and the distribution of blessed bread took place afterwards. Just before he took his own communion, the priest kissed the pax, which would then be taken out to the congregation so that everyone there could kiss it in turn.[25] Because it was kissed sequentially, the pax ritual could provoke disputes over precedence.[26] Perhaps this was the reason why Reginald Sele struck his fellow tailor, Edmund Strickland, and drew a knife on him during divine service on the feast of St William's translation in 1468. Sele claimed that Strickland had given him offence of some kind, and a dispute over precedence is a likely explanation.[27] In any case there are few recorded instances of violence within the minster even on feast days when the greater number of people in the minster increased the likelihood of disputes over precedence. On Sundays and less important feasts these issues of precedence were diffused over a whole number of parish chapels, each with its own pax. The lord in his own chapel, for example, would not have to fear anyone would usurp his place.[28] Kissing the pax was one substitute for taking communion, and the reception of a piece of blessed bread was another.[29] A different family customarily supplied the loaf to be blessed and distributed each week, though in Ripon perhaps more than one family per week supplied the bread since the congregation was so large. Like the pax ritual, the distribution of blessed bread would have taken place at the many chapels too.

Low masses at the minster's subsidiary altars were less elaborate, but far more numerous and frequent than high masses in the choir. They lacked the processions of the high mass, but they had their own pax rituals.[30] When all the perpetual chantries and temporary ones are combined together, there were easily more than a dozen such masses per day in the minster. These masses were much more accessible to the laity than the high mass, and must have provided the best opportunities for laypeople to see Christ's body. The minster's subsidiary altars probably had screens or other forms of enclosure that kept laypeople from standing next to the altar while at the same time still permitting them to witness the mass and elevation nearly as well as they would have been able to in ordinary parish churches, and far better than at the minster's high mass. Low masses took place at various times during the day, but never during high mass itself when the vicars and chaplains were supposed to be in the choir. It is entirely likely that masses were staggered as at other large churches so that

---

25   Duffy, *Stripping of the altars*, 125.

26   Bossy, 'The mass as a social institution', 56.

27   AoC, 128–30.

28   Colin Richmond, 'Religion and the fifteenth-century English gentleman', in Barrie Dobson (ed.), *The Church, politics, and patronage in the fifteenth century*, Gloucester 1984, 193–208 at p. 199.

29   Duffy, *Stripping of the altars*, 125; Rubin, *Corpus Christi*, 73–4.

30   Duffy, *Stripping of the altars*, 112, 114.

people could witness several elevations in succession.[31] The chaplain of the St Thomas chantry was supposed to celebrate mass 'between the hours of seven and eight o'clock'.[32] Servants, labourers and travellers especially benefitted from morrow masses said even earlier, at dawn, so they could hear them before setting of to work or on their journey.[33] Ripon's Holy Cross guild provided two of these daily from sometime in the middle of the fifteenth century.[34] The foundation of these chantries, especially by Ripon's guilds, was part of a wider process of increasing the number of masses said in the parish for the benefit of the living as well as the dead. The many chantry chapels on the estates of the lords and in the villages of the parish were the rural counterparts of the chantries founded in the minster.

The guilds

Guilds were more common in towns than in the countryside, providing a form of belonging to the transient populations moving into towns after the Black Death.[35] The fourteenth and fifteenth centuries also witnessed a great expansion in the number of English guilds due to the rigidity of the established parish system, which did not adapt to changing social conditions and therefore often became inadequate as a social framework.[36] The history of Ripon's medieval guilds is concentrated within this period, beginning with the description of two of them in Richard II's national survey of guilds in 1389. All Ripon's known guilds were based in the town, but some had a membership that extended into the surrounding countryside to link rural and urban elites together. The earliest documented Ripon guild was especially important in this respect.

The purpose of the Guild of SS Mary, Wilfrid and All Saints, as described in the late fourteenth-century guild survey, was to support a chaplain, maintain a chapel dedicated to St Mary and discipline its members.[37] The maintenance of discipline was especially important because it preserved the guild's public reputation and allowed for the moral development of its members.[38] This provision serves as a significant reminder that parishioners, in their own lay organisations, were as capable as the chapter court of upholding moral standards in the parish. The members of this fraternity founded a chantry in

[31]   Ibid. 98. See also Burgess, 'For increase of divine service', 59–60.

[32]   'inter horas septimam et octauam super le knoll': MR iv. 199.

[33]   Duffy, Stripping of the altars, 99.

[34]   TNA, E 178/2609, m 6.

[35]   Rosser, Art of solidarity, 50.

[36]   Idem, 'Communities of parish and guild in the late Middle Ages', in S. J. Wright (ed.), Parish, church, and people: local studies in lay religion, 1350–1750, London 1988, 29–55 at p. 33.

[37]   TNA, C 47/46/452; David Crouch, Piety, fraternity and power: religious guilds in late medieval Yorkshire, York 2000, 31.

[38]   Rosser, Art of solidarity, 69–71.

the Ladykirk sometime in the 1370s or 1380s, and many of its founders are identifiable in the 1379 poll tax. The assessment rates and number of servants listed in the poll tax provides a useful index of their wealth. The merchants John de Hawkeswick and Walter de Leeds were among the richest residents of the town of Ripon at that time. Wealthy brewers, a cook and a carpenter also contributed to the chantry endowment. The membership of the Guild of SS Mary, Wilfrid and All Saints also included some substantial rural property-owners. Their membership provides further evidence that one of the guild's main functions was to serve as an elite association. The franklin John de Morpath resided in the nearby suburb of Aismunderby-Bondgate between Ripon and Markenfield. To reach the chapel from his home, he would actually have had to pass by the minster, which lay directly on his route through the town to the Ladykirk. If he attended religious services there, it was not for the sake of convenience but rather so that he could meet with the wealthy merchants and other important burgesses who comprised the membership of the fraternity. The chantry founders selected John de Ingilby, from the family of knights based at Ripley, to be the patron of the chantry.[39] The Ingilby family were newcomers to the area, having inherited the lordship of Ripley through an heiress in the middle of the fourteenth century.[40] Sir Ralph Pigot, another one of the chantry founders, had similarly inherited the lordship of Clotherholme through his wife, Joan.[41] For Ingilby and Pigot the connections with Ripon's mercantile elite must have been one of the main benefits of membership. Ingilby lived even farther away from the Ladykirk than John de Morpath, and very close to other places of worship. His manor was very near to the parish church of Ripley, and not actually in the parish of Ripon at all. Pigot had his own domestic chapel at the manor of Clotherholme, although, according to the licence for this chapel, he and his family were supposed to attend the minster on Sundays. Although the names of the Wakemen are not recorded until after 1400, the list of fifteenth-century Wakemen displays the same mixture of wealthy craftsmen, merchants and local gentry who were evidently members of the SS Mary, Wilfrid and All Saints fraternity.[42] Like many other guilds with wide local membership, this guild gave members who lived outside of the town an identity within the town.[43] In particular, it helped Sir Ralph Pigot to strengthen his ties in the area after he inherited the lordship of Clotherholme. The Ladykirk was well equipped for guild conviviality on whatever occasions the guild used as its feast days. As described in the will of one of its late fifteenth-century chaplains, it had a hall, kitchen and cellar.[44]

---

[39]   MR iv. 139.

[40]   Jennings, *History of Nidderdale*, 107.

[41]   Gowland, 'The manors and liberties of Ripon', 61.

[42]   Ripon Cathedral, dean and chapter archives, MS Dep 1980/1 434, fos 21r–22r.

[43]   Rosser, *Art of solidarity*, 114.

[44]   AoC, 183–4.

The dedication of the guild suggests that there were many possible banqueting occasions: perhaps four for Mary, three for Wilfrid and one for All Saints. Indeed, as these included many of the feasts on which attendance at the minster was required even by gentry who had their own chapels, the guildhall might have served on all these occasions to combine meetings of the parish elite with feast days of general parochial obligation.

The Guild of SS Mary, Wilfrid and All Saints is the only Ripon guild known to have had its own separate chapel, but after 1400 a rising number of guilds celebrated patronal feast day masses and more regular chantry masses in the minster. This expansion can be charted in references to their patronal masses, which are recorded in the chamberlain's accounts. The earliest account dates to 1410, and names two guilds.[45] One of them was probably the unnamed fraternity from 1389, while the other was either more recent or not recorded by the surveyors. The next surviving account dates to 1439 and lists four: now the fraternities of Corpus Christi and Holy Cross join the older fraternities of St Wilfrid and the Assumption of the Blessed Virgin.[46] The nameless guild from the 1389 guild returns had, at the time of the survey, existed for ten years. Its purpose was to give alms and to support a chaplain performing a daily mass 'at an altar in the high church'.[47] This anonymous guild had no rents, properties, plate or vestments for the use of their chaplain.[48] If the fraternity was actually one of the named guilds that appear in the records after 1400, the most likely candidate is the Guild of the Assumption. This appears in the 1410 chamberlain's account, which records a collection of 3s. 8d. 'from gifts at a certain mass of a certain fraternity of St Mary on the feast of the Assumption of the same'.[49] Efforts to establish a chantry were already underway at this time, and are documented in the grant of lands by John de Fulford and Robert Kendale to the chaplain at the altar of the Assumption in 1406 or 1407.[50] Their names appear at the start of the 1416 chantry ordination and they were regarded as the chantry's founders, though the guild's members were certainly also involved.[51]

The Guild of the Assumption was dedicated to Mary's ascension into heaven, a feast, celebrated on 15 August that was a holiday throughout Christendom. Ripon's Assumption altar was probably located in the inner chapel of the south transept. A medieval wall painting depicting scenes from the life of the Virgin still appears on the north wall of this chapel. The Malory family concentrated their tombs around this altar in the late fifteenth century

[45] *MR* iii. 225-6.

[46] *MR* iii. 225-6, 228.

[47] 'a un autier en le haute esglise': TNA, C 47/46/452.

[48] Ibid.

[49] 'de obl. ad quandam missam cujusdam fraternitatis Beatæ Mariæ in festo Assumpcionis ejusdem': *MR* iii. 225.

[50] TNA, C 143/438/23.

[51] *MR* iv. 243

and it was probably also the parochial altar of Givendale. The founders of the Guild of the Assumption provided a comprehensive outline of their chaplain's responsibilities. He was expected to say mass daily for the brothers and sisters of the guild, living and dead, and also to perform the office of the dead on a daily basis.[52] He was required to dress in the same habit as a vicar of the minster, and to participate in divine services in the choir on what amounted to all Sundays and feast days, plus weekdays during Advent and Lent.[53] Naturally he was also required to participate in processions and in any type of mortuary foundation established by one of the guild's members.[54] Guild members intended their chaplain to augment the liturgy of the minster, to showcase its own contribution by having the chaplain take part in processions, and to safeguard the salvation of their souls. They stipulated also that the chaplain should visit any guild member who fell ill, thereby assisting somewhat with the cure of souls in the parish, though the primary purpose of this requirement was, of course, to guarantee that no guild member died without the last rites.[55] It is difficult to determine very much at all about the membership of the guild. The chantry foundation was paired with an annual obit to be held on 8 November for William de Lynton, John de Lynton and his wife Agnes, and John Feriby and his wife Margaret.[56] The de Lyntons were a merchant family from Ripon, and one John de Lynton was also a party to the foundation of the Guild of SS Mary, Wilfrid and All Saints in the late fourteenth century.[57] Beyond this obit there is little evidence for the membership of the guild.

The Guild of St Wilfrid and its annual mass, which took place on the feast of Wilfrid's translation (24 April), are mentioned in the 1410 chamberlain's account, making it the second-oldest of the guilds established in the minster.[58] In 1419 the guild co-founded a chantry to be based at the St Thomas altar of the minster.[59] Preparations for this foundation were already underway as early as 1409.[60] The Ripon Psalter was almost certainly made for the chaplain of this guild.[61] Its Easter table begins with the year 1418 and the calendar includes references to the family of Christopher Kendale, who was chaplain of the chantry from 1488 to 1491. The guild included a number of stipulations in its chantry ordination. One was that the chaplain should hold an annual obit for guild members on 23 July, encouraging wider clerical attendance with

---

[52] MR iv. 244–5.
[53] MR iv. 245.
[54] Ibid.
[55] Ibid.
[56] MR iv. 246.
[57] MR iv. 137.
[58] MR iii. 228.
[59] MR iv. 194–203.
[60] TNA, C 143/441/31.
[61] Ripon Cathedral Library, MS 8

cash incentives.[62] The chaplain was also in charge of the candles that should be carried in procession at the feasts of the Ascension, Corpus Christi and Wilfrid's nativity.[63] It was clearly a point of pride to guild members that these torches be carried in the processions, presumably by some of the members themselves. They also required their chaplain to place a candelabrum with five lit candles on the altar of St Thomas the Martyr every Sunday and double feast day for at least as long as the current members lived.[64] This too would have been a sign of the guild's status on important occasions. The chaplain was to attend divine services in the choir on Sundays and feast days, to participate in processions, and in general to model his conduct on that of the vicars.[65]

The Guild of the Holy Cross or Rood was Ripon's most widely supported fraternity during the fifteenth century. It concentrated its devotion on the sculpted crucifix that once sat atop a beam spanning the eastern end of the nave. Around the year 1400 the fabric wardens reached an agreement with the carpenter William Wright to replace the old rood loft for the sum of £3 6s. 8d.[66] This sum was only slightly less than the £4 3s. 4d. that the fabric wardens paid the carpenter Thomas Wright to replace an entire house in 1393.[67] The guild may have been founded around this time to raise money for candles to light the new rood. Exactly the same circumstances set in motion the foundation of a Guild of the Holy Cross at Grantham in Lincolnshire.[68] The new screen and rood loft came complete with at least one altar. The crucifix that sat upon this beam was Ripon's equivalent to the rood of the average parish church, which normally stood above the chancel screen. It was probably much larger than the roods of most parish churches, and its positioning was slightly different. Ordinarily the chancel screen marked the boundary between nave and chancel, thus demarcating the end of parochial space within a church. Ripon Minster had a choir and transepts, so the boundary was instead the stone screen on the eastern side of the central crossing. Ripon's parishioners could pass through the rood screen to reach the transepts, where some of the parochial altars were located. The rood was thus in the middle of parochial space rather than at its boundary, and its location was typical of former minsters rebuilt as large cruciform churches.[69] The guild's activities provide some of the best evidence for how the building was actually used by laypeople.

---

[62]   MR iv. 201.

[63]   Ibid.

[64]   Ibid.

[65]   MR iv. 199.

[66]   MR iii. 133.

[67]   MR iii. 116.

[68]   Rosser, Art of solidarity, 132.

[69]   John Blair, 'Clerical communities and parochial space: the planning of urban mother churches in the twelfth and thirteenth centuries', in T. R. Slater and Gervase Rosser (eds), The Church in the medieval town, Aldershot 1998, 272–94 at p. 283.

The Holy Cross guild's masses were performed at one or more altars set before the rood, and must therefore have been some of the most accessible of all in Ripon Minster. The altars, screen, rood and loft no longer exist. Only the rebates that held the ends of the rood beam remain, and they can be seen on the western faces of the two western crossing piers. Nevertheless, written sources provide enough evidence to form a basic idea of the arrangement of the screen and altars that once stood at the east end of the nave. In 1407 William Clynt and William de Leeds proposed to grant lands and rents to a perpetual chaplain who would serve an altar dedicated to the Exaltation of Holy Cross that had been recently installed in Ripon Minster.[70] The chamberlain's accounts reveal that later on the Holy Cross guild's main feast day was that of the Exaltation of Holy Cross (14 September) and that the minster clergy arranged a mass on the guild's behalf. The proposed perpetual chantry does not seem to have been connected to the guild because at the last minute the plans for the chantry were changed and its endowments diverted to the St James altar, located elsewhere.[71] This change of plan is the best indication that the Holy Cross guild was forming and had its own designs on the altar of the Exaltation of Holy Cross.

The Holy Cross guild owned properties and elected its own wardens by the 1440s, as demonstrated by a petition datable to between 1443 and 1450, in which John Thomson and John Williamson, two of the guild's former wardens, asked the chancellor of England to intervene in a dispute over a rent promised to their guild.[72] John Thomson's membership of this guild may help to explain the causes of one of the many cases of invasion of the liberty. On the day after the feast of the Exaltation in 1467, a shoemaker named John Thomson was assaulted in his home in Stonebridgegate.[73] It is possible that this was the same man who had been warden of the guild and that the feast of the Exaltation had, as feast days often did, brought social tensions into the open.[74] In any case, the Guild of the Holy Cross had established itself as Ripon's most broadly supported guild by that time. Testamentary bequests provide the best evidence for the membership of the Holy Cross guild, if it can be assumed that donation to the guild implied membership.[75] They become more noticeable from the middle of the fifteenth century primarily because this is the period covered by the chapter acts book that preserves the extant copies of most of Ripon's medieval wills. During this period the Holy Cross guild enjoyed a far greater number of bequests than any of the other guilds, which are rarely if

---

[70] TNA, C 143/438/7.

[71] *MR* i. 162–5.

[72] TNA, C 1/168/3.

[73] *AoC*, 192.

[74] Arnold, *Belief and unbelief*, 142.

[75] Norman Tanner and David Crouch have argued that they can be interpreted in this way: Norman P. Tanner, *The Church in late medieval Norwich, 1370–1532*, Toronto 1984, 75; Crouch, *Piety, fraternity and power*, 9.

Table 1. Bequests to the Guild of the Holy Cross

Date	Name	Profession	Bequest
1452/3	William Wrampayn, Sr		10s.
1453/4	John Rotherham		
1454	Robert Percival	smith	
1459	William Forster	chaplain	22s
1459	Thomas Hardwick	butcher	12d.
1461	William Todd	potter	2s.
1470	William Mylns		12d.
1473	Robert Middleton	master mason	12d.
1488	John Pigot	esquire	4 tenements
1494	Isabella Gye		1 tenement
1529	Robert Roos (Ingmanthorpe)	esquire	3s. 4d.

ever mentioned. The Holy Cross guild was the preferred choice of Ripon's late fifteenth-century will-makers, or in other words those who had a large amount of moveable goods.

Many of these same donors were instrumental in the repair of the central tower after its fall in 1450. The tower collapse caused the most damage to the southern and eastern arms of the church, but the rood loft, located under the western side of the tower, was also affected. A major component of the tower repairs was the strengthening of three of the crossing piers, including the south-western pier which supported one side of the rood beam. Among the donors to both the tower and the Holy Cross guild was the chaplain William Forster, who was also one of the two special fabric wardens who supervised the first phase of tower repairs between 1453 and 1457.[76] Robert Middleton, who bequeathed 12d. to the Guild of Holy Cross in 1473, was in fact the master mason around the year 1470, and perhaps the designer of the renovated tower and south transept.[77] Robert Percival gave the fraternity of Holy Cross 3s. 4d. and the work of the central tower 6s. 8d.[78] William Wrampayn, Sr, gave the guild 10s. and the tower 20s. in his will, dated 1452.[79] His son was an even more generous benefactor of the works, if not also a member of the Holy Cross guild. Wrampayn senior's meagre £1 was overshadowed by the £8 bequest of

[76] MR iii. 162.
[77] AoC, 174.
[78] AoC, 29.
[79] Borthwick Institute, probate register 2, fo. 262r.

William Wrampayn, Jr, fifteen years later. The only catch was that this sum was made up of various uncollected debts, which the minster clergy would have to recover before they could be applied to the tower renovation.[80] William, Jr was also present in June 1457 when the special fabric fund handed over the residue of its account to the ordinary fabric wardens.[81] The merchant's mark of an elaborate W that appears alongside the heraldry of other benefactors on the stone screen before the choir almost certainly belonged to the Wrampayns.

The Holy Cross guild supported its own chaplains without ever formally endowing a chantry. It must have used the mechanism of enfeoffment to disguise the payment of their chaplains. The lands and rents would have been used by the chaplains but legally the possession of other parties, thereby evading the statute of mortmain.[82] This tactic spared the guild the cost of a mortmain licence but makes it much more difficult to trace its activities. Some of the details of its arrangements were recorded in Elizabethan-era depositions. Recorded in about 1576, the witness statements recall the last days of the guild about thirty years earlier. They reveal that in the 1540s the guild actually had two chaplains simultaneously, and that they lived in a property in Annsgate known as the Rood House.[83] One witness, John Slater, called it the 'guild and Rood howse', with the implication that the house was not only the dwelling of the two chaplains but also the guildhall.[84] The property probably came into the guild's possession sometime after 1488, when John Pigot willed four tenements in Annsgate to his wife Katherine for her lifetime that after her decease should go to the Holy Cross guild.[85] There were guilds in Lichfield and Stratford-upon-Avon that also required their chaplains to reside in the guildhall. In those cases, and perhaps also in Ripon, this was so that the guild members could better supervise the behaviour of their chaplains.[86]

The Holy Cross guild seems to have maintained greater influence over the selection of its chaplains than other guilds, which named the chapter as patron. Furthermore, it does not appear to have intended its chaplains to be fully integrated into the round of religious services in the choir. When the other chantry chaplains were given assigned stalls in the choir in 1504, the rood priests, a term which was used to identify the Holy Cross guild's chaplains, were not mentioned.[87] Indeed the term implies that they were distinct from the rest of the minster's chaplains. They were also quite recognisable as they went about their business. The founders of the St George chantry did, after all, single

---

[80] Ibid. probate register 4, fo. 38r–v.
[81] MR iii. 164.
[82] Kreider, English chantries, 77–8.
[83] TNA, E 178/2609, mm 5–6.
[84] Ibid. m 5.
[85] AoC, 266.
[86] Rosser, Art of solidarity, 72.
[87] MR iv. 277–8.

out the vestments of the rood priests as the model for their chaplain's own vestments.[88] The Holy Cross guild's last two chaplains were Richard Terry and Richard Jefferson. They said their masses before the image of the rood, most likely at one or more altars set against the rood screen. Testifying in 1576, the sixty-year-old labourer John Alanson supplied an important detail about the function of the Holy Cross chaplains when he testified that they 'dyd morwe masse' for the guild.[89] Such masses were typical of guilds, which catered to the mobility of their more distant members by enabling them to hear mass before setting off on their travels.[90]

While it is impossible to be certain when the guild began hiring chaplains, there were already two in 1504 when Robert Nellot offered them 4d. apiece to attend his funeral.[91] It seems likely that the guild had at least one chaplain from an early point in its history if for no other reason than that there are so many chaplains in the Ripon records who do not appear to have been vicars or the chaplains of any of the known chantries. The best example is Christopher Kendale, who was a chaplain at the minster during four of the decades for which there is the greatest amount of surviving documentation, but who nevertheless cannot be assigned to any known benefice before he became chaplain of the St Thomas chantry in 1488. William Forster, who was his colleague as special fabric warden between 1453 and 1457, is equally difficult to trace in the records. Rood priests could eventually move to a different role at the minster. John Slater, who at eighty-eight was one of the oldest deponents in 1576, named John Steel as a former rood priest.[92] In 1546 he was the vicar of Givendale, while in 1535 that post had been held by William Anman.[93] Many other chaplains may have begun their careers as rood priests before moving to a stable benefice.

The Holy Cross guild is the best example of Ripon's laypeople taking ownership of the fabric of the church and its liturgy, at least as much as circumstances in Ripon would permit. It did so in a specific area of the building, which was at the east end of the nave before the rood screen. While the church fabric remained the responsibility of the minster's fabric wardens, the members of the Holy Cross guild invested heavily in the repair of the tower. Ripon Minster had no churchwardens, but the office of guild warden offered alternative leadership positions to the types of people who might ordinarily have been churchwardens. The guild appears to have been less concerned than other guilds with incorporating its chaplains into the communal liturgy of the minster. Instead, the role of its chaplains was to say mass at accessible altars

---

[88] MR i. 183.
[89] TNA, E 178/2609, m 6.
[90] Rosser, Art of solidarity, 49.
[91] AoC, 295.
[92] TNA, E 178/2609, m 5.
[93] MR iii. 4, 14.

in the nave for the benefit of anyone who wished to attend them. Insofar as it was possible to do so, the efforts of the Holy Cross guild converted the nave of Ripon Minster into a parochial space. Ripon's urban parishioners were most able to benefit, while the parishioners of the surrounding countryside already had chapels that they could attend.

Ripon's Corpus Christi guild is nowhere near as well documented as the others. It enjoyed a patronal mass at the minster from at least as early as 1439. If it had its own chaplain, it hired him on a stipendiary basis without ever endowing a chantry. There is good reason to believe that there were other, perhaps even less formal fraternities in late medieval Ripon. In 1506 a shoemaker named Geoffrey Sharroke bequeathed 4s. to the 'lights of the masters of the cordwainers' so that they could buy torches.[94] These large candles could have been intended for a variety of purposes, such as processions, funerals or lighting a saint's image. His bequest indicates the existence of a fund organised by other shoemakers to raise funds for these lights. Similarly, the 'young men' raised over £3 in 1520 to fund the installation 'of a certain cloud for the Holy Spirit' in the new nave.[95] There is good reason, based on evidence like Geoffrey Sharroke's will and the fundraising of the young men, to believe that many other such organisations existed in late medieval Ripon. Indeed, the many saints' images of the minster might once have been lit by candles funded by just such groups.

The cult of saints and their images

The cult of St Wilfrid was preeminent in medieval Ripon, but the minster's patron saint was not its only saint. There were other relics to be found in Ripon, even if none were as complete as Wilfrid's bodily remains, and it was also possible to appeal to the help of the saints through their images. The number of these images increased over the fifteenth century to include saints who had no feast day in the Ripon liturgical calendar and also new 'saints' who had not been canonised by the pope. Individual piety could find an outlet in gifts of money, jewellery or clothing to these images. Burial near these images symbolised a profound desire for the saints to intercede on behalf of the people whose tombs their images overlooked, and the monuments of such people might even have been carved with inscriptions asking for help from the saints.[96] Sharroke's burial by Wilfrid's image in the nave is an example which incidentally shows that even Ripon's patron saint was often approached *via* his image rather than his shrine. The chamberlain's rolls provide the best index of saints' images in Ripon Minster, though certainly not a comprehensive one.

---

[94] 'luminibus magistrorum de cordwaners': *AoC*, 306.

[95] 'garciones' and 'cujusdam nebulæ pro lee Holy Goost': *MR* iii. 180.

[96] Badham, *Seeking salvation*, 230–2.

They record only the images where people could leave money. The survival rate of the rolls is such that all the new images were added during gaps between extant accounts, and the exact dates of their introduction are unknown. The earliest roll (1410) refers only to gifts at the images of St Wilfrid and St Mary plus the rood 'in the body of the church'.[97] In 1439 there was also an image of St Loy, the patron saint of smiths.[98]

The number of saints' images grew during the decades after the rise in chantry and guild foundations, and all of these developments indicate that the minster was becoming the focus of more intense lay piety. Whereas in the early fifteenth century the saints' images were all in the nave, at the end of the 1470s some of them were in the more privileged space of the eastern arm of the building. They were not within the choir itself, but in the ambulatory behind the high altar. Here a second image of St Mary could be found, as well as an image of St Roche, a plague saint. Both were located near the Holy Trinity altar at the east end of the building.[99] In some instances the change evident in the account rolls was merely a matter of granting access to existing images. The image of St Mary behind the high altar was hardly new when it entered the accounts in the 1470s: John Ely, vicar of Monkton, had bequeathed 6s. 8d. to decorate the image and altar of St Mary behind the high altar in 1427.[100] The donations made before this image in the late fifteenth century document a devotion to the Virgin Mary that the *pietà* image alone was not sufficient to satisfy. The greater access to images behind the high altar also implies greater access to Wilfrid's relics.

The number of images in the nave increased at the same time as images in the east end of the building became more accessible. The Holy Trinity altar in the nave gained its own image, namely of Holy Trinity and St Leo, around the same time.[101] It must have been created for the Holy Trinity chantry founded in the nave by John Sendale in 1467. An image of Zita, an Italian woman who became the patron saint of servants, was added to the nave during this same half of the century.[102] The company of saints depicted in the minster grew larger still as regionally and nationally important saints joined their ranks in the later decades of the century. The cult of St Ninian, a Scottish saint, appears to have spread from York Minster, where it was adopted to symbolise the claims of the archbishop of York to have metropolitan jurisdiction over south-west Scotland as well as northern England.[103] St Ninian, with his shrine at Whithorn, had long been important to the political ambitions of rulers who

[97] 'in corpore ecclesiæ': MR iii. 226.
[98] MR iii. 229.
[99] MR iii. 252.
[100] MR i. 329.
[101] MR iii. 252.
[102] Ibid.
[103] Pollard, North-eastern England during the Wars of the Roses, 192.

wished to gain influence in the region. The Scottish kings Robert I and his successor David II had been devotees of St Ninian, and Robert even went to Ninian's shrine on pilgrimage in 1329 in an effort to bolster his support in the region.[104] In late fifteenth-century England, Richard of Gloucester venerated Ninian as one of his favourites.[105] Sir Thomas Markenfield III, who was one of the duke of Gloucester's retainers, named his son and heir Ninian.[106] The cult of St Ninian at Ripon Minster outlived Richard of Gloucester, and St Ninian's image appears along with that symbol of Richard's defeat, Henry VI, in the 1505 chamberlain's account.[107] Henry VI was never canonised, but he fitted into a long tradition of English political saints' cults and the wider model of the murdered king as a political martyr saint. Henry VII promoted the anti-Yorkist cult of Henry VI following his victory at the battle of Bosworth.[108] Other recently added images in the 1505 roll included St Brigitta, located with Henry VI near the organ, and St Anthony, on the south side of the choir door.[109] Brigitta of Sweden had been popular with some of the Yorkshire nobility at the beginning of the fifteenth century.[110] The images by the door to the choir and near the organ must have been situated on top of the new stone pulpitum or in its niches. This explains their late entry into the accounts, as the pulpitum was not built until sometime after 1450 and probably closer to 1480 when other renovations to the central tower, south transept and choir had been completed.[111]

None of these saints' images survived the abolition of the cult of saints. They would have been sculpted images and they were probably most easily identifiable by a traditional symbol held by the saint. Zita, for example, was very likely shown holding a key, pot or pan to symbolise her domesticity.[112] The most intriguing of the images is that of St George, described in detail by a co-founder of the St George chantry in an indenture dated 3 April 1518. John Radcliff of Hewick Bridge, esquire, contracted with the master carpenter William Bromfleet for the construction of a loft nine feet wide and as long as the space between the arcade piers 'next adioinyng vnto St Wilfrids closet', and

---

[104] Michael A. Penman, 'Christian days and knights: the religious devotions and court of David II of Scotland, 1329-71', *Historical Research* lxxv (2002), 249-72 at pp. 251, 258.

[105] Pollard, *North-eastern England during the Wars of the Roses*, 192.

[106] Ibid. 128-9.

[107] TNA, SC 6/HENVII/1031.

[108] Duffy, *Stripping of the altars*, 164-5.

[109] TNA, SC 6/HENVII/1031.

[110] Jonathan Hughes, *Pastors and visionaries: religion and secular life in late medieval Yorkshire*, Woodbridge 1988, 75.

[111] G. Gilbert Scott, 'Ripon Minster', *Archaeological Journal* xxxi (1874), 309-18 at p. 316; C. Hallett, *The cathedral church of Ripon: a short history of the church and a description of its fabric*, London 1901, 94.

[112] Katherine L. French, *The good women of the parish: gender and religion after the Black Death*, Philadelphia 2008, 24.

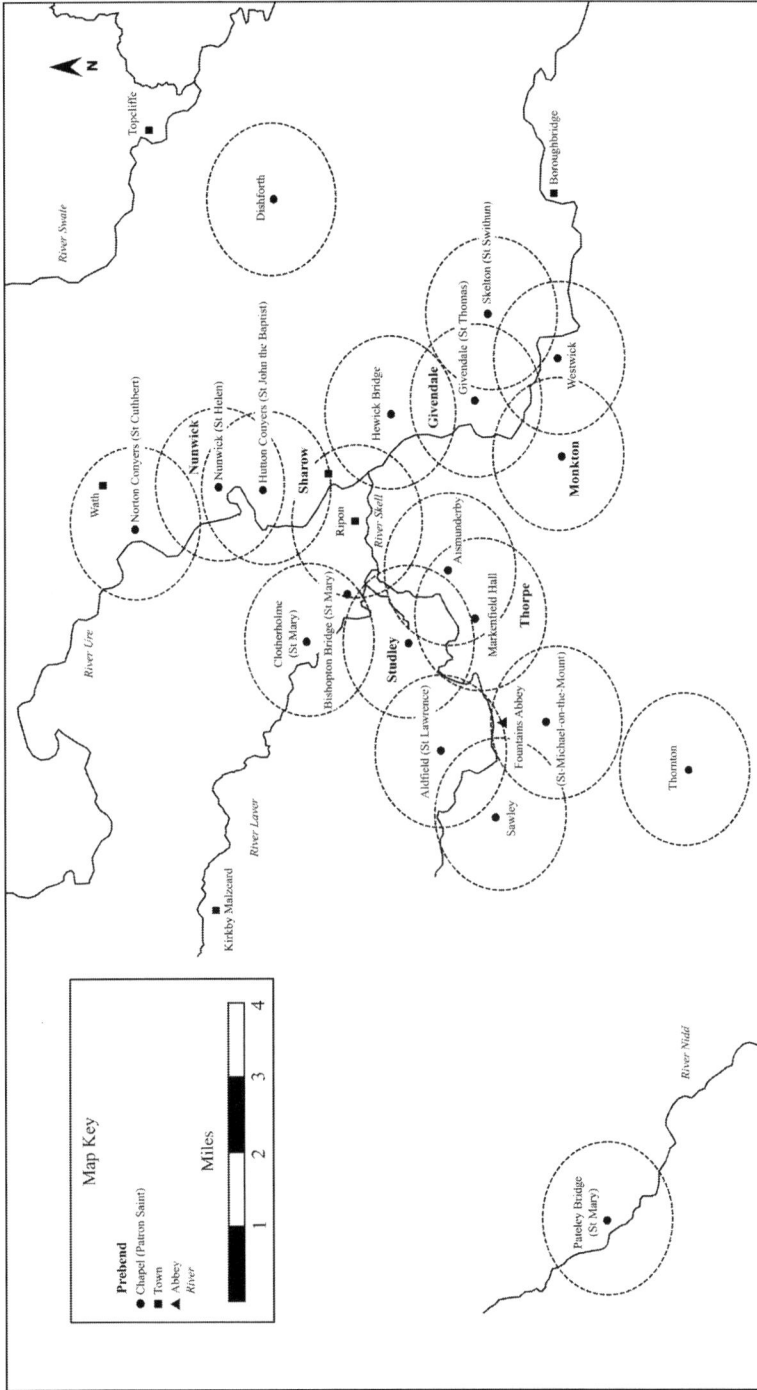

Map 3. Locations of chapels in the parish of Ripon in use during the fourteenth and fifteenth centuries

The circles around the chapels have a radius of one mile.

therefore evidently in the eastern part of the building near Wilfrid's shrine.[113] This project anticipated the rebuilding of the high altar which began a few years later.[114] Bromfleet was to carve a sculpture of St George on horseback as well as a dragon, both modelled on an image of St George at Kirkstall Abbey near Leeds.[115] Moreover, the statue was to have a total of two heads and three arms, so that they could be changed according to the day or season. One of the heads would wear a helmet while the other wore a chaplet.[116] Donations before the image of St George in 1525 show that the loft and sculpture were completed as planned, and all the witnesses in the inquest of 1576 remembered the loft as a feature of the St George chantry.[117] Of all the saints' images in medieval Ripon, only the origins of the St George image are known. The rest may have been introduced by the Ripon clergy or at the behest of parishioners. The chamberlain's accounts and Ripon wills can only demonstrate the popularity and functions of these images once they were installed. Whatever their origins, the saints' images made the saints and their help accessible even when their relics were not present.[118] Gifts of money and wax to the images were made as appeals to the saints for their help, or in thanksgiving for help received. The same help was likely available through saints' images in Ripon's many chapels, even if the chapel images themselves are not well documented.

Chapels of the parish

At one time or another there were more than two dozen different chapels in the parish of Ripon, and somewhere between ten and fifteen were in use at any given time in the fifteenth century. In his study of late medieval English parishes, Beat Kümin found that it was very common for chapels to be established in the distant parts of large parishes so that the people living there would have regular access to the sacraments. These people might well focus their fundraising and bequests on these chapels, but the parish church would ordinarily retain the tithes.[119] Nicholas Orme reached similar findings in his survey of chapels in Cornwall and Devon, where the scattered pattern of settlement most likely accounts for the great number of chapels there.[120] He has also argued that the groups of villagers who collectively supported their local chapels acted in many

---

[113] MR iv. 294.

[114] MR iii. 275.

[115] MR iv. 294.

[116] MR iv. 295.

[117] Ripon Cathedral, dean and chapter archivers, MS Dep 1980/1 183 no. 10; TNA, E 178/2609, m 6.

[118] Duffy, *Stripping of the altars*, 160.

[119] Kümin, *Shaping of a community*, 168–9.

[120] Nicholas Orme, 'The other parish churches: chapels in late medieval England', in Burgess and Duffy, *The parish in late medieval England*, 78–94 at p. 80.

ways as if they were guilds with wardens to organise their fundraising, regardless of whether or not they were fully organised as religious fraternities.[121] Ripon, like the large parishes of Devon and Cornwall, could easily accommodate a number of chapels, and the same patterns of foundation and use described by Kümin and Orme are observable in Ripon. For some of Ripon's chapels there is almost no evidence at all, so that only the better attested examples can be examined. Two of these chapels were attached to hospitals founded in Ripon by the archbishops of York in the twelfth century. Most of the rest were either domestic chapels founded by the gentry or village chapels supported collectively by their users. Some of the village chapels originated as the foundations of thirteenth-century families that no longer existed in the fifteenth century. In any case most of the early founders envisioned their chapels acting like parish churches for much of the year. The chapel of Sawley, about four miles west of Ripon, is a good example. Geoffrey de Larder witnessed the chapel's foundation charter, so it must have been founded in the early decades of the thirteenth century when the construction of the minster was being completed and new ideas about pastoral care were taking hold throughout Christendom.[122] The licence for Sawley shows how the chapter safeguarded the rights and incomes of the prebend in which each new chapel would be located and required the founders and their heirs to attend the minster at the feasts of Christmas, Easter and St Wilfrid.[123] The charter provides a second list of obligatory feasts for the rest of the parishioners who would use the Sawley chapel: Christmas, Candlemas, 'die Crucis adoratæ' (Good Friday), Easter, Ascension plus the three Rogation days, Pentecost, the feasts of St Wilfrid and All Saints.[124] The charter for Hewick Bridge chapel, datable to between 1272 and 1281, includes the same two-tiered set of restrictions; the charter from the Aldfield chapel from the same period simply refers to the customary obligations.[125] The charter for John de Clotherholme's chantry in 1351 required his household and the other parishioners to attend the minster on Sundays as well as the customary feast days.[126] The added requirement was due to proximity rather than a change in policy: Clotherholme was only about one mile from the minster while the rest of the chapels were more than two miles away.

In the fifteenth century there were fewer manorial lords in the parish than there had been two hundred years earlier. The treasurer's and chamberlain's accounts show that the most powerful families all had their own chapels, including the Markenfields, Wards, Pigots, Malories and Nortons. Extant licences for all the relevant chapels show that only the Pigots, as heirs to the

[121]   Ibid. 84–5.
[122]   *MR* i. 197, 200, 207.
[123]   *MR* i. 196.
[124]   *MR* i. 197.
[125]   *MR* i. 198, 202.
[126]   *MR* iv. 35–6.

Clotherholmes, were theoretically required to attend the minster on Sundays.[127] Their manor was closer to Ripon than any of the others and, perhaps even more importantly, they did not have to cross a river to reach Ripon and so could not cite bad weather and flooding as reasons to stay at home on Sundays. The Ripon gentry, except perhaps for the Pigot family, effectively withdrew from personal participation in the religious services of Ripon Minster for most of the year, having been more or less encouraged to do so by the chapter of canons when it licensed their chapels. These chapels were more parochial in nature than the average chapel – and the minster was correspondingly less so – due to the size of the parish of Ripon. In exchange for more widespread, regular and easily accessible masses for the parishioners of Ripon to attend, the thirteenth-century canons of Ripon allowed the seigneurial families of the parish to establish and maintain at their own cost a large number of chapels. A similar principle applied to the village chapels and the two types of chapel ultimately provided very good coverage of the most populated areas of the parish along the Skell and Ure. Most of Ripon's parishioners lived within a mile of one of these chapels.

Two of the best documented village chapels are Aldfield and Skelton, both more than three miles from Ripon. The chapel of St Swithun at Skelton flickers into view in the wills of four of its villagers. In 1470 William Turret donated 6d. to the chapel and another 6d. to its chaplain, John Kendale.[128] Nicholas Anderson made identical gifts to the chapel and chaplain of Skelton during the same year.[129] The following year the widow Joan Hewick bequeathed 2s. to the chapel for a torch, perhaps to light an image of St Swithun or the altar during mass.[130] In 1472 Thomas Stele bequeathed 'all the grain growing on a rod of his land' to the chaplain of the Skelton chapel.[131] As late as 1504 William Hewick bequeathed land to the chapel at Skelton and cash to support the rebuilding of the minster nave.[132] Their bequests show that they identified closely with their village chapel, though not to the exclusion of their parish church. Turret, Anderson, Hewick and probably Stele were buried in the churchyard of the minster. Moreover, Turret made bequests to the tomb of St Wilfrid and the altar of St Mary behind the high altar in the minster. William Sawley, his vicar, was one of the witnesses to his will.[133] John Kendale, the Skelton chaplain, composed his own will in 1477, and the scale of his bequests gives some indication of his income as chaplain. He gave two pounds of wax to burn at his vigil, 2s. for torches to burn around his body at his funeral, cash

---

[127]   MR iv. 35–6, 37–8, 40–1, 255–63.

[128]   AoC, 143.

[129]   AoC, 144.

[130]   AoC, 168.

[131]   'totum frumentum crescens super unam rodam terræ suæ': AoC, 103.

[132]   AoC, 297.

[133]   AoC, 143.

bequests to the minster clergy and chantry chaplains to attend his funeral, 6s. 8d. to the fabric of the minster, 3s. 4d. to the works at York Minster, 13s. 4d. to be divided between the mendicant houses in York, 20s. to be distributed on the day of his funeral and, of course 10s. to the chapel at Skelton.[134] These are not all of his bequests, but they are enough to illustrate his intention to be commemorated in the same way that any vicar or chantry chaplain of the minster might have chosen. The Skelton chaplain was far from poor, and the few scraps of surviving evidence show the chapel of Skelton was well supported by its villagers. It, like others of its type throughout England, may have benefitted from fundraisers organised by the local population.[135] Donations and any other funds must have been overseen by someone acting effectively in the capacity of churchwarden for the chapel.

The minster's main contribution to the religious life of the Skelton villagers was an annual patronal mass on the feast of St Swithun (2 July). The celebration of the patronal mass at Skelton is a significant link between the minster's treatment of guilds and chapels in the parish. Minster clergy celebrated patronal masses for all the minster guilds, and for the guilds at least the patronal mass and the accompanying banquet were the highlights of the year and central to the communal identity of the fraternity.[136] The same is likely true of the villages with chapels and patron saints. The communal veneration of a shared patron gave the villages an identity and made them into communities worth speaking of and not merely communities assumed to exist.[137] Aldfield was another chapel that celebrated a mass honouring its patron saint. The chapel of St Lawrence in Aldfield, founded by the Aldfield family sometime between 1272 and 1281, had become an important village chapel by the fifteenth century. The Aldfield family itself had ceased to exist and their lordship of Aldfield had been transferred to Fountains Abbey by 1474, when the chapter of Ripon made an agreement with the abbot and convent of Fountains for the monastery to staff the chapel on the feast of St Lawrence 'and other dayes in the yere', farming the gift income from the chapel to the abbey for an annual fee of 2s. 10d.[138] The Aldfield chapel was allegedly ruinous at that time, though it presented the minster's chamberlain with gifts from the feast of St Lawrence as late as 1439.[139] The monks of Fountains Abbey operated a second chapel, which they founded on How Hill in 1346. This, dedicated to St Michael, had been established by agreement between Ripon and Fountains.[140]

---

[134]   AoC, 177–8.

[135]   Orme, 'The other parish churches', 84–5.

[136]   Rosser, Art of solidarity, 122–3.

[137]   For the dangers of assuming the existence of 'communities' everywhere see Carpenter, 'Gentry and community', 340–4.

[138]   Ripon Cathedral, dean and chapter archives, MS Dep 1980/1 356, pp. 27–8.

[139]   Ibid. p. 27; MR iii. 228.

[140]   MR iv. 20–2.

The chapel of St Michael and the village of Aldfield were both around four miles to the south-west of Ripon. More than far enough away to merit their own chapels, they were still relatively close to Ripon when compared with the chapel of Pateley Bridge, which was over ten miles away in Nidderdale.

The most privileged chapel in the parish was indeed Pateley Bridge, but it was something of an aberration. The chapel once had aisles and arcades, making it somewhat grander architecturally than Ripon's other known chapels.[141] Ultimately more similar to the appropriated parishes of Nidd and Stanwick, Pateley Bridge had rights that reflected its distance from the minster and its rapid development as a town after its market was established by Archbishop Melton in 1320.[142] At the end of the fourteenth century the adjacent townships of Dacre and Bewerley were annexed to the prebend of Studley because their parishioners were attending the chapel of Pateley Bridge, which was technically part of that prebend, instead of their proper parish church.[143] The 1470 treasurer's roll shows that the chapel had a large number of rights. Christopher Kendale, sub-treasurer that year, wrote in his account that he had been unable to collect money coming from weddings, baptisms and churchings in Pateley Bridge because the chamberlain had unjustly taken these profits.[144] He accounted for them separately from the weddings, baptisms and churchings in the minster, so it seems that all three could occur at Pateley Bridge. Only the baptism of children at Pateley Bridge is really remarkable since weddings and churchings could be performed in any of the parish chapels.

In and around the town of Ripon were still more chapels, including at the hospitals of St John the Baptist and St Mary Magdalene, and the almshouse of St Anne. The hospital of St Mary Magdalene had been founded as a leper hospital by one of the archbishops of York, possibly Thurstan, around 1140; his successors – especially Wickwaine (r. 1279–85) and Romanus (r. 1286–96) – augmented its endowment and adapted it for the care of elderly priests and other corrodians.[145] The archbishops transformed St John the Baptist, their other Ripon hospital, from a pilgrim hospital into a school for poor students during this same period.[146] Both hospitals had a chapel and one or more chaplains, as did the almshouse of St Anne during the fifteenth century. The Ladykirk was yet another chapel in Ripon where laypeople could hear mass on a daily basis. Regardless of the fate of its guild, the chantry endured throughout the fifteenth century. There is good evidence that these chapels were increasingly being used by parishioners from the town of Ripon and the surrounding

---

[141] Peter Leach and Nikolaus Pevsner, *The buildings of England: Yorkshire West Riding: Leeds, Bradford, and the North*, New Haven 2014, 624.

[142] Gowland, 'The manors and liberties of Ripon', 60.

[143] Jennings, *History of Nidderdale*, 64.

[144] MR iii. 215.

[145] Stephen Werronen, 'The hospital of St Mary Magdalene and the archbishops of York, c. 1150–1335', *Nottingham Medieval Studies* lviii (2014), 115–36 at pp. 122–6.

[146] Ibid. 126–7.

area as alternatives to the minster. Like the more distant chapels of Skelton and Aldfield, the hospital chapels were licensed for use in marriage and churching ceremonies.

The chapter court of Ripon was responsible for enforcing religious observance. It appears to have done so only rarely. The case of Isabelle Greve is one of a few examples. On the Friday after Easter 1481 Isabelle was cited by the chapter court at the instance of her vicar, Thomas Braithwaite, who alleged that she had not made her confession or taken communion that year.[147] Isabelle claimed that she had done both at the Maisondieu, the chapel of St Anne on the bank of the River Skell near the minster. When the chaplain of the Maisondieu denied her claim, Isabelle changed her story, but to no avail. In July, after repeated failures to even attend the court, she was excommunicated.[148] Emota Plane was cited in 1453 because 'she does not lead a Catholic life ... she did not confess or receive the Eucharist in the feast of Easter last elapsed'.[149] She appeared in court in November 1453 after being suspended from the church, and she was then sentenced to be flogged for her negligence.[150] Three other cases all deal with improper observance of feast days. In 1453 Nicholas Sponer was cited for making nets on holidays; Joan Farand was flogged in 1468 for spinning and carding during the feast of St Matthew; the weaver William Laton received the same punishment for making textiles during the feast of St Mark in 1471.[151] There are no citations for non-attendance on Sundays. Whatever hypothetical restrictions may have existed, the chapter appears to have been content to let its parishioners attend their local chapels on Sundays provided that they properly observed the major feasts and received communion in the minster at Easter.

So far it is clear that chapels could be used to say prayers, hear mass and venerate the saints. They were essential to the proper functioning of the parish because it was entirely impractical to expect parishioners regularly to travel great distances to and from the minster. To judge from the chapel licences, anyone living more than about a mile from the minster was likely to have permission to attend a chapel most of the time. The obligations placed on ordinary laypeople were usually greater than those placed upon the gentry families who founded chapels. The gentry were thus able to withdraw from the communal religion of the parish, though not quite as much as might seem to have been the case if the minster was interpreted as the sole parish church. In practice, the chapels of the parish served as parish churches on many occasions and some of these – perhaps Clotherholme, Givendale and Hutton-Conyers – may have been shared

[147] AoC, 186.

[148] AoC, 187–8.

[149] 'non ducit vitam catholicam ... non confitebatur nec eucharistiam recipiebat in festo Paschæ ultimo elapso': AoC, 21.

[150] AoC, 26. Flogging was a common punishment for breaking the Sabbath: Swanson, Church and society in late medieval England, 178.

[151] AoC, 21, 134, 149.

by the gentry and other parishioners. None of them are well documented for the fifteenth century, and it seems unlikely that the Wards of Givendale were in fact sharing their chapel with neighbouring parishioners who could just as easily have attended the Skelton chapel. At any rate, there was more to a church and parish than just the mass, and the place of the chapels in the parish cannot be fully comprehended without an examination of their role in administering other sacraments, especially those that marked a change of status.

Sacraments and status

Five of the seven sacraments – baptism, confirmation, marriage, ordination and extreme unction – marked a change of status. They are now frequently interpreted as rites of passage, and as such it is reasonable to include a few additional rites that, although highly ritualised, were not strictly sacramental. These include the churching of women after childbirth and the veiling of widows who took vows of perpetual chastity.[152] It is also necessary to exclude a few of the actual sacraments: confirmation because it is the most poorly documented of them all, and many people may never have been confirmed;[153] ordination because it applied only to the clergy. Rituals are a lens through which to scrutinise more closely the relationship between the parishioners of Ripon and their clergy, chapels and the minster.

Marriage

According to the ideal, clerical model of marriage, prospective couples were supposed to exchange vows in the future tense, have the banns proclaimed, and only afterwards exchange vows in the present tense before a priest who would then celebrate the nuptial mass in church.[154] In practice, the couple could form a binding, sacramental marriage simply through the exchange of vows in the present tense without any witnesses or through the exchange of future-tense vows followed by consummation, as long as the couple was free to marry at the time that the vows were exchanged.[155] The proclamation of the banns was intended to detect any impediment to the marriage, yet many late medieval English couples exchanged present-tense vows and only afterward had the banns proclaimed and the marriage solemnised in church.[156] Although valid,

---

[152] Swanson, *Church and society in late medieval England*, 271; French, *Good women of the parish*, 50; Gilchrist, *Medieval life*, 182.

[153] Swanson, *Church and society in late medieval England*, 277.

[154] McSheffrey, 'Place, space, and situation', 965.

[155] Donahue, *Law, marriage, and society*, 1–2.

[156] McSheffrey, 'Place, space, and situation', 965–6.

marriage formed by the exchange of vows in this way was generally considered by laypeople and clergy alike to be in a liminal and imperfect state before its final solemnisation.[157] The minster clergy strongly encouraged their parishioners to complete the process with a church ceremony. The extant treasurer's rolls give annual figures for the number of weddings in Ripon. In 1401 there were thirty-six marriages with thirty-one the following year, thirty in 1470 and thirty-five in 1484.[158] These did not all occur in the minster because the chapter was willing to license the solemnisation of weddings in chapels throughout the parish. A few extant licences from around 1470 show the range of chapels that could be selected. In 1467 the chapter licensed William Sawley, vicar of Givendale, to marry Lady Joan Ward and Sir William Stapleton at her manorial chapel of Givendale.[159] Joan was the widow of Sir Roger Ward (d. 1453) and daughter of the lord of Markenfield.[160] As a widowed lady, Joan was able to have her new marriage solemnised in this chapel. If she had her own chaplain, he is not mentioned in the licence. Instead, William Sawley was responsible for presiding over the ceremony after first proclaiming the banns.[161] Joan is clearly identified as Sawley's parishioner in the licence and it seems likely that he would also have performed the ceremony if it had taken place at the minster.[162] The same rule was applied to all other licences to solemnise a marriage outside the minster, guaranteeing that Ripon's vicars knew the marital status of all their parishioners. They were therefore equipped to detect illicit sexual relationships as well as prevent couples from attempting to enter into invalid marriages.

The Walworth family celebrated two marriages in the space of three years at the chapel of St John the Baptist, Thornton. In 1467 the chapter authorised Robert Sherop, vicar of Studley, to solemnise the marriage of Henry Walworth and Katherine, widow of William Wythes.[163] Sherop's successor, Robert Castleford, was licensed to do the same for John Wythes and Margaret Walworth in 1470.[164] As with Joan Ward's marriage, the vicar of the relevant prebend was charged with proclaiming the banns and solemnising the two marriages at Thornton. Many of the Walworths mention the chapel of Thornton in their wills. John Walworth (d. 1519) bequeathed 'all such landes as I stande in estate of to the use of Thornton chapell, that they shall goo towardes the fyndyng of a prest to syng on the warke day at Ravynstofte, and on the holyday at Thornton chapell, as haith bene usede afore tyme'.[165] His bequest demonstrates his

---

157 Ibid. 966–7.
158 *MR* iii. 207, 211, 213, 219.
159 *MR* iv. 235.
160 *TE* ii. 165.
161 *MR* iv. 235.
162 Ibid.
163 *MR* iv. 236.
164 *MR* iv. 242.
165 *TE* v. 108–9.

support for both the Thornton chapel and the domestic chapel at Raventofts Hall, a house owned by the archbishops of York in which the Walworths lived. Margaret Walworth (d. 1521) wished to give the Thornton chapel £1 6s. 8d. to buy a chalice, provided that a priest would sing mass there twice a week and say prayers for her soul and the soul of her husband.[166] The village of Thornton is a significant distance from the minster, which accounts for the development of a chapel there. As far away as Thornton was from the minster, the Walworths still had some form of relationship with their vicar. Not only did Robert Sherop officiate at the wedding of Henry Walworth and Katherine Wythes, he was also bequeathed 20d. by John Walworth in 1458 to pray for his soul.[167] The patterns of devotion in Thornton during the late fifteenth century were evidently very similar to those in Skelton.

Although it was possible, it was risky to form a marriage without sufficient witnesses because one party might afterward deny the exchange of vows. The case of Alice Thomson is a good example. Marriage disputes of this type were more often than not initiated by women rather than men in late medieval York diocese.[168] It is impossible to know which party was lying in Alice Thomson's case, but the court eventually decided against her. The value of witnesses is demonstrated more positively by the case of the stonemason John Owlthwaite seventeen years later. In May 1471 he had the banns proclaimed for the forth-coming solemnisation of his marriage to Margaret Donning. Richard Donning and Thomas Rigongey objected, so Owlthwaite had them cited to appear in the chapter court. On 3 August Margaret testified that she had contracted a marriage with Thomas Swan before witnesses on 6 and 7 July of that year.[169] Owlthwaite alleged that his marriage to Margaret had been agreed between them privately at the feast of the Invention of Holy Cross (3 May) and made public three weeks later on the Friday after the feast of the Ascension (24 May 1471).[170] Owlthwaite could provide witnesses and, since his claim was prior to that of Thomas Swan, the court decided to hear his evidence first.[171] Owlthwaite's witnesses were Robert Middleton, Thomas Kendale and Thomas Braithwaite. They gave virtually identical testimony that illuminates the social context of the exchange of vows. Robert Middleton was sixty-four years old and master of the masons in Ripon. After the end of the working day on 24 May he and his servant, the nineteen-year-old Thomas Kendale, went to the house of Thomas Donning at the request of John Owlthwaite, who was one of his masons.[172] Thomas Braithwaite, a twenty-four-year-old deacon at the minster,

---

[166] *TE* v. 107n.

[167] Ibid.

[168] Donahue, *Law, marriage, and society*, 79, 85.

[169] AoC, 152.

[170] Ibid.

[171] AoC, 161.

[172] AoC, 162–3.

recalled that he had a conversation with Owlthwaite near the west door of the church at around seven o'clock, and that he too agreed to have a drink with Owlthwaite at the house of Thomas Donning.[173] Thomas Donning was Margaret's father, and he must have known of the contract but his opinion has not been recorded. Middleton, Kendale and Braithwaite all testified that Braithwaite was asked to wait outside while the vows were exchanged, and only invited in afterwards.[174] Middleton and Kendale both recalled the vows that had been exchanged and when asked who had provided the words for the vows, they agreed that it was Middleton who had done so.[175]

John Owlthwaite's marriage to Margaret Donning exemplifies the late medieval attitude toward marriage as a process to be begun with the exchange of vows before witnesses and perfected later by solemnisation in a church. Owlthwaite clearly intended to solemnise the marriage since the dispute only began once the banns had been published.[176] In many cases from fifteenth-century London, the woman's house was the site where vows were exchanged before reliable men who could testify afterwards if necessary.[177] Owlthwaite made such arrangements for his marriage to Margaret Donning, meeting her in her father's house with his witnesses. Owlthwaite was one of the masons who worked for Middleton on a daily basis, so the master mason was a significant choice. Moreover, by providing the vows for Owlthwaite and Donning to repeat, Middleton effectively presided over the ceremony. Owlthwaite probably asked Braithwaite to stand outside during the actual exchange of vows for fear that his presence might somehow preclude him from having the marriage solemnised in church. The outcome of the case is not recorded, but in all likelihood Owlthwaite won since he was called together with Thomas Donning's widow to administer his estate when Donning died intestate in 1472.[178] Many of the other marriages in the medieval parish of Ripon may have begun in a similar way but, since they were not disputed, there is no record of them.

The actual procedure used to solemnise marriages in Ripon Minster is not known. Only one wedding is described, and it was an exceptional one. In January 1516 the chapter produced a letter testimonial concerning the wedding of Thomas Waterton and Margery Pigot. The canons noted that it had taken place in May 1508, with about half of the minster clergy and over one hundred knights, esquires, gentlemen and other honest people in attendance.[179] On this occasion the bishop of Negropont, one of the archbishop of York's suffragans,

---

173 AoC, 164.
174 AoC, 162–5.
175 AoC, 163.
176 AoC, 151–2.
177 McSheffrey, 'Place, space, and situation', 973.
178 AoC, 173.
179 MR iv. 254.

presided over the ceremony.[180] The letter does not specify which altar was used, but no doubt it was the high altar. Most weddings in Ripon would have been much more modest in scale. As with communion at Easter, the altar used for the nuptial mass may have been the parochial altar of the couple, and the officiant was almost certainly their vicar. The Owlthwaite case indicates that marriages were formed in medieval Ripon as they were elsewhere in fifteenth-century England. It was a process that began outside the church and ended with the solemnisation of the wedding in the church or in one of the parish chapels. The Ripon clergy evidently wanted the process to be completed, as in the 1486 case of John Pigot and Katherine Heton, who had already been living as man and wife but without solemnising the marriage.[181]

Baptism and churching

Individual baptism in the parish font was customary in late medieval England. It was the first of the five sacraments now commonly interpreted as rites of passage.[182] Baptism marked the entry of the individual into the parish community as well as the wider community of Christendom.[183] The father and godparents brought the child to the church for the baptism, but the mother did not attend because she had not yet been ritually purified by means of the churching ceremony.[184] The selection of godparents allowed the family to form a bond of kinship with people, usually of a similar social standing, to whom they were not otherwise related.[185] The number of baptisms in Ripon each year would have been much higher than in most parishes. The treasurer's rolls record sixty in 1401, seventy-two in 1402 and ninety-four in 1470, for example.[186] There was only one font in the minster, so the prebendal altar scheme used for communion was not replicated for baptism, yet the vicars must have performed the baptisms according to prebend to guarantee that their knowledge of the baptismal status of their parishioners would be as accurate as that of their marital status.

The villagers of Skelton could not be baptised in their chapel, but the will of their chaplain shows that he could still take part in the baptismal ceremony. In his 1477 will John Kendale refers to Emma Hewick and Robert Smith as his godchildren (*filiola, filiolus*).[187] They can both be connected to the village

---

[180]   Ibid.
[181]   *TE* iii. 350.
[182]   French, *Good women of the parish*, 50; Gilchrist, *Medieval life*, 182.
[183]   Arnold, *Belief and unbelief*, 136–7.
[184]   French, *Good women of the parish*, 59.
[185]   Arnold, *Belief and unbelief*, 137.
[186]   *MR* iii. 207, 211, 213.
[187]   AoC, 177–8.

of Skelton and some of its other inhabitants. A Robert Smith is named as a witness in the will of the Skelton villager Nicholas Anderson, and Emma Hewick is almost certainly related to the Joan Hewick who died in 1471.[188] John Kendale thus had ties of spiritual affinity with some of the villagers whom he served as chaplain of Skelton. It was a habit that he had formed earlier in his career, when he was chaplain of Thornton. He was almost certainly a nephew or cousin of the chaplain Christopher Kendale, and the Kendales' manor of Markington was not far from Thornton. Another of John Kendale's godsons was John Walworth, son of the Kendales' neighbours the Walworths of Raventofts, and he probably acted as his godfather either when he was still chaplain of Thornton or because of the proximity of the two families. The practice may have been more widespread, as the only evidence here comes from John Kendale's desire to name all of his godchildren in his will.

The baptism of the new-born infant was followed at a later date by the ritual purification of the mother, or childwife, in the churching ceremony. This usually took place about four to six weeks after the birth, and included a procession composed of the childwife and her female family members, friends and associates.[189] This ceremony was important, though not a sacrament. The childwife, wearing a veil, received a blessing at the church door, offered a candle and penny at the altar during the offertory of the mass, and was the first to be given a piece of blessed bread after the mass.[190] In the parish of Ripon this ceremony appears to have taken place at whichever chapel the woman normally attended. Women who lived close to the minster would have been churched there. The only insights into the form of the ceremony in the minster come from the will of Elizabeth Brown (d. 1458). She gave to the 'altar of St Stephen in the same place one towel and one covering, for women to be purified thereafter'.[191] Her bequest indicates that even when women were churched at the minster, there was an element of separation by prebend. The wider practice of churching women in chapels close to their homes is crucial evidence that masses were regularly performed in these chapels and that the women churched there identified these chapels as their own.

Among the chapter records there is a series of licences granting permission for churchings at chapels throughout the parish. The licences name the woman, her prebend, the chapel licensed for her purification and the chaplain who was authorised to perform the ceremony. The licences were less restrictive than those for weddings, with the chaplain of the chapel rather than the vicar of the prebend performing the ceremony. In practice this included a variety of chantry chaplains and even monks from Fountains Abbey. These licences

---

[188] AoC, 144,167.

[189] French, *Good women of the parish*, 62–3.

[190] Ibid. 61–2.

[191] 'altari Sancti Stephani ibidem, j manitergium et j coopertorium pro mulieribus exinde purificandis': AoC, 75.

give the clearest impression of the chapels as centres of distinct communities within the parish. Henry Walworth and Katherine Wythes wed at Thornton chapel in the summer of 1467. A year later, Katherine gave birth to a child. Like her wedding, her churching was to take place in the chapel of Thornton. The chapter granted a licence to John Kendale, who had not yet moved to Skelton, to perform the ceremony.[192] In February 1468 the chapter allowed William Sam, a Cistercian monk, to church Alice West of Warsell in Nunwick prebend at the chapel of St Mary at the west gate of Fountains Abbey.[193] Two years later, in August 1470, another of the monks from Fountains was given permission to church a woman. This time the monk was Thomas Day, the woman was Agnes Burton of Thorpe prebend, and the chapel was that of St Michael-on-the-Mount.[194] Another licence dated 1468 permitted the chaplains of the hospital of St Mary Magdalene to church Agnes Walworth of Sharrow prebend.[195] There were in fact no obvious restrictions on where women could be churched provided that they obtained the chapter's licence. While the vicars needed to know whether or not their parishioners were married, only the chaplains of the chapels that the women attended needed to know if they had been ritually purified after childbirth. Moreover, the licences for the old leper hospital and two different chapels constructed by Fountains Abbey show that these chapels played a more important part in the parish than might be assumed based on all other surviving evidence, and they suggest that by the fifteenth century even many parishioners who lived within two miles of the minster attended chapels of ease more regularly than the minster itself.

Taking the veil

Like ritual purification after childbirth, the widow's vow of perpetual chastity was not a sacrament, but it did have a prescribed ceremony. Chastity was an essential feature of the ideal widow, the counterpart to the maiden's virginity and the wife's obedience.[196] A widow could remarry, but if she did not intend to, the vow of perpetual chastity helped her to perfect her status as a widow. The widow who wished to become a vowess received a mantle, veil and ring as symbols of her vow.[197] She remained a lay woman, but now had visible signs of her changed status. The symbols of the vowess were recognisable enough to identify the effigies of deceased women as widows rather than married

---

[192] *MR* iv. 241.

[193] *MR* iv. 238-9.

[194] *MR* iv. 220-1.

[195] *MR* iv. 240.

[196] Arnold, *Belief and unbelief*, 146.

[197] Hughes, *Pastors and visionaries*, 123.

women.[198] The confirmed widow had greater independence than maidens and married women because she was not subject to her father or husband as she had been during those two previous phases of her life. Even a widow who remarried was, in the interim, relatively freer from her male family members than at the time of her first marriage and thus contracted her new marriage in her own house.[199]

A bishop, abbot or prior ordinarily invested the vowess with the symbols of her new status, and the registers of the archbishops of York contain records of the veiling of widows throughout the diocese.[200] One example from Ripon parish is Margaret Pigot (d. 1485), widow of Sir Geoffrey II of Clotherholme. On 2 September 1466 she made her vow before the bishop of Dromore, one of the archbishop of York's suffragan bishops commonly tasked with receiving the vows of widows.[201] She subsequently lived as a vowess for nearly two decades until her death in 1485. The other identifiable Ripon vowess was Katherine Walworth (d. 1470), who took her vow before the abbot of Fountains after the death of her husband John in 1459.[202] Both women were from elite families and there is no evidence concerning the customs of widows of lower social standing. The ring, mantle and veil that Margaret Pigot and Katherine Walworth wore must have distinguished them not only from married women of high standing but even from widows of lower standing in the town and parish of Ripon.

The parish of Ripon was very large and complex. A single church, no matter how many altars it contained, could never really have served the whole parish. During the thirteenth century an array of wealthy landowners multiplied the number of masses performed in the parish by endowing chantry chapels. For the most part these were domestic chapels that doubled as chapels of ease for inhabitants of the surrounding area. A few of the larger villages had chapels that were later maintained by groups of local laypeople. Many chapels were still in use in the fourteenth and fifteenth centuries. The chapter does not appear to have made any great efforts to enforce church attendance on Sundays, but there is no way to determine from the available evidence whether this was because it did not need to or because it was not able to do so. The terms of the chapel licences suggest that anyone living more than a mile or so from Ripon would have been free to attend the nearest available chapel except on important feast days. The same licences reveal that the list of obligatory feast days was very short for the gentry, but somewhat longer for the rest of the parishioners. This two-tiered set of conditions raises the possibility that the gentry rarely attended

---

198 Saul, *English church monuments*, 299.
199 McSheffrey, 'Place, space, and situation', 974.
200 *TE* iii. 312.
201 *TE* iii. 340.
202 *TE* iii. 334.

the minster at all, perhaps less than half a dozen times per year. Did this mean that the gentry had withdrawn from the communal religion of Ripon? The answer to this question depends on how the community is defined.

The debate over the religion of the gentry looms large in the historiography of late medieval English religion. At stake are various interpretations of the causes of the Reformation. Eamon Duffy emphasises the vibrancy and inclusivity of late medieval religion, arguing that 'in most communities the gentry and the urban elites chose not to withdraw from communal worship, but to dominate it'.[203] He rejects Colin Richmond's argument that the gentry ensconced themselves in private pews with books, and cites Christine Carpenter's article on the Warwickshire gentry in support of his argument.[204] A few preliminary remarks on this issue may be made. Ripon's gentry were not unique in resorting to alternative chapels, and very many of the minster's parishioners would only rarely have attended the minster. What really set the gentry apart from the rest of the parish was that their list of obligatory feasts was shorter than that of their neighbours. It is difficult to say whether the gentry were still sharing their chapels with other parishioners in the fifteenth century. If they were, then these chapels functioned a lot like many of the small parish churches of medieval England, with the gentry dominating the religion of the community centred on these chapels. In any case, the gentry could not altogether forget about the minster, which largely retained control over baptism, marriage, churching and burial. Weddings and churchings could be licensed to take place in manorial chapels, but baptisms and burials could not. Moreover, since the attendance of all parishioners was required on the greatest feast days, Ripon Minster was periodically transformed into a place of competition over status between families who otherwise did not regularly encounter one another in a religious setting. The tombs and heraldic displays of the leading families helped to reinforce their status on these holidays, and to preserve their memory in their absence during the rest of the year. There were no private pews in the minster, but men of gentry families enjoyed the privilege of being permitted access to the choir during mass.

Clearly any attempt to understand religion and society in late medieval Ripon must take account of the fact that it was not a single, stable parish community. Even the ordinary parishioners living in the widely scattered villages of the parish might only attend the minster a dozen times in a year. Ripon's parishioners were baptised in the minster's font and buried in its churchyard, but for much of their lives, and much of any given year, they practised their religion in distant chapels. The most telling evidence that the chapels were the real centres of a number of small religious communities is that women underwent the ceremony of ritual purification after childbirth in their own chapels. They

---

[203] Duffy, *Stripping of the altars*, 122.

[204] Richmond, 'Religion and the fifteenth-century English gentleman', 193–208; Carpenter, 'Religion of the gentry', 53–74. Carpenter argues that fear of purgatory, veneration of saints and obsession with display were the hallmarks of conventional gentry religion.

were readmitted not into the big congregation of the minster, but the smaller and more familiar groups of friends, family and neighbours. Another set of licences shows that chapels were used for the solemnisation of weddings. This ceremony was the final stage of marriage formation, which was a process that often began with an exchange of vows in the house of the bride's father, the hall of the master, or a widow's own house depending on the status of the two parties to the marriage. In other words, even though the process had already begun in an environment familiar to the marriage partners, for many it ended in a religious setting that was hardly any less local. The chapel was in many ways the parish church, and meaningful local communities with a common identity would have centred on these chapels and the veneration of their patron saints, especially in the larger villages of Skelton, Thornton and Aldfield. Meanwhile the gentry always had their own family identities, preserved with the memory of their ancestors both in their manorial chapels and in the minster.

The dependent chapels of the countryside only account for the rural divisions of the parish of Ripon. The town of Ripon itself was too large and too populous to have only one church, and like the countryside it was garlanded with chapels. The Ladykirk with its Guild of SS Mary, Wilfrid and All Saints is the most obvious example, but the almshouse and hospitals of Ripon also had chapels which laypeople attended. Moreover, if the laypeople of the town attended the minster on Sundays, they would have heard much more than they saw during the mass. The elevation of the consecrated host, the most important moment in the mass, took place far away from them at the high altar. Few if any would have been able to see it without being present in the choir, and it was unlikely that they were admitted to the choir itself. The townspeople would have had to look elsewhere to actually witness the mass. After high mass they could attend the low masses at the subsidiary altars of the minster or the masses celebrated in the other chapels of the town. In the early fifteenth century the number of daily masses performed in the minster increased as new perpetual chantries were founded. Some of these were established by the new guilds that formed at the same time. From the middle of the fifteenth century, the Guild of the Holy Cross seems to have been the largest and most influential of Ripon's religious fraternities. It employed two chaplains to say masses every day before the rood at the east end of the nave. The timing and location of these masses show that this guild, more than any of the others, was transforming the nave into the type of parochial space that could be found in more conventional parish churches. Saints' images are another feature of such spaces, and they were increasing in number in Ripon Minster during the fifteenth century. Even those behind the high altar were becoming more accessible, which suggests that the clergy's grip on the building was loosening in order to accommodate lay piety.

4

The Ritual Year of the Minster and Parish

Two complementary types of evidence – a liturgical calendar from the fifteenth century and the financial accounts of the minster's officers – together conjure up the image of the ritual year in medieval Ripon. The calendar alone is its mere skeleton, unable to indicate much beyond the prescribed dates and rankings of the feasts. The financial accounts are like flesh stretched over the dry bones, giving more tangible form to the various customs of different holidays. The ritual year is the third mode of time, a natural complement to, first, the ordinary, constant repetition of the mass and, second, the life cycles of individual people whose changing place in the world was signalled by sacraments and rituals. It had two significant types of feast day. On the one hand, the guilds and chapels had their own special feast days that distinguished them from each other and from the parish as a whole. On the other hand, feast days interrupted the more mundane pattern of religious observances with special obligations to attend the minster rather than the nearest chapel. The latter were an integral part of parish society because nothing else drew the whole parish together at once. The major feast days at Ripon formed a cyclical and recursive annual routine in which people venerated the saints, elevated the great and good, and commemorated the dead with processions, banners, bells, chanting, flames, incense and smoke.

The Ripon Psalter is the only surviving manuscript witness to Ripon's medieval liturgy and thus contains its only liturgical calendar, a ranked chronological list of saints' feast days.[1] With leaves measuring 310 x 223 mm it is a very large manuscript, which would have been suitable for use by a priest in the choir or at one of the subsidiary altars in the minster.[2] In addition to the Psalms, which would have been necessary for performing the daily office, it contains sets of readings and other material proper to the performance of the office on Wilfrid's feast days. It is clear from the rubrics that accompany these texts that the manuscript was always intended for use in Ripon. The feast of St Wilfrid's nativity, celebrated nowhere else in Christendom, was a principal double feast 'within the church and parish of Ripon'.[3] Such feasts, with nine lessons, were the highest grade in a secular collegiate church. Christmas, Easter and other universally important feast days had the same rank.

---

[1] Ripon Cathedral Library, MS 8.

[2] Neil R. Kerr, *Medieval manuscripts in British libraries*, Oxford 1962-92, iv. 212.

[3] 'infra ecclesiam et parochiam Ripon': Ripon Cathedral Library, MS 8, fo. 162r.

The table provided to aid the calculation of Easter begins in 1418, so the manuscript was probably produced at around that time.[4] Given the number of new chantries that were founded in the early fifteenth century, it seems likely that the psalter was made for one of their chaplains. The most likely candidate is the chantry of St Thomas, founded in 1419. In 1488 Christopher Kendale became the chaplain of the St Thomas chantry, and the names of several of his kin appear in notes about marriages and births added to the psalter's calendar in the first years of the sixteenth century. These notes situate the memory of important life events within the annual cycle of saints' feasts in the parish of Ripon. The calendar of the Ripon psalter is not very elaborate. It lacks the illuminations that calendars in books of hours often possessed: the signs of the zodiac and the labours of the months. Only two colours of ink were used for its feast days. The less important feasts were written with black ink while the holidays were written with red. The new feast days of the Transfiguration (6 August) and the Holy Name (7 August), promulgated in the province of York in 1489, were never added to the calendar.[5] Indeed these new feasts came very late to Ripon, perhaps because they would have clashed frequently with the feast of St Wilfrid's nativity.

The chamberlain's and treasurer's accounts, and to a lesser extent the fabric rolls, are the other major source of evidence for Ripon's ritual year. Before he became chaplain of the St Thomas chantry in 1488, Christopher Kendale was the sub-treasurer of the minster. His account rolls from 1470-1 and 1484-5, the only two from the period of his tenure now extant, provide crucial information about the ritual year in medieval Ripon. Many sources of income, such as the plough money collected on the Sunday after Epiphany and wax donated at the feast of the Purification (2 February), were dependent on lay involvement in the ceremonies of important feast days. The expenses are equally revealing. In 1470-1 Kendale reckoned that it was necessary to purchase 11,400 communion wafers from Boroughbridge, at a cost of 1*d.* per hundred, and 14½ gallons of red wine from York for the regular use of the minster clergy.[6] For the annual communion of parishioners at Easter as well as for the *mandatum* on the preceding Thursday, Kendale purchased two bushels of fine white flour and two baskets of charcoal to bake the wafers.[7] The baking took two vestry clerks twelve days to complete.[8] The accounts of Ripon Minster's chamberlain have survived in greater number than those of the treasurer. While there are only four surviving treasurer's accounts from the fifteenth century, there are eleven chamberlain's accounts that have been edited, and there is a twelfth extant chamberlain's roll that was not edited because it was preserved unnoticed in

---

4 Kerr, *Medieval manuscripts in British libraries*, iv. 211-12.
5 Pfaff, *New liturgical feasts*, 30, 77.
6 *MR* iii. 216.
7 Ibid.
8 Ibid.

The National Archives rather than with the rest of the Ripon material.[9] The chamberlains, including Christopher Kendale in 1472-3, collected a much wider array of gifts than did the treasurers. Masses honouring important saints in the minster, the patronal feast days of guilds and dependent chapels, the images of the saints in the minster and the relics of St Wilfrid all generated gift income that filled his coffers. His expenses ranged from payments to clergy for all manner of special duties on major feast days to hiring minstrels for the Rogation procession and a man to carry the procession's dragon.

Dividing the year

Church custom and natural cycles mingled together to give meaning to the year, to forbid and permit activities, to impose obligations of feast and fast. The lavish books of hours that combine lists of saints' feast days with illustrations of the labours of the months and the signs of the zodiac eloquently depict this synthesis. The labours represented were mainly rural, and agricultural time was as important to the wealthy landowners who could afford to commission books of hours as it was to the many peasants who worked the land.[10] The natural year had two seasons: summer and winter.[11] Midwinter and midsummer, the year's shortest and longest days, were both solemnised by important feast days. Christmas, on 25 December, was the first in a series of feasts, liturgically termed the *temporale*, that commemorated the life, death and resurrection of Christ. Christmas and Epiphany had fixed dates, but the latter half of the series was filled with moveable feasts based on the date of Easter. The last of these, Corpus Christi, could fall as late as midsummer itself, on 24 June. The *sanctorale*, the counterpart to the *temporale*, was the schedule of saints' feasts. Unlike the *temporale*, it ran throughout the year. The two series blended together in an annually variable pattern wherein the static elements of the *temporale* and *sanctorale* were like the fixed stars and the moveable feasts wandered among them like the planets. The twelve days of Christmas were exceptional because they incorporated a number of saints' feasts (St Stephen, St John the Evangelist, Holy Innocents, Thomas Becket). The twelve days ended on 6 January with another *temporale* feast, Epiphany. Ordinarily Easter and its associated feast days were the only moveable feasts, but in Ripon there were two locally important feast days whose dates orbited around those of other feasts from the calendar. These were the feast of St William of York's translation in early January and the feast of St Wilfrid's nativity at the beginning of August.

[9]   MR iii. 224-91; TNA, SC 6/HENRYVII/1031.
[10] Le Goff, *Medieval civilization*, 179.
[11] Ibid.

Between midsummer and Christmas there were generally fewer saints' feasts than in the first half of the year, and among scholars of religion and folklore this fact has given rise to a debatable distinction between the year's two halves. Charles Phythian-Adams has described the six months from midsummer to Christmas as the secular season of the year, but Eamon Duffy argues that none of the year was truly secular because there was no secular mode of reckoning time.[12] As proof of the ritual significance of the midsummer to Christmas half of the year, he points to the major guild pageants, such as that staged in Lincoln at the feast of St Anne (26 July), and the tendency to establish regionally important feast days in October.[13] Ronald Hutton, with the slightly later start date of St Peter's eve (28 June), supports Phythian-Adams's division because of the lack of nationally important feast days that occurred during the contentious period.[14] In any case, these scholars agree that while the half of the year from Christmas to midsummer was dominated by universal feast days, there were far fewer of them and far more locally important ones during the latter part of the year.

This chapter concentrates here on the ritual year within the parish of Ripon, revealing how the feasts of patronal saints formed the devotional focus for the parish as a whole as well as for the smaller communities of guilds and chapels. Chapel licences show that the major feasts where attendance at the minster was compulsory were usually Christmas, the Purification of the Virgin Mary, Good Friday, Easter, Ascension, Pentecost, All Saints and the feasts of St Wilfrid. The division of the year into two halves is useful in some ways, because many of the major feast days when the people of the whole parish were obliged to attend services in the minster fell in the period of the year from Christmas to midsummer. The rest were feast days of universal importance that honoured the Virgin Mary and All Saints, plus the locally significant feasts of Ripon's patron saint. Wilfrid, like many other local patron saints, had major feasts outside of the *temporale* cycle. These were the feasts of his deposition (12 October) and, more important, the feast of his nativity in early August. Many, but not all, of the patronal feasts of guilds and chapels also occurred between midsummer and Christmas. Not all red-letter feast days were equally important, and there were many that did not require attendance at the minster. The calendar contains many such holidays dedicated to the Apostles and to significant York saints. On these days Ripon's parishioners would have been forbidden to work and presumably were expected to attend one of their local chapels. Failure to observe the holiday properly could be punished by the chapter court with public penance like that assigned to Joan Farand of Aismunderby for spinning and carding wool on the feast of St Matthew.[15] The

---

[12] Charles Phythian-Adams, *Local history and folklore: a new framework*, London 1975, 24, and 'Ritual constructions of society', 380–1; Duffy, *Stripping of the altars*, 41, 47.

[13] Duffy, *Stripping of the altars*, 47–8.

[14] Hutton, *Rise and fall of Merry England*, 46.

[15] AoC, 134.

rare feast days when parishioners were bound to attend the minster were truly exceptional. The minster's financial accounts show lavish expenditure during the twelve days of Christmas, Holy Week and the Rogation days leading up to the feast of the Ascension. Such expenditure was necessary to make these occasions into true spectacles unmatched anywhere else in the parish. If it were possible to make a community embracing the whole parish, its crucible was the minster on these feast days when crowds of parishioners filled the church.

The occasion of a feast day was indicated by more than merely increased attendance: light, smell, colour, clothing and spatial access all fluctuated according to the holiday. Candles augmented winter feasts, especially Christmas, Epiphany and Candlemas, and the extinguishing and kindling of candles were central to the rituals of Holy Week. Different types of incense were used for different grades of feast, meaning that the more important occasions smelled differently from the lesser ones. While on the double feasts and feasts of nine lessons the Ripon clergy censed the choir with incense made of resin, they used what the accounts refer to as *sclateincense* for the principal feasts.[16] Various liturgical seasons and feasts called for different coloured clerical vestments. In theory the colours were white (feasts related to Christ, the Virgin Mary, confessor and virgin saints), red (the Holy Spirit, Apostles, martyrs), black (the penitential seasons of Lent and Advent) and green (everything else).[17] In practice blue might have been used for Lent and Advent, and green could be replaced by yellow or tawny.[18] The clergy also wore special types of vestments to indicate the greater dignity of some feasts. Most notably the cope, normally worn by priests presiding over the mass and other ceremonies such as weddings, was worn by the whole of the Ripon clergy including acolytes and paten-bearers, at Christmas, Easter and on the feast of Wilfrid's nativity.[19] Even the usual prohibitions on lay access to the choir were temporarily suspended on two occasions: on Good Friday the clergy let the laity enter the choir so that they could creep to the cross, and again at dawn on Easter morning the laity could go into the choir for the ritual emptying of the Easter sepulchre.

From Christmas to Midsummer

Preparation for Christmas began with the penitential season of Advent, which commenced around the feast of St Andrew at the end of November. The feast of Christmas on 25 December brought to an end the fast and opened a twelve-day-long period of celebration that continued until the feast of Epiphany on 6 January. Between Christmas and Epiphany there were several other feast

[16]   MR iii. 216-17, 222.
[17]   Woolgar, *The senses in late medieval England*,168-9.
[18]   Badham, *Seeking salvation*, 125.
[19]   Janet Mayo, *A history of ecclesiastical dress*, London 1984, 55; MR iii. 231-2.

days: St Stephen (26 December), St John the Evangelist (27 December) Holy Innocents (28 December), Thomas Becket (29 December), St Sylvester (31 December) and the Circumcision of the Lord (1 January). The twelve days of Christmas were characterised by banqueting, a custom which had been transferred from pagan holidays such as Yule and Saturnalia to Christmas during the early centuries of Christianity.[20] Ripon's greatest Christmas banquets would no doubt have taken place in the halls of its wealthiest families who, although they were obliged to visit the minster on Christmas itself, could celebrate the rest of the midwinter saints' feasts in their own domestic chapels. The banqueting of the twelve days was in part an effort to counteract the bleakness of a season so dark that it became known as the time when apparitions of the dead were most likely to visit the earth.[21] The Christmas liturgy, with its emphasis on light, was also intended to offset the winter darkness.

Christmas was unusual in having three masses rather than one. The most important of the three took place at midnight because it was thought that Christ was born not just on the darkest day of the year but also at the darkest moment of the night.[22] At Ripon the chamberlain paid clerks to read lessons from the prophet Isaiah, the source of much of the light imagery.[23] These lessons and a recitation of the genealogy of Christ were customary features of the Christmas liturgy. The minster's wax star, lit at Christmas and Epiphany, was less common. They could ordinarily be found only in large urban churches like Ripon.[24] The star, the procession of all the clergy wearing their ceremonial copes, and the requirement that all parishioners attend the minster were the essential features of Christmas at the minster. It was one of the few moments in the year when the parishioners were assembled as a single parish. Afterwards they largely returned to their villages and manors to observe the rest of the twelve days of Christmas in more familiar company. The morrow masses held at dawn on the feast of St Stephen (26 December) might have been intended to allow those who had spent the night in Ripon to hear mass before travelling home.

Within the town of Ripon there is evidence, at least for the decades around 1400, of fundraising for the minster organised by laypeople. One of Ripon's religious fraternities raised money for the minster fabric at twilight on Christmas. In 1354 this sum was only 8s. 5d., but the 16s. 8d gathered in 1379 was more typical.[25] In 1424 and in the few other fifteenth-century accounts the collection is described as taking place on the night of the feast of St Stephen.[26]

---

[20]   Alexander Murray, 'Medieval Christmas', *History Today* xxxvi (1986), 31–9 at p. 32.

[21]   Schmitt, *Ghosts in the Middle Ages*, 174.

[22]   Murray, 'Medieval Christmas', 35.

[23]   MR iii. 232.

[24]   Hutton, *Rise and fall of Merry England*, 15–16.

[25]   MR iii. 88.

[26]   MR iii. 149.

The fabric wardens never specify which guild it was, and it is possible that it was a group whose only purpose was to collect money at Christmas or on the feast of St Stephen. Ronald Hutton discovered many similar groups in the church-wardens' accounts of medieval England. They were often called 'Hogans' or 'Hogglers', and they usually existed in rural parishes rather than in urban ones.[27] The custom appears to have fallen out of use in Ripon by the sixteenth century but it is none the less a noteworthy example of traditional parish fundraising in the minster accounts. Many of the others – such as Hocktide fines, May games and church ales – are absent from the records but may well have been employed to raise money for the maintenance of chapels and guilds. The townspeople of Ripon may also have seen the minster's Boy Bishop just after Christmas, a custom that was observed in Ripon although there is no clear evidence of its timing: it could just as easily have been taken place at the feast of St Nicholas (6 December) as at the feast of the Holy Innocents (28 December).

The Christmas holidays came to an end with Epiphany on 6 January, the feast which marked the coming of the kings, led by a special star, to visit the infant Christ. In Ripon a star made of wax candles was lit on Christmas and Epiphany to represent the star described in Scripture. Epiphany was not an obligatory feast in the parish, so parishioners were free to observe the holiday in their chapels. The treasurer of the minster distributed incense to those who did attend the minster, mirroring one of the gifts of the magi. It was the lower grade of incense, the resin type, used in the choir for lesser double feasts and feasts of nine lessons rather than *sclateincense*.[28] Its value should be interpreted in relation to the moral qualities attributed to smells at the time. Like the original gift of the magi, which fittingly replaced the stink of the stable where Christ was born with a sweet fragrance, the incense given to Ripon's parish-ioners at Epiphany could impart the smell of holiness to their dwellings.[29]

The date of Epiphany determined the date of the feast of the translation of St William, a regional saint and former archbishop of York. William's cult was the solution to a problem faced by York Minster in the 1170s, when it had no relics of any saintly former archbishops. The meteoric rise of Becket's cult following his murder in 1170 brought prestige to Canterbury and the southern church province of England and left York looking for its own holy bishop. The body of Archbishop William Fitzherbert had rested in York Minster since his death in 1154. Around Pentecost 1177 William performed a flurry of miracles, ultimately leading to his canonisation by Honorius III in 1226.[30] Ripon Minster had its own St William altar during the fifteenth century. Its location is unknown but it is frequently mentioned in connection with gift-giving on the

27   Hutton, *Rise and fall of Merry England*, 12–13.
28   MR iii. 222.
29   Woolgar, *The senses in late medieval England*, 119.
30   Christopher Norton, *St William of York*, York 2006, 149–64.

feast days of St Mary and St Wilfrid, though not on the feast days of St William. In Ripon the feast of St William's translation was ranked as a principal feast and took place on the Sunday after Epiphany, which was also Plough Sunday. It was customary for ploughs to be blessed on this Sunday, and the ploughing season began the next day.[31] Ripon's treasurer collected the donations made at this time, for example 9s. 2d. in 1401, 8s. the following year, and 13s. 8d. in 1470.[32] The collection of plough money for the church was common in rural parishes; the star at Epiphany was a feature of large urban churches.[33] Ripon Minster, as an urban great church at the centre of a vast rural parish, naturally had both.

Candlemas was another name for the feast of the Purification of the Virgin Mary (2 February); celebrated forty days after Christmas, it was effectively the last element of the Christmas component of the *temporale*.[34] After giving birth to Christ, Mary needed to be ritually purified at the Temple in Jerusalem just as Ripon's own women were purified and then readmitted to the church after childbirth. The evidence of chapel licences indicates that Candlemas, unlike the individual purifications of women of the parish, obliged most parishioners to attend the minster. As the name implies, there was a great emphasis on light provided by candles. Laypeople brought candles and wax to the minster, donating much of it as part of their parish dues, but they could return home with additional candles that had been blessed by a priest, and which were believed to have apotropaic powers.[35] The procession of laypeople with lit candles on this feast day was a happy occasion in contrast to the shaming of penitents ordered to carry lit candles in Sunday and feast day processions. The blessing of the paschal candle at Candlemas looked forward to Easter when it would burn beside the high altar.[36] Not long afterwards came the penitential season of Lent and all the other moveable feasts associated with Easter.

Lent began on the Wednesday forty days before Easter, and varied in date according to the movement of Easter itself. The rood and other crosses were veiled during this period as a sign of mourning.[37] When the fabric wardens replaced the rood in 1399, they paid John Payntour 2s. 10d. to decorate a great crimson veil 'to cover the cross standing in the body of the church during Lent' and another 8d. for the coverings of two 'other images', no doubt the figures of the Virgin and John the Evangelist that flanked the rood.[38] The

---

[31] Hutton, *Rise and fall of Merry England*, 16.

[32] MR iii. 207, 211, 215.

[33] Hutton, *Rise and fall of Merry England*, 15–17.

[34] Ibid. 15.

[35] Duffy, *Stripping of the altars*, 16–17.

[36] Ibid. 16.

[37] Hutton, *Rise and fall of Merry England*, 20.

[38] 'ad cooperiendum crucem stantem infra corpus ecclesiæ in Quadragesima' and 'alias ymagines': MR iii. 129.

preferred colour of clerical vestments during Lent was black, the same colour used for Advent and funerals, though they might in fact have been another dark colour such as violet, blue or russet.[39] The season imposed a condition of fast on everyone in preparation for Holy Week and Easter, a penitential season universal throughout Christendom. Failure to observe the fast could result in prosecution by the chapter court as in 1481, when the vicar Thomas Braithwaite reported one of his parishioners, Isabelle Greve, for not making her confession or taking communion, 'and not fearing to eat meat and meaty dishes, and dairy products, and other foods in all circumstances, with abstinence and the holy fast having been forgotten'.[40] In addition to their tithes, the parishioners paid, as part of their parish dues, annual Lenten fines that included many of the things that were forbidden during Lent, such as calves, eggs, butter, milk and cheese. Some of the fines may have been commuted to a cash payment, but tithe calves at least seem to have been given in kind rather than cash.[41] In 1502 the chamberlain paid Richard Olle 4d. per day for six days to collect them; the rate was the same in 1505 but that year it only took four days to collect the calves.[42] Non-payment of tithes, like neglect of religious duties, was a matter for the chapter court. In April 1460 it cited the fuller John Walker for not paying Lenten tithes worth 5d. and threatened him with a sentence of greater excommunication if he did not pay.[43] The enforcement of the fast and the collection of tithes remained the prerogative of the minster throughout the fifteenth century.

The Sunday before Easter was Palm Sunday, which commemorated Christ's entry into Jerusalem with one of the year's grandest processions. It was an important feast day and yet, like Epiphany before it and Maundy Thursday afterward, it was not an obligatory feast day for any category of the minster's parishioners. Nevertheless, it seems very likely that the spectacle of the occasion attracted people who did not usually go to Sunday mass in Ripon. In some English churches Palm Sunday included not only processions with relics and consecrated hosts but even men hired to play Old Testament prophets.[44] Ripon's Palm Sunday processions do not appear to have involved the relics of St Wilfrid or hired actors but they were still more elaborate than the average Sunday procession. The York Minster procession would have provided the model. Blessed palms, which could be one of a number of types of foliage, including willow, sallow, box, yew and evergreens,[45] were distributed to the

---

[39] Woolgar, *The senses in late medieval England*, 168; Badham, *Seeking salvation*, 125.

[40] 'et tum carnes et carnea ac lacticinia et cetera alimenta, omnimodo abstinencia et jejunio sacro oblita, non veretur comedere': AoC, 186–7.

[41] MR iii. 224.

[42] MR iii. 267; TNA, SC 6/HENRYVII/1031.

[43] AoC, 50.

[44] Duffy, *Stripping of the altars*, 24.

[45] Hutton, *Rise and fall of Merry England*, 20.

laity at the beginning of this procession.[46] In 1439 Henry Cook, the minster chamberlain, paid the archbishop's parker 2s. 'for palms and ivy' and spent another 6d. on the costs of gathering and transporting them.[47] After the distribution, the main processional body then went outside the church where it was met by a smaller procession that brought out a consecrated host for veneration before returning it to the church. The meeting occurred at a station marked by a permanent cross in the churchyard. Many churches had such crosses, usually somewhere near the north-eastern end of the church.[48] Agnes Hawton (d. 1512) mentioned the Ripon palm cross in her will, evidently hoping to be buried nearby.[49] After the departure of the host procession, the main procession continued around the church to the western portal where more verses and responses were sung.[50] The next major station was the rood itself which was unveiled when the procession reached it so that it too could be venerated.[51] Ripon's rood, screen and adjacent altars of Holy Trinity and Exaltation of the Holy Cross were the subject of intense devotion throughout the year. The Holy Cross guild focused on the rood and the Holy Trinity altar was, from 1467, the site of John Sendale's chantry and tomb. From about the same time it was also the place where the younger William Wrampayn was buried.[52] After the unveiling of the rood the clergy would then enter the choir for the mass, during which, in place of the normal Gospel passage, they would sing the whole of the passion story from the book of Matthew.[53] According to popular belief crosses made during the singing of the passion story would have the power to protect their owners from evil influences.[54] They thus had properties that were similar to the Candlemas candles and the Epiphany incense.

Holy Thursday commemorated the Last Supper, after which Christ was betrayed by Judas and arrested in the garden of Gethsemane. Like Epiphany and Palm Sunday, Maundy Thursday was a significant feast when there were strong incentives for Ripon's parishioners to attend the minster even though they were not necessarily required to do so. The earliest extant treasurer's account (1401–2) notes the purchase of forty-six gallons of ale, three-quarters of a pound of ginger, one pound of sugar, as well as cloves and anise for the event.[55] The spices purchased by the treasurer would not have been out of place

---

[46] *Manuale et processionale ad usum insignis Ecclesiæ Eboracensis*, ed. W. G. Henderson, Durham 1875, 148.

[47] 'pro palmis et edrea': MR iii. 234.

[48] Badham, *Seeking salvation*, 209.

[49] The copy of her will is damaged but the reference to the cross occurs at the point where the testator normally specifies a burial place: AoC, 334.

[50] *Manuale et processionale*, 149–51.

[51] Hutton, *Rise and fall of Merry England*, 21; Duffy, *Stripping of the altars*, 25.

[52] Borthwick Institute, probate register 4, fo. 38v.

[53] Duffy, *Stripping of the altars*, 25–6.

[54] Ibid. 26.

[55] MR iii. 208.

in the accounts of a gentry household preparing for a banquet in the fifteenth century.[56] The huge amount of ale purchased in 1402 was no fluke. For Holy Thursday 1403 the treasurer bought forty-eight gallons of ale.[57] The same rolls record the purchase of sweetmeats. The amount seems too great to have been intended only for distribution to a small but symbolic number of poor men, so the spiced ale and sweetmeats must have been part of a wider distribution to laypeople who attended the Holy Thursday service. It was the fourth and final instance in the liturgical year when the minster clergy gave gifts of symbolic significance to the laity. After the Holy Thursday mass, the clergy stripped and cleaned all the altars in the church. In York the archbishop blessed the holy oil used for the sacraments of baptism and extreme unction, some of which would later be distributed to Ripon.[58] The tenebrae service, in which a series of candles were extinguished, was a feature of not only Holy Thursday but also the days before and after.[59] In 1402 the sub-treasurer spent 3s. 4d. on a new candelabrum for this very purpose.[60]

Holy Friday commemorated Christ's crucifixion. In place of a mass it had a reading of the entire passion sequence from the Gospel of John.[61] The tenebrae service was repeated for the third time. Unlike the preceding Wednesday and Thursday, when one candle remained lit, all the candles were extinguished on Good Friday and only afterwards was the large paschal candle lit.[62] For the laity, one of the key elements of the Holy Friday service was the creeping to the cross. The usual boundaries between lay and clerical space were temporarily dissolved to permit this ritual. The laity could enter the choir to venerate the cross, and afterwards they made gifts there. On Holy Friday in 1411 the chamberlain accumulated more than 3s. in gifts given 'in the choir to adore the cross on Good Friday'.[63] The monks of Durham had a similar practice, allowing the laity to come and venerate a crucifix; yet the Durham monks kept the laity out of their choir and only allowed them to venerate the cross at its west door before they held their own monastic ceremony of creeping to the cross within the choir.[64] The custom had a long history in Ripon: chapel licences of the late thirteenth century even identify the feast as the 'day of adoring the cross'.[65] This penitential act defined Holy Friday, which was one of the obligatory

---

[56] Woolgar, *The senses in late medieval England*, 108-9.

[57] MR iii. 212.

[58] Duffy, *Stripping of the altars*, 28; Hutton, *Rise and fall of Merry England*, 22.

[59] Hutton, *Rise and fall of Merry England*, 21, 23-4.

[60] MR iii. 212.

[61] Duffy, *Stripping of the altars*, 29.

[62] Hutton, *Rise and fall of Merry England*, 24.

[63] 'in choro ad crucem adorandam in die Parasceven': MR iii. 227.

[64] John McKinnell, 'For the people/by the people: public and private spaces in the Durham sequence of the sacrament', in Frances Andrews (ed.), *Ritual and space in the Middle Ages*, Donington 2009, 213-31 at p. 220.

[65] 'die Crucis adorandæ': MR i. 202. The Bridge Hewick chapel licence is typical.

annual feast days for the majority of Ripon's parishioners, though it was left to the discretion of the gentry families whether they wished to attend or not.

The other significant feature of the Good Friday liturgy was the Easter sepulchre. This represented the tomb in which Christ was buried after the cruci-fixion. It could be a permanent fixture of the church or a moveable object made of wood. Sepulchres were common features of parish churches in medieval England, and many had their own light and guild whose members would watch over the sepulchre during the two nights before Easter.[66] They were usually located on the north side of the high altar. The base of the structure could be a table tomb with a flat top, thereby linking the deceased person whose tomb it was to one of the most important rituals of the year.[67] The gifts made 'in the choir at the Resurrection of the Lord at dawn on Easter' indicate that Ripon's Easter sepulchre was located in the choir, though no physical traces of it remain.[68] The burial of a crucifix in the Easter sepulchre followed the ritual creeping to the cross, and the celebration of Easter would normally begin with its removal.[69] According to the York processional, the church bells were rung to gather the clergy and people who then knelt in prayer, after which a priest censed the sepulchre, opened it, and removed the items buried within.[70]

Easter was the great moveable feast upon which so many other feast days depended. It could fall as early as 22 March and as late as 25 April. It was a feast day of the highest rank and one of the three occasions when the minster clergy processed in their copes, not to mention one of the few feast days when Ripon's gentry families were supposed to attend the minster with everyone else. Furthermore it was the occasion when laypeople were expected to make their annual communion, having already prepared by making their annual confession. They were expected to confess their mortal sins to their parish priest in their parish church and although individual, these confessions were not as private as they would become in the sixteenth century when the private confessional booth was developed.[71] Without confession the sacrament would be ineffective because the recipient would not be in the proper spiritual state. The Lenten fast only ended after reception of the sacrament.[72] Confession was also a vehicle for religious instruction. In the province of York, when Archbishop Thoresby (r. 1353–73) held the see in the late fourteenth century, it became one of the most important means of examining and instructing the laity about religion.[73] Those who failed to fulfil the obligation of confession

---

[66]   Hutton, *Rise and fall of Merry England*, 23–4.

[67]   Duffy, *Stripping of the altars*, 32.

[68]   'in choro ad Resurreccionem Domini in die Pasch. in aurora': MR iii. 227.

[69]   Duffy, *Stripping of the altars*, 29–30; Hutton, *Rise and fall of Merry England*, 25.

[70]   *Manuale et processionale*, 170.

[71]   Arnold, *Belief and unbelief*, 170.

[72]   Duffy, *Stripping of the altars*, 93.

[73]   Hughes, *Pastors and visionaries*, 143.

and communion would be excommunicated, so it was important to be able to determine whether or not a parishioner had done so. The parish of Ripon was so large that it would have been impossible for the clergy to administer the sacraments without dividing it into smaller spheres of responsibility, namely the prebends overseen by the six vicars.

The 1546 chantry certificate records that Ripon's vicars were 'to have Cure of Sowle and mynystracon of Sacrements at vj severall Alters to all the parochians of the said prebendariez'.[74] It summarises the essential scheme by which the parish was divided. Each prebend, which was the geographical unit that provided the income for one of the minster's prebendaries, had its own altar in the minster. In lieu of the canon, a vicar was charged with the cure of souls within the prebend. The practice of using six altars was already well established by 1439, when the chamberlain paid 'diverse ministers helping with the communion of parishioners at six altars at the feast of Easter ... a deacon serving the wine, two acolytes holding the houselling cloth, and two porters for keeping the door'.[75] This scheme of division may have limited the possibility for disputes over precedence by separating many of the most powerful families from one another. It certainly gave them wider scope to demonstrate lordship over a particular part of the parish by installing monuments near their own parochial altars. The Markenfields and probably the Malories developed the spaces around their parochial altars into family mortuary chapels. The result was that they took communion in the presence of their ancestors, whose monuments would also have impressed the status of these families upon their neighbours at that time. It was as difficult to avoid these symbols of lordship as it was to neglect the annual religious obligations.

The next major feast day was the first feast of St Wilfrid after Christmas. On 24 April, in a week congested with feast days – it was preceded by the feast of St George and followed by the feast of St Mark – the cult of St Wilfrid drew together the urban and the rural elements of the parish for commercial as well as religious reasons. Henry I had long ago granted the archbishop of York the right to hold an annual fair of four days at the feast of Wilfrid's translation.[76] The three feasts periodically coincided with Easter, and the potential clash had in fact caused a rearrangement of the feast days of St Wilfrid much earlier in the history of his cult.[77] It is almost certain that Wilfrid died on 24 April 710 and that his April feast was therefore originally the feast commemorating his earthly death and heavenly birth.[78] Later it was swapped with the feast on 12

---

[74] MR iii. 14.

[75] 'diversis ministris ad sex altaria ibidem axiliantibus ad communicand. parochianos ibidem ad f. Paschæ ... uni diacono ministranti vinum, duobus tentoribus tuallia, duobus portariis pro ostio custodiendo': MR iii. 234.

[76] MR i. 94.

[77] This happened five times between 1370 and 1520: on 23 April 1413, 1424, 1508; on 24 April 1519; and on 25 April 1451.

[78] Stancliffe, 'Dating Wilfrid's death and Stephen's Life', 18–19.

October. The feast of Wilfrid's translation was evidently the least important of Wilfrid's feast days and had only three lessons. The third lesson incorporates Archbishop Walter de Grey's indulgence from 1224 and also describes the earlier translation of Wilfrid's relics by Archbishop Oswald in the late tenth century.[79] Both of these episodes affirmed the presence of Wilfrid's relics in Ripon and rejected the alternative tradition according to which he had been translated to Canterbury. Ripon's Guild of St Wilfrid celebrated the feast of Wilfrid's translation as its annual patronal feast, and beginning around 1410 the minster clergy held a mass for the benefit of the guild on this feast day.[80] It is the best example of a feast day between Christmas and midsummer that was important to the communal identity of a distinct group within the parish. By contrast the other guilds, and also the dependent chapels of some of the villages, largely had their major feast days during the other half of the year.

St Wilfrid's summer fair provided an opportunity for the minster to market any Lenten tithes that it had collected in kind, such as calves. Presumably the marketplace was the site of these fairs and the name of the Horsefair, a street to the north-west of the marketplace, indicates its role in the marketing of livestock, an important element in medieval fairs. The feast of the Invention of Holy Cross on 3 May was a related landmark in the agricultural year. When the ploughing season began in January, the sheep and cattle were still at their low-lying winter stations. In March, probably around the feast of the Annunciation (25 March), the lambing season began.[81] Now, at the start of May, it was time for the annual transhumance of the flocks. The ewes that had lambed were kept close to the granges where they could be milked to produce cheese, and their lambs remained there with them. The rest of the flocks were moved up into the higher reaches of the dales where they would graze for the summer. Pastoral agriculture was the predominant type in the upland portions of the parish to the west and north of Ripon. Those employed to look after the livestock would have been increasingly busy in places far from the minster once the grazing season began. It seems doubtful that they would all have returned to the minster for the feast of the Ascension, but some of the shepherds might have seen the Rogation procession as it trooped along the moorland boundary of the parish in Nidderdale.

The Thursday forty days after Easter was the feast of the Ascension, preceded by three days of processions, the Rogation or cross days. It was Ripon's most important annual procession, and the one in which the Marmion tenants were supposed to carry Wilfrid's relics. Rogation and Ascension together formed a highly significant moment in the liturgical year when the parish was represented as a single community presided over by Wilfrid, the minster clergy and the parish elite. Rogation Monday could be any date between 27 April and 31

---

[79] Ripon Cathedral, MS 8, fos 168r–169r.

[80] MR iii. 228.

[81] Winchester, *Harvest of the hills*, 58.

May depending on the date of Easter. In many parishes the procession that took place then and on the following two days was a beating of the bounds that followed the parish boundary. Such a procession thus inscribed this boundary on the memories of its participants while seeking divine blessing for the year's crops and giving ritual expression to the identity of the parish.[82] Rogation thus ranked among the most important annual rituals, with great power to form parochial identity.[83] Notwithstanding its immense size, Ripon had its own beating of the bounds. The boundary is described in an itinerary from 1481. Furthermore, the minster's account rolls show that the procession was an annual event with various types of income and expenses. The chamberlain spent 10s. on hiring minstrels for the processions on the three Rogation days and on the feast of the Ascension in 1439, and paid a man 16d. (4d. per day) to carry the dragon which was a customary feature of Rogation processions.[84] The fabric wardens paid the minster's sacristan 2d. per day to raise and lower a tent, most likely to shelter Wilfrid's relics wherever the procession stopped for the night.[85]

The itinerary for the 1481 Rogation procession lists its major participants, both the clergy and the laymen who carried Wilfrid's relics. The list is significant since processions like this one were part of the process by which the hierarchical order of the parish was established and affirmed.[86] It was a counterpart to the major feast days in the minster, and provides the clearest insight into the ideal parish structure envisioned by the clergy of Ripon. The most important participant was Wilfrid himself, and in theory he should have been accompanied by the Marmion tenants and the most important clergy. The 1481 list of participants shows that practice and theory had diverged somewhat by the late fifteenth century. The first cleric named is none other than Christopher Kendale, sub-treasurer and commissary of the chapter.[87] The 'twelve ministers of the choir' were actually Kendale and three chantry chaplains from the minster, three chaplains from elsewhere in the town, the chaplain of Pateley Bridge, the chapter's bailiff and three clerks.[88] None of the canons is named in this list, even though the canon of Stanwick at least should have been present in Ripon since he was bound to perpetual residence. The formula 'twelve ministers of the choir' evidently records an earlier practice that had been modified by 1481. More startling still is the absence of all known Marmion tenants. In their places were twenty-four other laymen, all from the parish. The

[82] Ronald Hutton, *The stations of the sun: a history of the ritual year in Britain*, Oxford 1996, 277–8.

[83] Duffy, *Stripping of the altars*, 136.

[84] MR iii. 233–4.

[85] MR iii. 171.

[86] Arnold, *Belief and unbelief*, 106.

[87] AoC, 338.

[88] 'duodecim ministros chori': ibid.

itinerary states the residence and profession of many of the twenty-four, most of whom were husbandmen and yeomen from the many villages surrounding Ripon. Thornton was well represented with five, including the brothers John and William Walworth. John was the forester of the archbishop of York's free chase in Thornton and Nidderdale while William was a former archiepiscopal bailiff of Ripon.[89] The other villages with representatives escorting the relics were Copt Hewick, Grantley, Markington, Monkton, Nunwick, Pateley Bridge, Sharrow, Skelton, Thorpe, Wallerthwaite and Westwick. The only notable exception is Aldfield. The procession thereby incorporated many of the major settlements of the parish through their representatives, but where were the Marmion tenants?

The chapter acts show that throughout the fifteenth century Ripon's Marmion tenants continued to swear fealty to the chapter when they inherited their lands. The act book contains a list of thirteen Marmion tenants admitted between 1466 and 1476, but not one of them was listed among the twenty-four 'good, free, and lawful men living within the franchise' who escorted Wilfrid's relics in the 1481 procession.[90] The resident canons, often named as recipients of the oath of fealty from the Marmion tenants, are likewise absent from the list of clerical participants. In fact, some Marmion tenants were actually swearing their oath of fealty in the presence of the resident canon while the procession was marching along the parish boundary far away from the minster. John Scrope, lord of Bolton, was admitted as a Marmion tenant on Cross Tuesday in 1476. He was admitted by proxy, but the canons who received the oath were present in the chapter house rather than accompanying Wilfrid's relics.[91] Likewise on Cross Tuesday 1490, when Robert Kendale swore his oath in person.[92] The majority of the Marmion tenants swore their oaths of fealty on one of the Rogation days, most commonly on the Monday, so the ceremony remained connected to Rogation and Ascension. Nevertheless, the Marmion tenant's oath had become separated from the service of carrying the relics, and this service was taken up by men of lesser gentry status and below. These men were residents of the parish and therefore represented it in a way that some of the Marmion tenants could not. At least five of the thirteen men on the 1466-76 list of Marmion tenants resided outside the parish. Relieved of their duty to carry the relics, the Marmion tenants from within the parish probably took no part in the procession after they had sworn their oaths. The knights, esquires and their families who had their own chapels were exempt according to the terms of their chapel licences: Rogation and Ascension only feature in the long list of obligations for ordinary parishioners. Whether or not the rest of the parishioners attended is a different matter. As was generally the

---

[89]   AoC, 339.

[90]   'probos, liberos, et legales homines infra franchesias ... inhabitantes': ibid.

[91]   AoC, 247.

[92]   AoC, 248.

case throughout medieval England, there were not many instances of Ripon's parishioners being punished for not attending, and it is not clear whether this was because they all attended or because attendance was not enforced.[93] Only one category of person, the permanent sanctuary seekers (*gyrthmen*) who took refuge within the liberty of St Wilfrid, were ever cited by the chapter court for failing in their duty to accompany Wilfrid's relics.

There is no mention of *gyrthmen* in the 1481 itinerary, but they were expected to take part in the procession. It was their obligation

> to carry their rods or banners on the three days of Rogation, and on the feast of the Ascension in the general procession in the same place, in the presence of St Wilfrid's reliquary, according to the ancient custom, and also to that which they were bound by their corporal oaths, when they touched the holy Gospels at their first admission to the said liberty.[94]

When they failed to do so, the chapter court cited them and imposed its penance. In 1505 it suspended four men for not fulfilling their obligations.[95] Around fifty years earlier, just after the feast of the Ascension in 1453, the chapter cited six sanctuary men. Thomas Plumber alleged that he had attended the processions every day except for Monday; Robert Morton claimed that he had not dared to attend for fear of his creditors and imprisonment; William Topshawe said that he would have been ready if the choir had left the church in the usual fashion.[96] Canon William Scrope rejected all excuses and sentenced the three to be beaten before the procession on four forthcoming major feast days: Pentecost, Holy Trinity, Corpus Christi and the Nativity of St Wilfrid.[97] Henry Johnson and Edmund Skaythlok appeared later and were also assigned penance, but John Skaythlok was pardoned because of his age and mental incapacity.[98] The sanctuary seekers with their banners were integral to the pageantry of the Rogation procession. The occasion demanded their participation and as the case of Robert Morton shows, they enjoyed additional protections to guarantee that they processed. Morton could not have sought sanctuary from debt, so his protection from harassment by creditors was a special privilege just for the days of Rogation and Ascension. The sanctuary seekers proved that Wilfrid not only had the power to bind knights and gentlemen to him by oath of fealty but also that he could quash vendettas and

---

[93] Hutton, *Rise and fall of Merry England*, 35.

[94] 'ad portand' rodas suas sive vexillas tribus diebus Rogacionum, et in festo Assencionis Dominicæ in processione generali ibidem, coram capsula Beati Wilfridi, secundum morem antiquum, et eciam ad quod per eorum corporalia juramenta, tactis per ipsos sacrosanctis Dei evangeliis in prima sua admissione ad dictam libertatem sunt astricti': AoC, 315.

[95] AoC, 315–16.

[96] AoC, 72.

[97] AoC, 72–3.

[98] AoC, 73.

turn aside the wrath of kings from the felons who sought his aid. There could be no more powerful symbol of the minster's authority over the parish than the annual Rogation procession.

The boundary needed to be preserved in memory in order to prevent the chapter from losing jurisdiction over any of Wilfrid's rightful territory. According to the itinerary, the circuit had been 'continually known and used from the time of the noble princes Oswiu the father and Alfred the son, kings of Northumbria, and of the most holy confessor and bishop Wilfrid the Great, archbishop of York, up to now'.[99] This claim cannot be literally true, since the custom of making Rogation processions was not introduced in England until the Council of Cloveshoo in 747, thirty-some years after Wilfrid's death.[100] Nevertheless, the antiquity of the boundary and the continuity of its memorialisation by annual procession were both guarantees of its legitimacy. Repetition gave the Ripon Rogation procession, like others of its type, a timeless quality and lent it almost irrefutable authority.[101] Should anyone choose to contest the boundary, the minster clergy were well supplied with men who could defend it in court. The itinerary implies as much when it describes the twenty-four laymen who escorted Wilfrid's relics as 'good, free, and lawful men', which are the same words normally used to describe jurors summoned to give evidence in an inquest.[102]

The 1481 perambulation reveals the extent of the parish, using landmarks like towns and villages as well as roads, bridges, rivers, streams, ditches, walls, hedges, fallen trees and large stones. Reliance on features that have changed over the last five hundred years, especially hedges and trees, makes it difficult for the exact route to be plotted today. Moreover, many of the villages mentioned in the perambulation were not visited directly, but appear in connection with their surrounding fields through which the procession passed. For example, one passage describes the party 'going across the said water of the Ure up to the Reed Bank in the pasture of North Stainley between the liberties of Ripon on the one hand and the lordship of the liberty of St Cuthbert of Durham and the lordship of Allerton on the other'.[103] This is typical of the description, which is concerned first and foremost with boundaries. When the procession followed the course of rivers and roads, it was because these marked the limits of the parish in many places. Stones are mentioned at a variety of points in the course of the procession. Some of these stones may have been

[99] 'a tempore nobilium principum Oswii patris et Alfridi filii, regum Northumbrorum, et sanctissimi confessoris et pontificis Wilfridi Magni Ebor. archiepiscopi, usque nunc continue cognitos et usitatos': AoC, 338.

[100] Hutton, *Stations of the sun*, 277.

[101] Arnold, *Belief and unbelief*, 107.

[102] 'probos, liberos, et legales homines': AoC, 339.

[103] 'ex transverso prædictæ aquæ de Yoore usqe le Reed Banck in pastura de North Stainley inter libertates de Ripon ex una parte et dominium libertatis Sancti Cuthberti Dunelm. et de dominio de Alverton ex altera parte': AoC, 344.

natural geological features but others were artificial. Early in its progress to the west the procession met a large stone named for St Wilfrid in the bank of Holbeck. Later there were stones marked with the symbols of the archbishop of York and Fountains Abbey on the high moor near Thornton. The area of open country between Kettlestang Hill and the River Skell was probably devoid of the landmarks that defined much of the rest of the parish and the series of three stones that the procession encountered there must have been essential to show the route. Standing stones like these were typical boundary markers in moorland areas.[104] The area around Skelton and Hutton Conyers was similarly marked by a number of other stones, including 'a great stone placed since antiquity in the earth upon the moor'.[105] The estimation of the length of time that the stone had stood there is tantalisingly vague. The relationship between the ritual landscape of the fifteenth century and that of prehistoric times deserves much greater attention than is possible here, but the presence of henges near Hutton Conyers and just beyond the northern edge of the parish at Thornborough leaves no doubt that an elaborate ritual landscape existed along the River Ure long before Wilfrid founded his monastery on its banks.[106]

Ascension Thursday witnessed the culmination of the procession with the return of Wilfrid's relics to the minster and a large-scale high mass procession within the church itself. The chamberlain's accounts hint that smaller processions from a few of the key chapels of the parish preceded this larger procession. The 1439–40 account records donations from the Skelton chapel 'on Ascension day'.[107] The parishioners of Skelton would have been required to attend the minster on the same day, so the best explanation for these donations is that they were collected at a morrow mass and then brought to the minster by a procession comprised of the villagers of Skelton. As such it was a direct link between chapel and minster, which was not provided by the beating of the bounds on the previous three days. Many other participants of the Rogation procession also returned for the Ascension Day ceremonies. The man carrying the dragon and the town's Wakeman were both in attendance on Wilfrid's shrine, just as they had been for the preceding three days.[108] The minstrels who provided musical accompaniment were likewise hired for all four days.[109] It is conceivable that the Marmion tenants and canons, having eschewed the arduous trek of the preceding three days, put in an appearance at the procession in the minster on the feast of the Ascension itself. Some Marmion tenants, notably those from other parishes who may have had Rogation duties

---

[104] Stephen A. Moorhouse, 'Boundaries', in S. A. Moorhouse and M. L. Faull (eds), *West Yorkshire: an archaeological survey to AD 1500*, Wakefield 1981, ii. 265–89 at p. 266.

[105] 'magnum lapidem ab antiquo in terra positum super moram': AoC, 347.

[106] Hall and Whyman, 'Settlement and monasticism at Ripon', 63.

[107] 'in die Ascensionis': MR iii. 228.

[108] Ripon Cathedral, dean and chapter archives, MS Dep 1980/1 183 nos 5, 6, 7, 8, 9, 10; TNA, SC 6/HENVII/1031.

[109] TNA, SC 6/HENVII/1031.

there, swore their oaths of fealty on the feast of the Ascension rather than Cross Monday. Sir Richard Aldborough did so in 1466 as did Robert Byrnaman of Knaresborough the following year.[110]

Pentecost, or Whitsun, commemorated the descent from heaven of the third person of the Holy Trinity, the Holy Spirit. It came ten days after the feast of the Ascension, and fifty days after Easter. It could therefore be on any date between 10 May and 13 June. It was the last feast day in the long list of obligations before midsummer. The feast had special significance in Ripon because of the apostolic elements of Wilfrid's cult. Wilfrid's biographers highlighted his steadfast obedience to the see of St Peter and his veneration of Peter himself, to whom he dedicated his church at Ripon. Writing around the year 1200, Peter of Blois developed the themes of Stephanus' original to cast Wilfrid, blazing with the Holy Spirit, as the 'light of all Britain'.[111] The monks of Durham commemorated Wilfrid's predecessor, St Cuthbert, in ways that were comparable. Processing with Cuthbert's banner during Rogation and on the feasts of the Ascension and Pentecost, they too viewed their patron as an apostle of northern England.[112] In Ripon, popular enthusiasm for the Holy Spirit found an outlet during the closing phase of construction on the minster's new nave in 1520, when £3 18s was gathered 'by the young men of the town of Ripon ... both for the new timberwork of a part of the roof in the nave and for the new construction of a certain cloud for the Holy Ghost'.[113] The occasions when the Ripon cloud would be raised and lowered were Ascension and Pentecost, most likely during the procession before the high mass.[114] Devices of this sort were most common in large urban churches in the eastern part of England.[115] One other notable feature of Pentecost was that it was one of the few feast days besides Easter when people took communion.[116] Some of Ripon's parishioners evidently did so, though probably not very many in total. In 1472 the communicants at Pentecost only gave 4½d. in gifts.[117]

The feast of Holy Trinity was yet another moveable feast dependent on the date of Easter. It was the Sunday after Whitsun and so its date varied between 17 May and 20 June. Although attendance at the minster was not required, it was customary for mass be said at one or both of the Holy Trinity altars on the feast of Holy Trinity. In the earliest chamberlain's accounts the celebration of the mass must have been focused on the Holy Trinity altar in the east end of

---

[110] AoC, 244–5.

[111] 'tocius britannie lumen': Ripon Cathedral Library, MS 8, fo. 163r.

[112] McKinnell, 'Public and private spaces', 227.

[113] 'per garciones villæ Ripon hoc anno ... tam ad novam cellaturam parcell' del Roof in navi ecclesiæ prædictæ quam pro nova factura cujusdam nebulæ pro lee Holy Ghost': MR iii. 180.

[114] MR iii. 182.

[115] Hutton, *Stations of the sun*, 279.

[116] Rubin, *Corpus Christi*, 147–8.

[117] MR iii. 242.

the building, where William Plumpton had founded a chantry in 1345.[118] This altar had probably been dedicated to the Holy Trinity since the start of the thirteenth century, when one of the earliest documented lights was founded in the minster.[119] In the 1447 chamberlain's account the collection had broadened to include 'an altar of Holy Trinity on the feast of the same in the body of the church of Ripon and elsewhere in the same place'.[120] The 1472 account is even clearer, referring to the altars 'both in the choir and in the nave of the church'.[121] The second Holy Trinity altar was located next to the Holy Cross altar, and both of them stood before the rood screen at the east end of the nave. John Sendale would have considered the ceremonies associated with the altar as much as its dedication when selecting it as his burial place and the site of his chantry in the late 1460s. Likewise William Wrampayn, Jr, asked to be buried 'before the altar of Holy Trinity and All Saints'.[122] The younger Joan Ward (d. 1474) also wanted to be buried by one of the two Holy Trinity altars.[123]

Corpus Christi was the last of the moveable feasts whose date was determined by Easter, and it was always the Thursday after Holy Trinity Sunday. It could be as early as 21 May or as late as 24 June. It only took hold in England in the early fourteenth century, so of course the Ripon chapel licences make no mention of it.[124] Modern scholars, following Mervyn James, often concentrate on Corpus Christi as a key moment to represent civic identity. James argued that the populations of the larger towns lacked symbols like lordship and lineage that structured rural society, and that instead they made their hierarchies visible in relation to the host carried in Corpus Christi processions.[125] The body of Christ served as a powerful metaphor to incorporate different members, especially in large towns with numerous craft guilds. Medieval York, with its cycle of plays, each performed by a different guild, is an especially good example. Ripon and York were very different in this respect, for although Ripon may have had some craft guilds, they did not perform a cycle of plays on Corpus Christi. The only documented example of a Ripon craft guild is the cordwainers' guild mentioned in Geoffrey Scharroke's will.[126] Moreover, it seems unlikely that the town of Ripon had a very developed civic identity. Throughout the fourteenth and fifteenth centuries it remained a town with

---

[118] MR iii. 226, 228; *CPR Edward III*, vi. 455.

[119] MR i. 293–4.

[120] 'ad altare Sanctæ Trinitatis in festo ejusdem in corpore ecclesiæ Ripon et alibi ibidem': MR iii. 236.

[121] 'tam in choro quam in navi ecclesiæ': MR iii. 243.

[122] 'coram altari Sancte Trinitatis et omnium Sanctorum', Borthwick Institute, probate register 4, fo. 38v.

[123] Ibid. probate register 2, fo. 7r.

[124] Rubin, *Corpus Christi*, 199.

[125] Mervyn James, 'Ritual, drama, and social body in the late medieval English town', *P&P* xcviii (Feb. 1983), 3–29 at pp. 3–5.

[126] AoC, 306.

two ecclesiastical lords and a minimal system of civic government. Its highest civic office was the Wakeman, who together with an unknown number of aldermen exercised a limited degree of authority in the town.[127] At the end of the sixteenth century, shortly before the city government was reformed, the Wakeman's duties amounted to setting the watch each night and effectively running an insurance scheme that guaranteed property owners in the town against loss *via* burglary.[128] The Wakeman could be a resident of the town, like the master carpenter William Bromfleet (alias Carver) in 1511, or could be drawn from one of the gentry families of the parish, like Ralph Pigot in 1471.[129] A few of them appear to have been drawn from even further afield. The William Pullayn, gentleman, who was Wakeman in 1454, probably came from Scotton near Knaresborough.[130] The lay elites of the parish could therefore also be the figurehead leaders of the town, although in practice the archbishop of York and the chapter never relinquished their status as Ripon's real lords. Many of the elites were Marmion tenants, and so as Wilfrid's vassals they were members of a body whose head was Wilfrid and the chapter. The oath of fealty for the new Marmion tenants just before the feast of the Ascension connected them to the chapter, and though they may not have actually taken part in the procession, the Wakeman ordinarily did. Indeed, in the late fifteenth and early sixteenth centuries the chamberlain ordinarily paid the Wakeman 2s. for attending Wilfrid's feretory at Rogation, the feast of the Ascension and the feast of Wilfrid's nativity in August.[131] Corpus Christi appears never to have had the same importance in Ripon as it did in towns like York or Coventry, and instead the Rogation procession, obligatory feast days and Sunday processions at the minster gave ritual expression to the society of the town and parish. These were the occasions when the parish hierarchy was contested and displayed.

Corpus Christi was in fact significant in Ripon primarily as the patronal feast day of one of its guilds and as an occasion when the guilds were more involved than usual in the church procession. Ripon's Corpus Christi guild is first mentioned in the 1439 chamberlain's account. The roll offers little beyond the barest evidence for the existence 'of a certain guild of Corpus Christi' whose members did not donate any money during the mass celebrated for them in the minster on Corpus Christi day that year.[132] There is no way to gauge the membership of this guild and it did not profit from a flood of bequests like the Holy Cross guild at this time. However, there was an important ecclesiastical procession in Ripon on Corpus Christi even if it did not have a play cycle. The

---

127 Gowland, 'The manors and liberties of Ripon', 82–3.

128 Walbran, *Guide to Ripon*, 17.

129 Ripon Cathedral, dean and chapter archives, MS Dep 1980/1 434, fos 21v–22r; William Harrison, *Ripon millenary: a record of the festival; also a history of the city, arranged under its wakemen and mayors from the year 1400*, Ripon 1892, ii. 10, 18.

130 Ripon Cathedral, dean and chapter archives, MS Dep 1980/1 434, fo. 21r.

131 Ibid. 183, nos 5, 6, 7, 8, 9, 10; TNA, SC 6/HENVII/1031.

132 'cujusdam fraternitatis Corporis Christi': *MR* iii. 228.

chaplain of the St Thomas chantry was required to make certain that a light of six torches was carried in the procession, one of the conditions imposed by the Guild of St Wilfrid, co-founders of the chantry.[133] The minster's chamberlain and treasurer did not spend any money on special provisions for the feast, so whatever other elaboration there was on Corpus Christi came from the guilds, whose records have not survived.

At last, six months after Christmas, on 24 June it was midsummer and also the feast of the nativity of St John the Baptist. It was the latest possible date for the feast of Corpus Christi (they coincided in 1451), and therefore marked the end of the *temporale*, the cycle of feasts that began with Advent and Christmas and commemorated the intervention of Christ in the history of the world, as well as celebrating the Holy Spirit and the Holy Trinity. Many of these universally important feast days were obligatory feasts that bound the parish together as a single entity by requiring attendance at the minster by all except the gentry, and even they had to attend at Christmas, Easter and the feast of Wilfrid's translation. In the second half of the year, when agricultural labour kept many of the distant villagers busy, the important feast days were mainly those of local patrons in the village chapels or of guild patrons in Ripon. Midsummer in Ripon is not well documented and while the practice of lighting bonfires was widespread in medieval England, it was not a church custom nor was it used to raise funds for the parish and therefore is not recorded in the accounts of Ripon's sub-treasurers, chamberlains or fabric wardens.[134] Midsummer was of course the patronal feast of the hospital of St John the Baptist, which was located south of the town just beyond the River Skell. The chamberlain's accounts mention gifts on its patronal feast day, so it is likely that a mass was celebrated there to mark the occasion. It was used for a wedding in 1486, and probably had become the accustomed chapel for people in the Bondgate suburb of Ripon.[135] St Peter's Eve, on 28 June, was another occasion for games and bonfires, and in some places it was preferred over the feast of St John four days earlier.[136] St Peter was co-patron of the minster, but the accounts give no clear indication that his feast was any more important than midsummer in Ripon.

From Midsummer to Christmas

The first half of the year, because it was filled with the great feasts of the *temporale*, was characterised by the regular gathering together of the many smaller congregations of the parish, and even the gentry families were expected to attend on a few of these occasions. This series of feasts culminated with

---

[133]   MR iv. 201.
[134]   Hutton, *Rise and fall of Merry England*, 37–9.
[135]   TE iii. 350.
[136]   Hutton, *Rise and fall of Merry England*, 44.

the greatest ritual expression of the parish, the Rogation procession. In this procession the many parts of the parish were incorporated together in much the same way that the Corpus Christi processions or mystery play cycles of other English towns and cities brought together their citizens and enabled them to articulate their social hierarchy. Easter, with its similar emphasis on the body of Christ, was the other great incorporative feast in medieval Ripon, and here again the parts of the parish did not merge seamlessly together but were in fact still discernible in the six altars scheme used for communion, not to mention the precedence of elites in actually receiving the host. The period of the year from midsummer to Christmas, in contrast, was a time of differentiation within the parish when its guilds and chapel congregations had their own distinctive holidays. There were only three obligatory feasts in this half of the year, and two of them were feasts of St Wilfrid. Wilfrid's important feast days owed their position in the year to the same factor that made it ideal for locally important feasts, namely the relative emptiness of the calendar during these months. The cult of St Wilfrid, including his feast days, was part of what made Ripon a distinct place. The same principle applied to chapels that only had images of their patron saints, where devotion to a particular saint was still something that set off one place from another.[137] As with the minster and St Wilfrid, the feast days of these chapels were significant features of their identities.

The feast of St Swithun (2 July) was the first of the village patronal feasts to take place in the parish of Ripon after midsummer. Swithun was a ninth-century bishop and, among other things, the patron of the chapel of Skelton. This chapel gave the village of Skelton its own identity within the larger parish, and the feast of its patron was a local holiday. The chamberlain's accounts show that it was customary for a mass to be said in the chapel on Swithun's feast day. The rest of the chapel's support was supplied by the villagers of Skelton. Skelton was important enough to have its own representative among the twenty-four who carried Wilfrid's relics at Rogation. In 1481 it was the yeoman Thomas Turret, whose father Robert (d. 1470) had made bequests to the chapel in his will.[138] The Skelton chapel could also be used for weddings, as it was on one occasion in 1467.[139] It was their investment in the chapel and their communal veneration of St Swithun, not to mention their routine use of the chapel of Skelton for mass and other sacraments, which made the villagers of Skelton into a distinct community. There were many other villages in the parish with locally important feast days. One of these was the chapel of St Mary Magdalene, which became the preferred chapel of the villagers of nearby Sharow.

Mary Magdalene was a biblical saint and the patron of Ripon's old leper hospital, which was located near the stone bridge over the River Ure less than a mile north of the town, but had been adapted during the thirteenth century

---

[137]   Arnold, *Belief and unbelief*, 89; Bartlett, *Why can the dead do such great things?*, 129.

[138]   *AoC*, 143, 339.

[139]   *TE* iii. 338.

to house corrodians, especially elderly priests. The hospital honoured its patron by distributing food to the poor on her feast day.[140] A number of chantries had been founded there over the years, and the chapel still had two chaplains in the 1540s.[141] As a result there would have been more than one daily mass for people to attend. Travellers crossing the Ure and the residents of Sharow were among those most likely to have had recourse to this chapel. It may in fact have become the main chapel for parishioners living in Sharow, who had no chapel of their own (the next closest was that of St John the Baptist at the manor of Hutton Conyers). In any case, the chapter permitted Agnes Walworth, parishioner of Sharow, to be churched in the St Mary Magdalene chapel in 1468, implying that this chapel had its own regular congregation and that Agnes was a member of it.[142] The Ripon chamberlains' accounts include an entry for gifts received from the chapel of St Mary Magdalene, which is a good indication that it celebrated a patronal feast on 22 July.

The first day of August was a feast day of St Peter, co-patron of the minster, and it was swiftly followed by the greatest of the three feasts of St Wilfrid. The feast of St Peter *ad vincula* celebrated an episode in the life of the Apostle when he was miraculously released from prison. The feast was fixed on 1 August and customarily opened the harvest season, earning it the name Lammas or Loaf Mass.[143] Wilfrid had greatly admired St Peter and dedicated his church at Ripon to him. In the course of his stormy career Wilfrid himself was not immune to imprisonment, but like Peter he was miraculously delivered from his tribulations.[144] Wilfrid's admiration for Peter was later translated into the association between the feast of St Peter *ad vincula* and the feast of his own nativity. They were coordinated so that Wilfrid's nativity was celebrated on the first Sunday after Lammas, and thus Wilfrid followed Peter in the calendar just as he had followed him in his terrestrial career.[145] The timing of Wilfrid's nativity meant that his feast day joined that of St Peter *ad vincula* in initiating the harvest, thereby forging another link in the chain of associations between York saints and the agricultural year. As an added peculiarity, the feast of Wilfrid's nativity was truly a celebration of the saint's birth and not a *dies natalis* in the usual sense of the entry into celestial life that followed a saint's death on earth. Wilfrid already had a feast day on 12 October to mark that occasion. The feast emphasised Wilfrid's importance as the patron of Ripon, since in most parts of Christendom only Christ, the Virgin Mary and John the Baptist had natal feasts.[146]

---

[140] MR i. 225; Werronen, 'The hospital of St Mary Magdalene', 116–17.
[141] *Chantry certificates*, ii. 368.
[142] MR iv. 240.
[143] Hutton, *Rise and fall of Merry England*, 44.
[144] See Ripon Cathedral Library, MS 8, fos 186v–187r.
[145] Ibid. fo. 162r.
[146] Le Goff, *À la Recherche du temps sacré*, 165.

The feast of Wilfrid's nativity was a rare type of feast during the summer months. It was one of the few occasions when the manorial lords were obliged to attend the minster and it was the last of three feast days when the minster clergy wore their copes in procession. The records do not indicate the holiday's liturgical colour, but presumably it was white as on Christmas, Easter and the feast days of other confessor saints. Because of its rank as a principal feast day, the better type of incense would have been burned. Another special feature of the feast day was the music of hired minstrels, perhaps in even greater numbers than at Rogation. In 1505, for example, the chamberlain hired them for a total of 10s. for three days of procession at Rogation plus the feast of the Ascension.[147] He spent 6s. 8d. on minstrels for the single feast day procession of St Wilfrid in August, suggesting either that he hired more minstrels or more expensive ones for Wilfrid's feast day.[148] Another element shared by the Rogation, Ascension and Wilfrid's nativity processions was the Wakeman's attendance on the feretory, which implies that the procession before the mass on the feast of Wilfrid's nativity included the saint's relics.[149] Indeed, the 1354 fabric roll, which contains the earliest surviving reference to the feast, records the collection of 8s. 5d. in gifts at the door of the choir 'because the shrine was then borne around the church'.[150] After 1419 the Wilfrid guild's contribution to this procession was six torches, carried in the procession no doubt by some of the guild's members. Their chantry chaplain was to guarantee that the torches were ready for the processions at Ascension, Corpus Christi and the feast of St Wilfrid *in Autumpno*, which should be interpreted as meaning 'harvest' rather than autumn in the modern sense.[151] They clearly did not mean the feast of St Wilfrid on 12 October, which is generally referred to as the feast of St Wilfrid in winter. The timing of Wilfrid's nativity remained unproblematic until the introduction of two new feast days in the late fifteenth century. These were the feasts of the Transfiguration (6 August) and the Holy Name (7 August). They were both promulgated in the province of York in 1489.[152] They posed an issue for the church of Ripon because they would frequently have clashed with the feast of Wilfrid's nativity (2 to 8 August, depending on the year). The new feasts do not appear in any sources of evidence from Ripon before 1540, and though Richard Pfaff thought that they must have been introduced sooner, the potential clash with the feast of Wilfrid's nativity helps to explain why they were not.[153]

[147] TNA, SC 6/HENVII/1031.
[148] Ibid.
[149] Ripon Cathedral Library, dean and chapter archives, MS Dep 1980/1 183, nos 5, 6, 7, 8, 9, 10; TNA, SC 6/HENVII/1031.
[150] 'quia feretrum tunc ferebatur circa ecclesiam': MR iii. 88.
[151] MR iv. 201.
[152] Pfaff, *New liturgical feasts*, 4.
[153] Ibid. 130; MR iii. 287.

The feast of St Lawrence (10 August) followed not long after the feast of Wilfrid's nativity. It was the patronal feast day of the chapel at Aldfield, and the saint's popularity there is demonstrated by the 15s. 3d. collected there on his feast day in 1410.[154] In 1474 the chapter of Ripon and the abbot and convent of Fountains reached an agreement to provide the chapel with masses on the feast of St Lawrence and other holidays. The charter alleges that the chapel had fallen into disuse, but the building itself must have endured because no arrangements were made to rebuild or repair it.[155] Only five days later came another holiday, the feast of the Assumption of the Virgin Mary, which was one of many feast days commemorating different episodes of her life. On this feast, the minster clergy provided for a special mass for the Assumption guild at its altar in the inner chapel of the south transept. By the end of the fifteenth century this had become the burial place of the Malory family, who thus made a claim on the thoughts and prayers of guild members. Like all the other guilds of the town, the members of the guild would have processed to the minster wearing their guild livery for the mass, and afterwards they would have processed to whatever location they used for their guild banquet.[156] Fraternal guild meals were an important occasion to meet other members and form new relationships and it was also the opportunity for the admission of new members.[157] In this respect the patronal feast days of the guilds were different from those of the chapels, because there was no equivalent means of becoming a member of the village community.

Devotion to the Virgin Mary had another outlet not long after on 8 September with the feast of the Nativity of the Virgin. Within the minster church devotion to St Mary on this feast day focused on the chapel of St Mary and the altar of St William. The exact location of St William's altar is unknown, but it is often mentioned in the chamberlain's accounts on feast days of St Mary and St Wilfrid. Far away in Nidderdale, the feast of the Nativity of the Virgin was the major annual feast day at Pateley Bridge. On the bank of the River Nidd, which was once the western boundary of the parish of Ripon, Pateley Bridge was an important economic centre.[158] Archbishop Melton (r. 1317–40), lord of the town, increased its profitability in 1320 when he obtained from King Edward II the right to hold a weekly market and an annual fair there. The fair lasted for four days, and it corresponded to the feast of the Nativity of the Virgin, whose September date was desirable because of its relation to the harvest.[159] This feast day was thus the distinguishing local feature of the

---

[154] MR iii. 225. The sums in the other two surviving chamberlain's accounts were 6s. 2d. in 1439 and only 10d. in 1447: MR iii. 228, 236.

[155] Ripon Cathedral, dean and chapter archives, MS Dep 1980/1 356, p. 27.

[156] Rosser, Art of solidarity, 125.

[157] Ibid. 135, 142–3.

[158] Jennings, History of Nidderdale, 113.

[159] Calendar of charter rolls, London 1906–27, iii. 422; Jennings, History of Nidderdale, 178.

ritual year in Pateley Bridge, and by the late fourteenth century more widely in Nidderdale. At that time the people of the townships of Dacre and Bewerley, adjacent to Pateley Bridge on the western side of the Nidd, began attending the Pateley Bridge chapel instead of their proper but more distant parish church of Kirkby Malzeard.[160] This shift provoked a tithe dispute, eventually settled by annexing Dacre and Bewerley to the Ripon prebend of Studley, which already contained Pateley Bridge.[161] Pateley Bridge was so far distant from Ripon and enjoyed so many more rights and privileges than the other chapels that it seems unlikely that its parishioners attended the minster very often at all, and it was fitting that it was the only other town in the parish to have its own fair.

There were two more significant feast days in September. The Holy Cross guild, which had the widest base of support of any guild in Ripon after the middle of the fifteenth century, celebrated its patronal feast day – the Exaltation of Holy Cross – on 14 September. The earliest documented instance of the guild's mass in the minster is from 1439, when the chamberlain collected 5s. 2d. worth of gifts.[162] Its altar was situated before the great rood at the east end of the nave. The graves of William Wrampayn, Jr, and John Sendale were installed in this area of the building after 1467.[163] Neither one of them mentions the fraternity in his will, but William Wrampayn, Sr, gave it 10s. and may also have been buried nearby.[164] Whether or not they were members, their memory became woven into the fabric of the guild's annual mass. After the mass in the minster, guild members would have attended their annual banquet in their guildhall, the Rood House, which was situated just to the south of the minster churchyard in Annsgate and described by later witnesses as the residence of the guild's chaplains.[165] The name of the property implies that it was also used by the guild for its meetings.

After the harvest, the feast of St Michael on 29 September was a common date for the payment of debts. Together with the feast of St John the Baptist (24 June), Christmas and the feast of the Annunciation (25 March), it was one of the four dates on which the vicars were paid their salaries. One of the dependent chapels of the parish was dedicated to St Michael. It perched atop How Hill, about a mile south of Fountains Abbey and was thus inside the parish of Ripon while also on the grounds of the abbey.[166] In 1346 the chapter of Ripon made an agreement with Fountains Abbey about the use of the chapel and the division of its income. On the feast of St Michael and other unnamed feast days the monks of Fountains could celebrate mass in the chapel and

[160] Jennings, *History of Nidderdale*, 64.
[161] Ibid.
[162] MR iii. 228.
[163] Borthwick Institute, probate register 4, fo. 38r; AoC, 230.
[164] Borthwick Institute, probate register 2, fo. 262r.
[165] TNA, E 178/2609 mm 5–6.
[166] Walbran, *Guide to Ripon*, 87n.

retain all the gifts given there in exchange for an annual fee of 2s. 6d..[167] This agreement endured. The 1502 chamberlain's account, for example, records the payment of the fee with the other farmed income.[168] In August 1470 the chapter gave Thomas Day, one of the Fountains Abbey monks, permission to church Agnes Burton, wife of the gentleman Thomas Burton, in the chapel of St Michael.[169] This licence suggests that the chapel of St Michael, like the chapel of St Mary Magdalene and others, was the centre of a small congregation of local people who had their own special patron saint. It was the latest of the known chapel and guild feast days. In total, there were at least half a dozen of these in the period between midsummer and Christmas.

The feast of Wilfrid's deposition, or death, was one of a series of York diocese feasts in October, including St Paulinus (10 October), relics of York (19 October) and the translation of John of Beverley (25 October). Only the feast of St Wilfrid on 12 October was especially important in Ripon; it was the first feast since Wilfrid's nativity when parishioners, gentry included, were required to come to the minster. Many other people were probably also present in Ripon for the winter fair of St Wilfrid. Like its counterpart in April, the winter fair was an important opportunity to market livestock. Following the feast of St Michael the cattle and sheep that had been grazing on the high summer pastures were brought down to their winter stations. Those destined for slaughter could be sold at Ripon's winter fair. With the conclusion of October the customary season for fairs ended, and November was the period in which livestock were butchered in preparation for winter.[170] The first day of November was the feast of All Saints, a universal feast day when most parishioners were again obliged to attend the minster. The minster clergy celebrated a high mass in honour of All Saints, but the financial accounts show no evidence of special expenditures of the type made at Christmas, Epiphany, Purification, Holy Week, Easter, Rogation, Ascension and Pentecost. The general commemoration of the dead at the feast of All Souls followed on 2 November. The month's other feast days were St Nicholas (6 November), St Martin (11 November), St Katherine (25 November) and St Andrew (30 November), but none of them carried an obligation to attend the minster. The feast of St Andrew heralded the beginning of the year's shorter penitential season, Advent. The fast of Advent ended with Christmas and the cycle of feasts and fasts began again.

Christ and St Wilfrid were the two strongest forces that shaped the ritual year in late medieval Ripon. The *temporale* cycle from Christmas to Corpus Christi was a universal feature of the Christian calendar, while the *sanctorale* emphasised the major saints of the province of York, especially Ripon's own saint, Wilfrid.

---

[167] MR iv. 21.

[168] MR iii. 262.

[169] MR iv. 220–1.

[170] Hutton, *Rise and fall of Merry England*, 45; Winchester, *Harvest of the hills*, 56, 61.

No place in Christendom had more feasts of St Wilfrid, and the feast of his nativity was unique to Ripon. This feast, trailing the feast of St Peter *ad vincula* around the first week of August, was the greatest of the three feasts of St Wilfrid and it began the annual cycle of feasts commemorating the life, death and translation of the minster's patron saint. The *temporale* and the Wilfrid cycle dovetailed in the Rogation procession and the feast of the Ascension. These four days witnessed an uncanny blending of past and present. The procession was both timeless and current, and since it carried Wilfrid's relics along with it, the saint himself preserved the boundaries of the parish that he had, in a sense, created. The whole history of the saint led to that moment every year. The minster clergy certainly owed their authority to Wilfrid and the sanctuary men who carried rods and banners owed their protection to him. The Holy Spirit fused together the feasts of the Ascension and Pentecost. The mechanical cloud installed in the new nave in the 1520s most powerfully manifested this connection, but the liturgy for the feast of Wilfrid's nativity makes clear that Wilfrid had always been presented as an apostle and therefore successor to the ministry of Christ. Long ago Britain had been the field of his apostolic mission. Ripon, though it was only one island in the vast archipelago of minsters that Wilfrid had founded, was foremost among those that preserved his memory in the fifteenth century.

Devotion to Christ was by no means lacking, but its forms and their incorporating power are worth considering in some detail. The emphasis on Ripon's Rogation procession undercut the potential for the feast of Corpus Christi to be the main processional holiday. More important, Corpus Christi was an important civic holiday only in towns with more developed civic authorities and a greater number of established craft guilds than existed in Ripon. Durham Cathedral and Beverley Minster, both of which were major churches in the ecclesiastical province of York, offer interesting comparative examples. Beverley, like Ripon, was a minster church with an enormous parish. Its patron was St John of Beverley, whose relics were carried in procession to key places within the parish during Rogation.[171] Cross Monday, the first of the three Rogation days, was an important day for Beverley's many guilds. Guild members, dressed in their guild livery, watched the procession of the relics from within the guild castles that they constructed along the processional route. Only the recognised guilds were permitted to build castles, and the location of its castle was a sign of a guild's rank.[172] Beverley originally had eight men whose hereditary obligation was to carry St John's relics during Rogation. The service was last mentioned in 1362, and by 1431 the hereditary relic bearers had been replaced by a guild formed for the purpose.[173] As in Ripon, Beverley's Rogation procession ritual

---

[171]   R. E. Horrox, 'Medieval Beverley', in K. J. Allison (ed.), VCH, *East Riding*, VI: *The borough and liberties of Beverley*, Oxford 1989, 2–62 at p. 10.

[172]   Ibid. 45–6.

[173]   Ibid. 10–1.

culminated with the feast of the Ascension when John of Beverley's relics were carried around Beverley Minster before high mass.[174]

The cathedral and priory of Durham dominated their town in the same way that the minster dominated Ripon. Durham lacked powerful civic authorities and the ceremonies of its liturgical year were designed to make a community out of the priory and city together.[175] The banner of St Cuthbert, patron saint of Durham, was carried in processions around the priory precinct at the feast of St Mark (25 April), to different parish churches on each of the three Rogation days, and around the cathedral on the feast of the Ascension.[176] At Pentecost the diocese of Durham as a whole was drawn together when its parishes descended on Durham with their own banners.[177] All these processions arguably culminated with the procession at Corpus Christi, when the guilds marched with the consecrated host to the door of Durham Cathedral where they were joined by the monks for a further procession that made a circuit around the cathedral's interior and St Cuthbert's shrine.[178] Durham and Beverley both had a sufficiently large number of guilds for Corpus Christi to be a more important element of their ritual year than it was in Ripon, though they were both still dwarfed by the mystery play cycle and guild structure of late medieval York.

Divided between two ecclesiastical lords throughout the fourteenth and fifteenth centuries, it is almost unremarkable that the patronage of the minster and chapter predominated in Ripon. The archbishop of York and indeed many other manorial lords exercised their power in their courts, but the chapter had no base of power outside the parish, and relied heavily on its connection to Wilfrid to keep the peace within the saint's liberty. Where Corpus Christi might have organised the society of the town, the Marmion tenants' oaths of fealty to St Wilfrid and the annual Rogation procession drew together the elite of the whole parish under the banner of St Wilfrid. Christocentric piety and conviviality coincided in the veneration of Ripon's great rood at the east end of the nave. What may have begun as a fund for lighting the rood had become by the middle of the fifteenth century one of Ripon's most important religious fraternities. While there are only traces of evidence for Ripon's Corpus Christi guild, a number of wills in the second half of the fifteenth century mention the Guild of Holy Cross. The ceremonies of Good Friday and Easter allowed laypeople to have special access to the choir of the minster in order to participate in creeping to the cross and the ritual of opening the Easter sepulchre at dawn on Easter morning. There is very little evidence to show that the new forms of

[174] Ibid. 10.

[175] McKinnell, 'Public and private spaces', 213–14.

[176] Phythian-Adams, 'Ritual constructions of society', 377; McKinnell, 'Public and private spaces', 224–5.

[177] McKinnell, 'Public and private spaces', 226.

[178] Phythian-Adams, 'Ritual constructions of society', 378.

devotion to Christ were popular in Ripon. The cult of the Holy Name, spurred on in part by the Yorkshire mystic Richard Rolle in the fourteenth century, had become increasingly popular among the nobility,[179] while in the late fifteenth century the August feast days of the Holy Name and Transfiguration were added to the York calendar. It would have been difficult, however, to include these feasts in Ripon's calendar because they would have clashed regularly with the feast of Wilfrid's nativity, and they remained unobserved there until sometime between 1525 and 1540.

A community of the entire parish of Ripon could only exist if it was forged from the whole parish population on the major feast days in the minster. The occasions when this could happen were the feasts of obligation, most of which were within the Christmas to midsummer half of the year. The crowds of communicants at Easter would have been unmanageably large if they had not been subdivided by prebend. This geographical scheme of organisation did not take into account difference of status, but the minster's parishioners had ample opportunity to display their social status and piety on these very public occasions when villagers and the neighbouring lord's household all came together in the minster. The status of the gentry was bolstered in some cases by the presence of the fine tombs of their ancestors near the parochial altars where they received communion. Although the great feasts of the *temporale* plus the feasts of Wilfrid's nativity and All Saints demanded the attendance of laypeople at the minster, during most of the year they were free to attend their local chapels. Here they gathered together in humbler surroundings with their neighbours; in many ways these chapels were their parish churches. The manorial lords had their own chapels, separate from those of nearby villages and remote from the other powerful families. Moreover, the licences for manorial lords freed them from attendance at the minster on all but a few very important feast days. They may of course have chosen to attend more regularly, but they were not expected to do so. The substitution of twenty-four men of the parish for the Marmion tenants on the Rogation days shows that even ancient custom could not prevent the gentry from being relieved of the obligations of ordinary laypeople. Of all the people of the parish, the gentry families were the most privileged.

The dependent chapels had their own dedications and through the veneration of these saints they became places in their own right with distinct identities within the parish. The chapel of St Swithun in Skelton is one of the best examples. No other chapel or altar anywhere in the parish was dedicated to Swithun, who thus belonged only to the villagers of Skelton. It is evident from a variety of wills that villagers, such as Robert Turret (d. 1470), funded the chapel and its chaplain out of their own resources. Each year 2 July was their holiday alone: St Swithun's feast was not even a red-letter feast day in the Ripon calendar.[180] Moreover, the Skelton villagers did not share the saint with their

[179] Hughes, *Pastors and visionaries*, 90–1.
[180] Ripon Cathedral Library, MS 8, fo. 10r.

neighbours, the lords of Givendale. The Ward family had its own manorial chapel dedicated to St Thomas, where Lady Joan Ward married her second husband, though they were certainly aware of the nearby Skelton chapel. The younger Joan Ward, for example, bequeathed the chapel 3s. 4d. in 1474.[181] At Easter the Ward family and the Skelton villagers were all parishioners of the prebend of Givendale. In the 1481 Rogation procession Thomas Turret, yeoman, was Skelton's representative among the twenty-four men who carried Wilfrid's relics.[182] Sir Christopher Ward, who had been admitted to his manor as one of the chapter's Marmion tenants in 1474, is not mentioned at all.[183] It is more difficult to determine how important St Thomas was to the identity of the Ward family, though he must have ranked fairly high in their devotions. Family lineage already provided a common identity for blood relations in these families, and they do not appear to have enjoyed patronal masses provided for them in their chapels by the minster clergy. They did not need them because they could endow their own chantries and therefore decide on the liturgy for feast days, just as the guilds that founded chantries in the minster were able to influence the types of masses performed by their chaplains.

The *sanctorale* sequence of saints' feasts gave opportunities for the guilds to venerate their patrons and host their banquets. They were also occasions for remembering dead members, keeping the peace among living members, and admitting new brothers and sisters to the guild. The guilds could just as easily join in the ceremonies of other feast days, as the members of the St Wilfrid guild intended when they decided that their chantry priest should make sure that a light of six torches was carried in procession on the feasts of Ascension, Corpus Christi and Wilfrid's nativity.[184] As far as it is possible to determine their membership, Ripon's guilds appear to have been an urban phenomenon that also attracted the gentry of the wider parish. The Guild of SS Mary, Wilfrid and All Saints, with its chapel and hall at the Ladykirk in Ripon, was well suited for this purpose. It may in fact have been intended as the site of regular conviviality between the rural and urban elite following many of the more important feast days in the calendar. In the countryside the villagers who funded their own chapels were guilds in all but name. Their major deficiency when compared to the guilds of the town and minster was that they lacked the full range of means to commemorate the dead.

[181] Borthwick Institute, probate register 4, fo. 7r.
[182] AoC, 339.
[183] AoC, 246.
[184] MR iv. 201.

5

The Minster and its Parishioners: The Dead

No matter their station in life, all Ripon's parishioners and clergy knew that death was inevitable. This was a theme graphically represented in medieval paintings of the dance of death, showing men, women, knights, ladies, kings and bishops clasping hands with leering skeletons. Ripon's parishioners knew also that it was unlikely that they would pass straight from earth to heaven. Instead, they were bound to spend a period of time in purgatory. Fortunately, the sufferings of the dead in purgatory could be reduced by the living. Masses, prayers and alms all helped the dead, and people could arrange during their own lifetimes for these works to be performed for them once they had died. Heraldry, merchants' marks and inscriptions could be used to identify objects like chalices, plate, vestments, windows and tombs in order to remind the living of particular dead people who needed their prayers. Monuments in particular, if they were installed near altars and saints' images, had the potential to generate huge numbers of prayers by becoming inescapable parts of the liturgical round of a church. While there were many ways to be remembered, there were also a number of limiting factors. One problem was that all these arrangements cost money. Another major difficulty was that with the passage of time any given deceased person was ever more likely to be forgotten. The most effective methods of being remembered for the longest time were naturally the most expensive. Only the elite could aspire to be remembered forever, though whether or not these aspirations could truly be realised was another matter. The most durable and visible type of object was a tomb, and the most enduring institution was the chantry. Yet as the number of the dead endlessly increased, old tombs might be replaced by new ones and the rents and properties donated to pay for chantry masses might eventually fail due to reductions in their value.

The memory of the dead could also benefit the living, especially when it affirmed the status of their descendants. Ripon's gentry families were very concerned with the commemoration of their ancestors. Some of them transformed chapels in the minster into their own mausolea, making the altars and surrounding spaces into family monuments. During much of the year the tombs of the gentry represented them in the minster while living family members heard mass in their own domestic chapels. Ripon's clergy had no heirs, but they too wished to be remembered and prayed for, if possible, in the vicinity of the altars that they had served in life or in other places where their graves were likely to be seen. The gentry, clergy and other parishioners who could afford to be buried within the building all competed for the most desirable burial places. This competition was only one part of a wider contest for the attention of the living, which the dead hoped to attract as often as possible for as long as possible. Different groups of clergy and parishioners could employ different commemorative strategies, which in turn could bring benefits to the living, including improved liturgy in the minster, greater access to the mass and affirmation of status.

Death and burial in late medieval Ripon

In 1453 the chapter's commissioner uncovered an especially serious infraction: the unshriven death of a carpenter referred to simply as W. Walter. Although he sought to confess to the priest T. Forsett, he was not able to do so because Forsett did not visit him at the hour of his death.[1] Walter died in a manner greatly feared by medieval people, who wanted the opportunity to confess their sins to a priest before they died.[2] The living also feared that those who died bad deaths or lived evil lives could return to haunt their friends and relations. A group of stories recorded by a monk from Byland Abbey in the early fifteenth century illustrates these fears in a Yorkshire setting. Driven by a need for absolution and pious intercession, the apparitions in these tales manifested to the living in places like Ampleforth, Gilling and Killburn, only about twenty miles from Ripon.[3] The great size of Ripon's parish must have magnified the menace of sudden death without the sacraments. The spread of chapels and chaplains through the parish diminished the risk and must have been one reason for the villagers, gentry families and guilds supporting them. The anxieties of the founders of the Guild of the Assumption are evident in their requirement that their chaplain visit the guild's brothers and sisters whenever they fell into ill health.[4] They hoped, like all Ripon's parishioners, that they would be able to confess, take communion and be anointed with holy oil before they died. These were the sacraments that marked the last transition, from life to death.

The dead also needed a proper funeral to help speed them through purgatory. Unless it was very elaborate, the funeral would normally take place a few days after a person died,[5] ordinarily in the church where the deceased would be buried. In the parish of Ripon this was usually the minster. Many of the dead therefore had to be transported a considerable distance to reach the church and funeral processions from the many villages must have been a fairly common sight. They would have been led by clerics carrying lights,

---

[1] AoC, 22.

[2] Duffy, *Stripping of the altars*, 310.

[3] Schmitt, *Ghosts in the Middle Ages*, 144–6; M. R. James, 'Twelve medieval ghost stories', *EHR* xxxvii (1922), 413–22 at p. 414.

[4] *MR* iv. 245.

[5] Badham, *Seeking salvation*, 185.

bells and a cross, while the body itself would have been carried by men of the same social standing as the deceased.[6] The body might have been brought to the church the night beforehand for the vigil, but this could also have taken place at home or perhaps in a local chapel.[7] The usual colour for vestments at funerals was black, like the chasuble purchased for the exequies of Ripon's dead in 1399.[8] In Yorkshire white was also associated with mourning as in the case of Lady Margaret Pigot (d. 1485), a widow and vowess.[9] She wished for six old men to stand around her coffin at her funeral, 'ylkoone holdyng a torche in his hand, and ilkoone of thaym to have for his labour a white gowne and j d'.[10] Bell-ringing normally marked the arrival of a funeral procession and later signalled the moving of the body from church to grave after the requiem mass. The number of peals indicated the age and sex of the deceased, thereby transmitting this information far and wide and alerting many people who would otherwise be unaware of the funeral.[11] Testators from Ripon often mentioned the minster's bells in their wills and the sacristan rang them for anniversaries as well as funerals. The ringing of the bells was intended to publicise the funeral, exhort the living to pray for the dead, invoke the help of the saints' whose names were inscribed on the bells, and ward off demons.

It is not entirely clear where in the minster funeral services actually took place; it probably varied depending on the person. Some wills mention the choir, but this practice must have been exceptional because otherwise funerals would have frequently disrupted the minster clergy's observance of the divine office. One or more of the subsidiary altars must have been used for the majority of funerals, and they could have been divided up according to prebend like communion and marriage. One particular altar was used for the funerals of the poor, whose funerals were evidently funded by others. John Pigot (d. 1429) gave a missal and ornaments to this altar in his will, but unfortunately he did not state the altar's dedication.[12] Guild members probably had their funerals at their guild's altar. In any case the guilds guaranteed good attendance and a set of torches to burn around the body during the funerals of their members. The torches, like the sound of the bells, were intended to keep away evil spirits.[13] The brothers and sisters of the St Wilfrid guild had their funerals and the annual guild obit at the altar of St Thomas the Martyr, the site of their chantry. Six torches, which were also carried in processions at Ascension, Corpus Christi and Wilfrid's nativity, were to stand lit before the bodies of guild

6   Ibid. 188.
7   Ibid.
8   MR iii. 133.
9   Badham, *Seeking salvation*, 31.
10   AoC, 278.
11   Gilchrist, *Medieval life*, 191; Graves, *Form and fabric of belief*, 72.
12   Borthwick Institute, probate register 2, fo. 544v.
13   Badham, *Seeking salvation*, 187.

members at their funerals.[14] The fraternity spared its members the cost of the candles at the treasurer's expense, and apparently they were not the only guild that did so. Christopher Kendale complained in his 1470-1 account roll that 'the wardens of the lights of diverse fraternities within the said church place their own torches at burials or obits', causing a serious reduction in income from wax since the wardens kept these torches for other guild ceremonies.[15]

The minster churchyard was large, ancient and rooted in the mortuary landscape of St Wilfrid's monastery. Before the reorganisation of the settlement of Ripon this landscape may have been defined by multiple chapels or oratories, each with its own graveyard.[16] In the late twelfth or early thirteenth century, at the same time as the minster church was rebuilt, the old monastic precinct was reduced in size and the minster's later medieval churchyard took shape.[17] At this time the precinct of the chapel known as the Ladykirk was separated from the minster by the new street of St Marygate, but continued to be used as a churchyard. Although the churchyards of the Ladykirk, the leper hospital of St Mary Magdalene and the Cistercian abbey of Fountains were sometimes used for the burial of Ripon's parishioners, the minster churchyard was the main parish cemetery. The churchyard's pattern of organisation is now only vaguely discernible, but it is clear from wills, antiquarian accounts and minor excavations that individual graves remained identifiable for at least one generation and sometimes for much longer.

In his 1468 will Robert Chamber, chaplain of the St James chantry, declared his intent to be buried 'in the churchyard of the collegiate church of Ripon, by the bodies of my parents'.[18] In the case of John Ely and John Brompton, when the latter died in 1471 he knew the location of Ely's grave even though Ely had been dead for over forty years. Moreover, Brompton paid for himself and Ely to have a new grave marker with a joint epitaph to honour them both, thereby extending the length of time that they would both be remembered.[19] Graves situated in the churchyard near the entrances to the minster were sometimes marked, including the high status graves near the north transept door.[20] There were similar graves just outside the door of the south transept. Leland recorded 'a Tumbe of one of the Malories in the Southe Parte of the Crosse in a Chapell: and without, as I herd, lyethe dyvers of them under flat stones'.[21] In Leland's description the graves of the Malory family seem to have

[14]   MR iv. 201.

[15]   'custodes luminum diversarum fraternitatum infra ecclesiam prædictam locant torchias suas ad sepulturas sive obitus': MR iii. 214.

[16]   Hall and Whyman, 'Settlement and monasticism at Ripon', 142-3.

[17]   Whyman, 'Excavations in Deanery Gardens and Low St Agnesgate', 160.

[18]   'in cimiterio ecclesiæ collegiatæ Ripon', juxta corpora parentum meorum': AoC, 135.

[19]   AoC, 153.

[20]   Bryan Antoni and David Brinklow, Minster Road, Ripon, North Yorkshire: report on an archaeological watching brief (York Archaeological Trust 1999 Field Reports, xix), 13-14.

[21]   Itinerary of Leland, v. 142-3.

spilled from the minster after space within the south transept ran out. The churchyard's Palm Cross, one of the stations of the Palm Sunday procession, was the site where Agnes Hawton wanted to be buried in 1512. [22] Such marked graves were intended to preserve the memory of the dead and incite the living to pray for them. The evidence for identifiable graves in the minster churchyard corresponds to findings from studies of wills and excavations of churchyards elsewhere in England.[23] While the pattern of burials within the minster churchyard is more obscure, it should not be assumed that it was homogenous or that everyone buried there entered immediately into oblivion. Their memories could of course be preserved just as well by prayers and masses as by grave markers.

Masses, prayers and the memory of the dead

There were many different kinds of masses and prayers that parishioners, mindful of their own approaching deaths, could try to obtain for themselves. Whether or not they succeeded had a lot to do with their heirs and executors. If the bequests and distributions stipulated by a will were too expensive, the executors might renounce it to avoid becoming liable for all its provisions.[24] Christopher Kendale was a reliable executor for a number of Ripon's parishioners, but when he died in 1491 his sister-in-law and nephew refused to undertake their duties as his executors.[25] As a consequence, his possessions were left to the administration of the chapter court and his will was not copied into the register. Other notable parishioners suffered the same fate. Cecilia Markenfield's goods were left to the administration of the court at York in 1391, and so too were Thomas Walworth's in 1437.[26] While this would spare them expense, by not properly honouring their ancestors heirs risked damaging their family's reputation.[27] Even when executors accepted the will, it is still safer to interpret its provisions as the aspirations of the testator, some of which may not have been fulfilled.[28] Bequests for huge numbers of masses to be said in a short span of time are frequently interpreted as being more aspirational than realistic because a priest could only say one mass per day, and many churches would have had too few chaplains to perform hundreds of masses within a week or month.[29] Realistic or not, people asked for these huge numbers of

---

[22] AoC, 334.

[23] Gilchrist, *Medieval life*, 205; Badham, *Seeking salvation*, 209.

[24] Swanson, *Church and society in late medieval England*, 268.

[25] AoC, 267.

[26] Borthwick Institute, probate register 1, fo. 32r; probate register 3, fo. 499v.

[27] Carpenter, 'Religion of the gentry', 68–9.

[28] Swanson, *Church and society in late medieval England*, 268.

[29] Badham, *Seeking salvation*, 148–9.

masses because maximising the initial number of masses had the twin advantages of setting the deceased off to a good start and counteracting the tendency for resources to run out over time.

All attempts at securing perpetual memory are paradoxical in nature if viewed from a purely spiritual perspective. Jean-Claude Schmitt has argued on this basis that making a foundation perpetual was contrary to its purpose of freeing the founder from purgatory as rapidly as possible, and he has also interpreted the rituals performed for the dead as a 'social means of forgetting'.[30] The consequences of not performing them properly could include warnings from apparitions as in the Byland Abbey ghost stories, but the danger diminished after about a year.[31] Within this period it was common to re-enact the funeral on its day, week and month anniversaries before the one-year anniversary that marked its conclusion. Schmitt had the great era of monastic responsibility for the dead in mind when he wrote that 'inscription in the *liber memorialis* did not promise that the deceased would be glorified forever – this was reserved for saints and kings – but that the deceased would rapidly be included in the anonymity of past generations'.[32] What other possibilities were there when, for example, the confraternity list of Reichenau ran to more than 40,000 names by the early eleventh century?[33] Writing about the parish bede roll, which was essentially the monastic *liber memorialis* adapted for a parish context, Duffy has argued that the desire to be remembered forever was genuine, that the efforts of the living to remember the parish dead were sincere, and that the parish bede roll made it possible for an individual to have 'a continuing place in the consciousness of the parish in which he or she had once lived, not as one of the anonymous multitude of the dead, but as the named provider of a familiar object'.[34] To illustrate the care and attention to detail sometimes employed in compiling bede-rolls, Duffy cites the example of All Saints, Bristol, where the list eventually grew to over 150 folios in length.[35] Good intentions notwithstanding, it is difficult to see how in a list of that length the individual did not sink into virtual anonymity as in the *libri memoriales* of the early medieval monasteries discussed by Jean-Claude Schmitt.[36] The objects given to the church might also later be replaced or, in the case where a parish accumulated numerous chalices and patens, they might even be sold to raise funds.[37] The main problem was not sincerity of intention but rather limited resources. The

---

[30] Schmitt, *Ghosts in the Middle Ages*, 5.

[31] Ibid. 172.

[32] Ibid. 5.

[33] Joachim Wollasch, 'Les Obituaires, témoins de la vie clunisienne', *Cahiers de civilisation médiévale* xxii (1979), 139–77 at p. 143.

[34] Duffy, *Stripping of the altars*, 335.

[35] Ibid. For this debate see Gilchrist, *Medieval life*, 190–1.

[36] Schmitt, *Ghosts in the Middle Ages*, 5.

[37] Badham, *Seeking salvation*, 120.

liber memorialis and the bede roll inevitably failed to guarantee the memory of all those named within them because there was limited time available to recall the names of an ever increasing number of the dead. If the dead were to be remembered perpetually, then each one needed his or her place in the cycle of the liturgical year. Since the cycle itself was finite, it was only a matter of time before any given institution was swamped, like Reichenau, by tens of thousands with a claim to be remembered. As Duffy himself notes, when parish bede rolls grew as large as that of Bristol, there was no longer adequate time to read out the names.[38] Other types of perpetual memorials – namely chantries, anniversaries and tombs – were likewise limited by the availability of funds, time and space.

The monasteries of the high Middle Ages, creaking under the weight of perpetual chantries, could never meet the growing demand for daily commemoration.[39] From the thirteenth century the chantry allowed knights to combine burial with commemoration in their parish churches and thus emulate the noble patrons and founders of monasteries.[40] In the same century intramural burial was becoming a widespread commemorative practice and an effective means of representing status.[41] Knights were identifying more closely with their manors, fortifying their manor houses, acquiring licences for domestic chapels and abandoning the monastic churchyards of their lords to make their parish churches into places for their families to be buried and remembered.[42] The gentry could never guarantee that their chantries would truly be perpetual just as they could not guarantee that their lineage would endure forever, but their financial resources enabled them to try. Moreover, their founders did not draw a sharp distinction between the spiritual and social sides of these practices, clearly intending their perpetual foundations to preserve family memory and affirm the status of descendants while also profiting the souls of dead ancestors.[43]

The perpetual chantry and its cousin the anniversary were so much more expensive than the donations required for being named in the bede roll that they thereby overcame the bede roll's anonymising tendency, allowing the founders to hope that they could be remembered, like Schmitt's saints and kings, forever. An anniversary was more affordable than a chantry, but the perpetual anniversary faced the same issue of resources running out over time. The anniversary also lacked the sustained presence of a tomb or chantry, and the ostentation necessary to garner adequate attendance and prayers added to

[38]   Duffy, *Stripping of the altars*, 335.

[39]   Howard Colvin, 'The origin of chantries', *Journal of Medieval History* xxvi (2000), 163–73 at pp. 168–9; Crouch, 'The origin of chantries: some further Anglo-Norman evidence', 170.

[40]   Saul, 'The gentry and the parish', 248.

[41]   Binski, *Medieval death*, 56; Saul, *English church monuments*, 26.

[42]   Saul, *For honour and fame*, 68.

[43]   Idem, *English church monuments*, 136.

the anniversary's expense. There was also a limit to how many obits the litur-gical calendar could sustain because anniversaries needed to avoid clashing with feasts of nine lessons.[44] In Ripon there were annually about sixty feast days of this type, when the memory of the 'very special dead' took precedence over the memory of the more common classes of the dead.

Ripon's oldest chantry was founded at the St Andrew altar in the early decades of the thirteenth century. It was subsequently re-founded by David de Wollore, prebendary of Studley, in 1370 to remedy its desolation due to insufficient property.[45] It was the penultimate act in a wave of foundations that had begun almost a decade earlier when he and John Sherwood obtained permission from the crown to endow a chantry at the hospital of St John the Baptist in Ripon.[46] David de Wollore had been master of the hospital in the early 1340s, owing his appointment there to his status as a royal clerk.[47] When he began to prepare his numerous endowments in 1361 he had already been master of the rolls for about fifteen years.[48] He and Sherwood changed their minds about the hospital and instead used the property to re-endow the chantry of St John the Evangelist in the minster in 1364.[49] At first glance this endowment looks like the creation of a new chantry, but in fact one William de Sherwood had obtained the chantry's original mortmain licence in November 1325, thereby establishing a chantry for himself and his wife, Isabelle, in Ripon Minster.[50] It seems very likely that John Sherwood was William de Sherwood's descendant, and that he was more anxious to preserve his ancestor's foundation than to create a second chantry.

By April of 1367 David de Wollore had taken possession of the properties that he would eventually use to augment the St Andrew chantry in Ripon Minster, and in November of that year he acquired the necessary licence for this endowment as well as for a gift of two messuages to the fabric fund of the minster.[51] He gave two more messuages to the chantry of St Mary (the Ladyloft) in March 1369.[52] Like the other donations that he arranged, this was intended to augment an existing endowment. He expressed his concern to improve the liturgy of the minster when he required the chaplain 'to be continually present in the choir of the said collegiate church at matins, vespers, and other canonical

---

[44] David Lepine, '"Their name liveth forevermore?": obits at Exeter Cathedral in the later Middle Ages', in Caroline M. Barron and Clive Burgess (eds), *Memory and commemoration in medieval England*, Donington 2010, 58-74 at p. 64.

[45] *MR* iv. 131.

[46] *MR* i. 241-4.

[47] *MR* i. 212-13, 322-8.

[48] 'Masters of the rolls (1286-2012)', *ODNB*; *MR* i. 203-5.

[49] *CPR Edward III*, xiii. 45-6.

[50] TNA, C 143/185/9; *CPR Edward II*, v. 190-1.

[51] *MR* i. 161-2, 194-5.

[52] *MR* iv. 170-1.

hours'.[53] Finally, in September 1370, he turned his attention to the hospital of St John the Baptist again. Instead of a new chantry, he now gave it five horses, a dozen oxen, two cows, a few hundred sheep, two muniment chests, various metal utensils for the hospital kitchen, a missal, a portable breviary, a paten, a chalice, a pair of vestments and some altarcloths.[54] These donations gave the hospital material support and equipped it to properly perform the mass and office. The masses performed by the hospital's chaplain were primarily for its inmates, but they were probably also attended by people who lived nearby. David de Wollore possessed the necessary connections to obtain the licences for his endowments with less difficulty than others may have had.[55] In doing so he was clearly influenced by what he perceived as shortcomings in the clerical provision of the parish, especially within the town of Ripon. It is also clear that other parties were involved in these foundations and benefited from his connections to royal administration.

In all his activities David de Wollore shows a clear awareness that dwindling resources could curb the effectiveness of perpetual institutions. Even in their revived forms, many of these chantries may not have effectively remembered all their original beneficiaries. The St Andrew chantry is a case in point. When Geoffrey de Larder had his deacon ordained as a priest and installed as the first chaplain of the chantry, it was worth 3 marks (£2) annually.[56] This sum was clearly adequate at the time, but somewhat lower than the £4 salaries that Yorkshire chantry chaplains could ordinarily expect by the end of the fourteenth century.[57] By that time repeated outbreaks of plague had diminished the number of available clergy, permitting the survivors to seek more profitable posts.[58] Geoffrey de Larder was still recognised as the chantry's founder in 1370, even though more than a century had passed since he created it, and thanks to David de Wollore he was still regarded as co-founder in the 1540s, meaning that the chantry had preserved his memory for about three centuries.[59] The list of beneficiaries in 1370 included a number of men who were still living, namely David himself, Henry de Ingilby and William de Dalton, both canons of York, and the Lincoln cathedral canon Thomas de Newby.[60] They would of course benefit from the chaplain's prayers and masses after they died, as would their unnamed parents and friends, Geoffrey de Larder, and another of the original beneficiaries, Archbishop Geoffrey

---

[53] 'matutinis, vesperis, et alijs horis canonicis in Choro dicte ecclesie continue intersit': MR iv. 171.

[54] MR ii. 130.

[55] Kreider, *English chantries*, 80.

[56] MR iv. 64.

[57] Swanson, *Church and society in late medieval England*, 47.

[58] Hughes, *Pastors and visionaries*, 136–7; Swanson, *Church and society in late medieval England*, 51.

[59] MR iii. 19; iv. 131.

[60] MR iv. 133.

Plantagenet.[61] These names were to be included in special collects during the chantry masses, and the chaplain was obliged to perform the office of the dead on ordinary days.[62] Archbishop Geoffrey and Geoffrey de Larder are the only named beneficiaries from the original foundation to be included in the new list. William and Nigel Mowbray, listed in the thirteenth-century foundation document, had been dropped.[63]

David de Wollore's late fourteenth-century re-endowments set the stage for the creation of a number of new perpetual chantries in the minster around the year 1400. This pattern runs against the general trend for Yorkshire, where Alan Kreider found that more than a quarter of the intercessory foundations dissolved in 1548 had been founded in the first half of the fourteenth century, and that there was a relative dip in foundations in the first half of the fifteenth century.[64] The peculiar circumstances of the town and parish explain Ripon's deviation from the wider pattern. Ripon's new guilds founded the majority of the minster's early fifteenth-century chantries when they were established in the town at about the same time. Some of the later chantries were founded by gentry families who already had domestic chantry chapels, and the rest of the chantries were founded by Ripon's clergy. In every instance the decision to endow a chantry in the minster must have been made with the knowledge that because its masses were more accessible than the minster's high masses, plenty of people would be likely to attend. Their attendance would then ideally be converted into prayers for the chantry's founders. The same principle applied even to the temporary chantries that were much cheaper and easier to arrange than their perpetual counterparts. They are also less well documented than perpetual chantries, which can cause their impact to be underestimated.

Wills offer the best evidence for Ripon's temporary chantries. They indicate that many of the temporary chantries in Ripon were for durations of between one and four years and were funded at a rate of about £4 annually. They were often paid for with lump sums of cash, but some of the longer term ones were funded by rents, and clerical founders sometimes augmented their endowments with books and vestments. Even from the scant surviving records of the temporary chantries it begins to become clear why the treasurers purchased so many communion wafers each year and just how many unbeneficed chaplains might have been supported by these foundations. In the last decades of the fourteenth century there was already a large number of unbeneficed clergy earning their keep in this way at Ripon Minster: fifteen in 1377 and eleven in 1381.[65] Temporary chantries, like perpetual ones, were not limited to the minster. Some were established in dependent chapels, and others were split over

61   Ibid.
62   MR iv. 134.
63   MR iv. 72.
64   Kreider, *English chantries*, 88–9.
65   TNA, E 179/63/6 m 1; E 179/63/12 m 1.

two locations. In 1466 Sir Ralph Pigot II established one of the more long-lived temporary chantries, intended to last for twenty-eight years. For the first four years the chantry was to be performed in the minster, and then for the remaining twenty-four years the chaplain would intercede for the souls of Ralph and his late wife Margaret in the family's chapel of the Virgin Mary at Clotherholme.[66] Like many of the Ripon gentry, he prioritised his manorial chapel for his intercessory foundations even though his grave was with those of his family in the minster. Margaret Walworth (d. 1521) preferred her local chapel for the whole duration of her temporary chantry.[67] Temporary chantries and other sets of masses, such as trentals, supplied income for unbeneficed priests, and their founders sometimes named the priest who was to perform the masses.[68] William Stable, John Pigot's designated chaplain, was one of the more successful of these when he went on to become chaplain of the Assumption chantry in the 1530s.[69]

More affordable than the chantry, the anniversary was another commemorative option. They were founded in great numbers but are often difficult to study because they are not as well documented as perpetual chantries.[70] The anniversary or obit was a re-enactment of the funeral that reproduced its basic liturgy and might, if the founder arranged it, also provide for distributions to encourage the attendance of the most valued types of intercessors: the poor and the clergy. The commemorative strategy of the obit was thus predominantly temporal, giving the founder a moment in time with the characteristics of a funeral but repeated annually to sustain its impact over a longer period. Anniversaries lacked the constancy of a daily, perpetual chantry or an ever-present funerary monument, and so to make them most effective they needed to be widely publicised. As was common throughout medieval England, Ripon's anniversaries were advertised by a combination of ringing the minster's bells and paying the bellman, a type of town crier, to announce the obit. Bell-ringing of this sort guaranteed an increase in the number of prayers not only from those who actually attended the anniversary, but also from those who said a prayer for the deceased upon hearing the sound of the bells.[71] The bells themselves, with their inscriptions imploring the saints for intercession, invoked the help of the Virgin Mary and St Wilfrid.

Obits are rarely included in studies of tombs and chapels that focus primarily on the spatial aspects of religious practices. This is partly because the location where obits took place is often as obscure as that of funerals. In general, it

---

[66] *TE* iii. 158.

[67] *TE* v. 107n.

[68] Swanson, *Church and society in late medieval England*, 50.

[69] *AoC*, 262.

[70] Lepine, 'Obits at Exeter Cathedral', 58. For an overview of the anniversary in an urban parish context see Clive Burgess, 'A service for the dead: the form and function of the anniversary in late medieval Bristol', *Transactions of the Bristol and Gloucestershire Archaeological Society* cv (1987), 183–211.

[71] Badham, *Seeking salvation*, 152.

may be assumed that both took place before the rood screen of most parish churches.[72] Ripon's anniversaries, like its funerals, probably took place in different locations depending on the person commemorated. In other words, a variety of subsidiary altars was used and the choice of altar depended on the prebend of the deceased or their status as a guild member. As a result, many anniversaries and funerals took place among the monuments of other dead parishioners whose own need for intercession was made manifest on the same occasions. The second major difficulty with obits is that a lack of evidence often forces them out of a wider analysis. Ripon is fortunate in this respect. After their incorporation in 1415, its vicars were responsible for most annual obits and part of their cartulary survives.[73] The surviving section of the obit roll reveals the beneficiaries, conditions and dates of annual obits at Ripon Minster. Most foundations were made for either one individual or a man and wife together. The individual male founders were clerics; the individual female founders may have been widows, but none of them mentions a husband. Among the more exceptional foundations were two multi-generational anniversaries. The anniversary of John Frankish, Jr, included provision for his son William, and the Walthewe anniversary was established by the sons William and John for themselves and their parents.[74] When William Walthewe, Jr, founded the anniversary, he chose the date of his father's death, meaning that the memory of his mother, brother and himself would later be attached to that same date.[75] These anniversaries could, like chantries and tombs, stand for the memory and identity of an extended family. The instructions for the Walthewe anniversary are more detailed than most, and are the only set that names a location for the obit. William Walthewe, Jr, wanted the anniversary to be held in the choir, perhaps because it could best accommodate the grand re-enactment of the funeral that he envisioned. He offered cash incentives to encourage the minster clergy to attend the office of the dead and requiem mass, including 4d. for each chantry chaplain, 2d. for each deacon and 1d. for each chorister or acolyte.[76] This amounted to a total of twenty-six clerics whom he foresaw attending the obit.

Other obits were connected to chantry endowments and were thus the chantry chaplain's responsibility rather than that of the vicars. Details from the vicars' cartulary, together with other sources, demonstrate the annual distribution of the obits and their chronological sequence of foundation (see Table 2). The Assumption guild funded an anniversary for some members of the Feriby and Lynton families, including Agnes de Lynton, whose will is dated 1384.[77] This combined multi-family obit is similar to the Walthewe

---

[72] Ibid. 153.

[73] Ripon Cathedral, dean and chapter archives, MS Dep 1980/1 40, fos 103a–103j.

[74] MR i. 130, 147.

[75] MR i. 130.

[76] Ibid.

[77] MR iv. 108, 246.

Table 2. Anniversaries in the partial obit roll and other sources (in calendrical order)

Name	Surname	Obit date	Foundation
William	Walthewe, Sr		1437
Isolde	Walthewe		1437
William	Walthewe, Jr		1437
John	Walthewe		1437
Thomas	Pakhardy	Saturday before Ascension	1386
Agnes	Pakhardy	Saturday before Ascension	1386
William	Vawsour	13 July	
Alan	Balyeman	22 June	
Agnes	Balyeman	22 June	
Hugh	de Roderham	27 June	
Agnes	Skrevyne	9 July	
Margaret	de Mylne	13 July	
St Wilfrid Guild		23 July	1419
Henry	Plumpton	2 August	1369
John	Frankish, Sr	4 August	1391
Wynand	de Rodes	4 August	1391
John	de Hawkeswick	4 August	1391
Julian		4 August	1391
Pauline	Warde	7 August	1349
Walter	Sutor	23 August	1349
Agnes	Sutor	23 August	1349
John	Frankish, Jr	Saturday before Michaelmas	1399
Margaret	Frankish	Saturday before Michaelmas	1399
William	Frankish	Saturday before Michaelmas	1399
Archbishop	Bowet	20 October	1415
Nicholas	Dall	27 October	1391
Matilda	Dall	27 October	1391
William	de Lynton	18 November	1416
John	de Lynton	18 November	1416
Agnes	de Lynton	18 November	1416
John	Feriby	18 November	1416
Margaret	Feriby	18 November	1416

anniversary (1437) and both of those founded by the Frankish family (1391 and 1399). The St Wilfrid guild, as part of its role in founding the St Thomas chantry, set 23 July as the date of the general anniversary for guild members with the same bell-ringing as any other obit.[78] The cash incentives for clerical attendance were the same as for the later Walthewe anniversary, except that in place of the chaplains, the vicars were offered 1s. each to take part.[79] Naturally the guild members would participate, and the guild would supply the lights for the funerals and anniversaries of its members.[80] Obits could preserve the collective memory of the parish and minster as well as that of a guild. The chapter grasped this in 1401 when it decided that there should be a regular obit for the soul of King Æthelstan, the alleged source of many of their privileges, and those 'of the other kings and bishops and canons and all benefactors of our church'.[81] It was essentially the same group of people commemorated regularly in the bidding prayers at high mass. This anniversary was to take place four times a year in correspondence with the Ember Days. The office of the dead would begin on Thursday evening, and the requiem mass would be performed on the Friday.[82] It was the only obit that the sanctuary men who took shelter in the liberty of St Wilfrid, were required to attend. Since they owed their safety to Æthelstan, it was appropriate that they ring the bells and attend his requiem mass.[83] As with many of the other anniversaries, the bellman was to go around the town and loudly beseech his listeners to pray for Æthelstan and the others.[84]

On the basis of the available evidence it is difficult to assess the durability of Ripon's obits. Those that were preserved until the incorporation of the vicars were probably very likely to be maintained in some form thereafter. In the comparable case of Exeter Cathedral, anniversaries whose resources became too limited to observe annually were made triennial to preserve them from total extinction.[85] Whether or not the Ripon vicars ever resorted to this solution cannot be determined from extant sources.

The other danger facing perpetual anniversaries was that the calendar would eventually become too crowded to accommodate any more. The known Ripon anniversaries would not have had to compete with each other or, for the most part, with major feast days. They might occasionally have faced competition from actual funerals since there was no way for obit founders to plan around

---

[78] MR iv. 201.

[79] Ibid.

[80] Ibid.

[81] 'aliorum regum et pontificum ac canonicorum et omnium benefactorum Eccl'ie n're': MR iv. 283.

[82] Ibid.

[83] MR iv. 281-2.

[84] MR iv. 283.

[85] Lepine, 'Obits at Exeter Cathedral', 69.

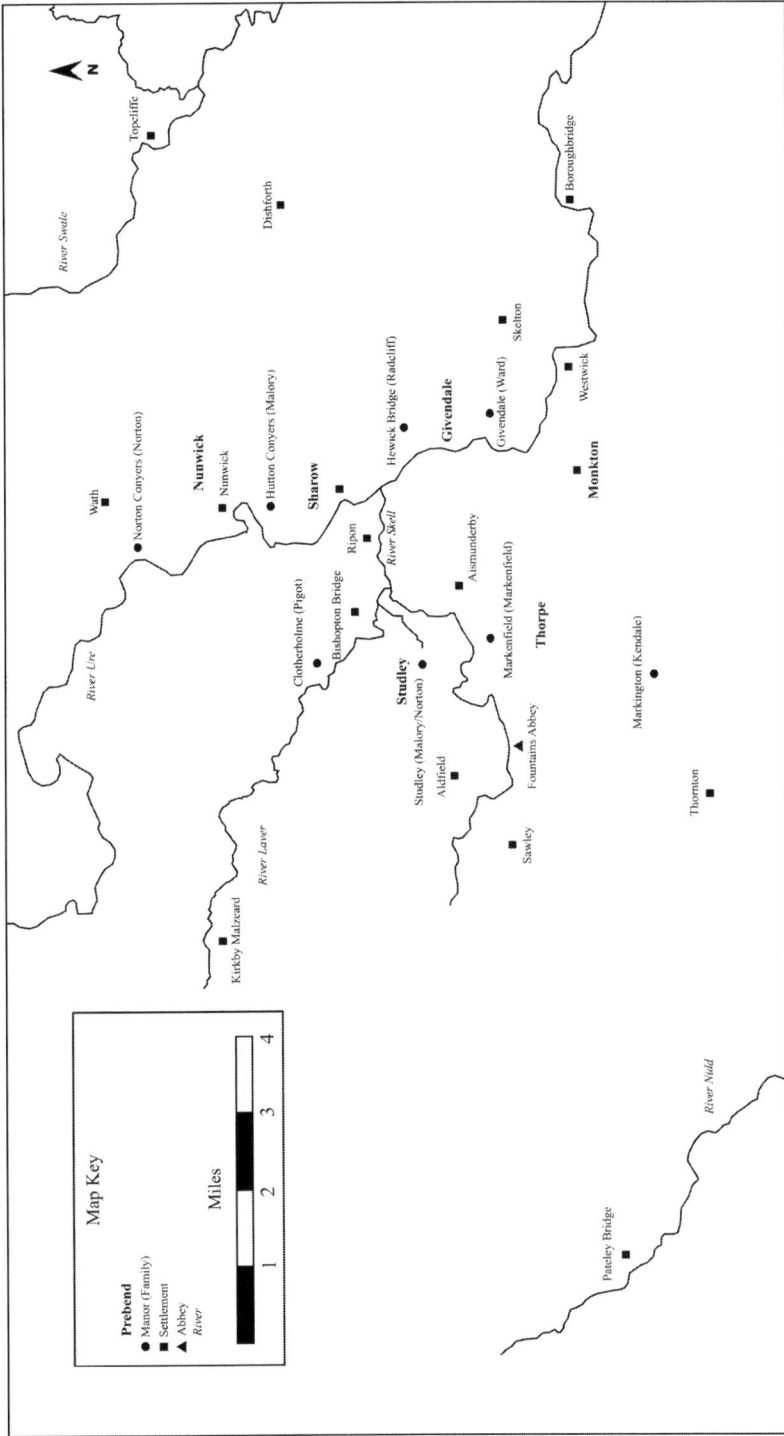

Map 4. Important manors surrounding Ripon, and the families that held them in the second half of the fifteenth century

them. Many other anniversaries may have been established in the chapels of the parish, where calendar congestion was less of an issue and the potential attendants were a smaller but more familiar group of people. Anniversaries and chantries alike, when they were founded within the minster, were intended to attract the attention of a large number of people. The same is true of the funerary monuments installed there. Tombs and chantries in particular could be combined to great effect so that a perpetual chantry was a defining feature of a space rather than a single event like an anniversary.[86]

Posthumous commemoration of Ripon's clergy

The minster's canons founded its earliest chantries to benefit themselves and other ecclesiastics, and the majority of the eight perpetual chantries recorded in 1546 were originally founded by minster canons. As Ripon's wealthiest clergy, the canons were most likely to be able to afford the costs of a perpetual chantry or a funerary monument. Geoffrey de Larder founded the first chantry at the altar of St Andrew in the north transept in about 1233. He was one of the minster's most industrious canons, establishing the lights of St Wilfrid's tomb around this time and making a spirited defence of the chapter's rights in 1229. Not all canons were so attached to Ripon, and those who were pluralists often distributed their resources around other churches. In particular, those with a benefice at York Minster often concentrated their bequests there, and even residence at Ripon was not always a deciding factor. John de Dene (d. 1435) and John Sendale (d. 1467) wanted to be buried at Ripon, but William Scrope (d. 1463), who was a residentiary canon at the end of his life, preferred to be buried with his kin in the St Stephen chapel at York Minster.[87] Here Scrope would be in the company of the lords of Masham, their wives and children, and Archbishop Richard Scrope.[88] William Cawood, who was prebendary of Thorpe from around 1393 until his death in 1419, expressed his devotion to Wilfrid by helping the St Wilfrid guild of Ripon to found a chantry there as well as by founding another chantry at the St Wilfrid altar in York Minster.[89] Even John Sendale wanted his perpetual obit established at York so that he would have a place in the memory of both institutions, and he bequeathed a sum of money to be spent on Archbishop Scrope's shrine in the event that he was canonised.[90]

Resident canons who chose to be buried at Ripon generally wanted tombs within the church building. Intramural burial was a sign of status for the clergy

---

[86]   Saul, *English church monuments*, 122.

[87]   *TE* ii. 43; *AoC*, 230; *MR* ii. 239.

[88]   Christopher Norton, 'Richard Scrope and York Minster', in P. J. P Goldberg (ed.), *Richard Scrope: archbishop, rebel, martyr*, Donington 2007, 138–213 at p. 184.

[89]   *CPR Henry IV*, iv. 260; *MR* ii. 212–13.

[90]   *AoC*, 231.

as much as for the laity, but the limited available space often affected who could be buried there as well as what type of monuments could be installed in the church.[91] The exact location of a grave was frequently symbolic. In a monastic context, abbots were often buried in the chapter house where in life they had exercised their authority.[92] The closest equivalent to an abbot at Ripon was a resident canon, but they could not be buried under the chapter house floor because of the undercroft. The other obvious location was the choir, but burial there appears to have been rare. John de Dene is the only individual known to have requested burial there, writing in his will that he wanted 'to be buried in the choir of the collegiate church of St Peter, Ripon, without any kind of secular pomp'.[93] His monument was a flat brass with an inscription to identify him.[94] In its location in the choir, Dene's monument was visible primarily to his fellow clergy.

The nave, with its population of saints' images and high traffic of parishioners, must have seemed attractive to John Sendale, who had been prebendary of Thorpe at Ripon since 1458 when George Neville, the previous holder, was elected bishop of Exeter.[95] Sendale founded a chantry dedicated to the Holy Trinity at an altar in the nave in 1467, preferring that altar to the parochial altar of Thorpe in a north transept arm already cluttered with chantries and Markenfield monuments.[96] He endowed his chantry not with local properties like most other Ripon chantries, but with an annual stipend from the Cluniac house at Pontefract.[97] This arrangement protected his chantry better than if he had merely assigned rental incomes for its support, since rental properties would have needed to be maintained and might sometimes be unoccupied. To distinguish it from the Plumpton Holy Trinity chantry in the choir, Sendale's chantry was often described in the records as being below or beneath the choir. It was not located underground, but in the nave by the junction of the rood screen and the south-west pier of the central crossing. There is a piscina in the remaining portion of the south wall of the old nave, which means that there was an altar nearby. The altar was probably enclosed by some type of structure, as is indicated by the roof scar in the western face of the southwest crossing

---

[91]   Binski, *Medieval death*, 74, 77.

[92]   Megan Cassidy-Welch, *Monastic spaces and their meanings: thirteenth-century English Cistercian monasteries*, Turnhout 2001, 115–16.

[93]   'ad sepeliendum in choro ecclesiæ Collegiatæ Beati Petri Ripon sine pompa aliqua seculari': *TE* ii. 43. The minster was variously referred to as the church of St Wilfrid, the church of St Peter, and the church of both Peter and Wilfrid.

[94]   *MR* ii. 249.

[95]   *MR* ii. 216.

[96]   For a summary of Sendale's career see *MR* ii. 217. His will can be found in Ripon Cathedral, dean and chapter archives, MS Dep 1980/1 40, fos 95–6, and printed in *AoC*, 229–36.

[97]   *MR* i. 172; iv. 263–6. This was intended to guarantee income and avoid the decay in value liable to affect rents.

pier. The scar cuts into the remnant of the c. 1175 pier and the masonry added after 1450. The altar may have been enclosed at the time of the chantry's foundation in 1467 or when the nave was rebuilt in the early sixteenth century. Sendale wished to be buried 'on the north side of the same [altar]', and this fits with the location of the altar by the south-west crossing pier.[98]

John Sendale knew from experience how and when the building was used, and he calculated that the site of his grave and chantry would be highly beneficial to his soul. His new chantry was situated directly before the rood and adjacent to the altar of the Exaltation of Holy Cross. Sendale might have hoped that when the Holy Cross guild's chaplains used this neighbouring altar for their own masses, they would pray for him too. The high mass processions would have paused to bless his Holy Trinity altar as part of their progress through the minster, and his monument was effectively in the midst of one of most dramatic of the Palm Sunday procession stations. On the latter occasion, the veil was raised from the rood and the procession halted to venerate it. Not long afterward, on the feast of Holy Trinity, Sendale's altar was used for an extra mass that pious laypeople could attend. These were its practical benefits, though Sendale may also have been influenced by the powerful symbolism of the location. Since it was believed that Adam was buried at Golgotha, the place of Christ's crucifixion, burials before the rood were an imitation of Adam and linked with the power of Christ's blood to redeem humankind from original sin.[99] These same factors made it an attractive burial place for others, such as the merchant William Wrampayn, Jr, and possibly also Joan Ward.[100]

Sendale also hoped that Christ's sacrifice, repeated in the form of a thousand masses, would wash away much of his incompleted penance. He asked for them 'to be performed as quickly as possible, in the manner of the trental of St Gregory, and to end within a month from the day of my death'.[101] These masses were to benefit Sendale's own soul, that of his friend John Marshall, and those of the late archbishops of York, John Kemp and William Booth.[102] His request is peculiar because the trental of St Gregory normally required a year to complete and only amounted to thirty masses. The usual custom for the St Gregory trental was to say three masses apiece within the octaves of ten major annual feasts: Christmas, Epiphany, Candlemas, Annunciation, Easter, Ascension, Pentecost, Holy Trinity, Assumption and the Nativity of the Virgin.[103] Perhaps what Sendale intended was to vary the forms

---

[98] 'ex parte boriali ejusdem': AoC, 230.

[99] Kornelia Imesch, 'The altar of the Holy Cross and the ideal of Adam's progeny: "ut paradysiace loca possideat regionis"', in Edelgard E. DuBruch and Barbara I. Gusich (eds), Death and dying in the Middle Ages, New York 1999, 73–106 at pp. 78–9.

[100] Borthwick Institute, probate register 2, fo. 7r; probate register 4, fo. 38v.

[101] 'quam cito fieri poterit, et ad ultimum infra mensem a die obitus mea, celebrandis more trentalis Sancti Gregorii': AoC, 230.

[102] Ibid.

[103] Duffy, Stripping of the altars, 370–1.

of the mass, using those of the major feast days that normally featured in a trental, and thereby concentrate the intercessory power of just over thirty-three years' worth of trentals into a single month. To judge from his other bequests, he probably envisioned the trentals being spread over a wide area, which is just as well because it is unlikely that requests for a thousand masses in a month could be accommodated in a single church.[104]

Vicars employed their own distinct strategies for posthumous commemoration, often relying on the whole corporation of vicars or their particular successors to remember them. Some vicars chose to be buried close to their altars in an effort to guarantee that they would be difficult to forget or ignore. The altar of St Andrew, which served the prebend of Monkton, is the best documented example of this practice. A number of interests converged on this altar and rendered the area around it a highly contested place of burial. Robert Brompton (d. 1471), vicar of Monkton, was one link in a chain of vicars and chaplains that stretches from the 1470s back to the last years of the fourteenth century. He desired 'to be buried in the churchyard of St Wilfrid of Ripon, by the wall of the church, at the boundary of the altar of St Andrew', which he further described as 'my altar of St Andrew the Apostle'.[105] This was the place 'where rests the body of John Ely, lately vicar of the said prebend', and Brompton asked for a joint epitaph over their adjacent graves.[106] Ely's will refers to burial in the churchyard but makes no mention of any monument.[107] Although he died in 1427, his burial place was still known forty-four years later when Brompton asked to be buried by him. The monument that Brompton shared with his long-dead predecessor demonstrates that dead vicars might expect to be remembered by those still living even if, as seems possible in this case, they had never met in life.

The vicars had less wealth than the canons to spend on fine tombs. Nevertheless, the personal monument for Ely and Brompton set them apart from the many laypeople unable to afford any monument. Their graves may have been in a prominent location near the north door, where high status burials were uncovered during a watching brief in 1999.[108] The altar of St Andrew was located in the outer chapel of the transept, not far from the north door. Some of the graves uncovered in 1999 appeared to have once had covers that were meant to be seen above ground.[109] Nevertheless, it is remarkable that these vicars were buried outside in the churchyard when intramural burial was preferred by most of the minster clergy. They had apparently

---

[104] Badham, *Seeking salvation*, 148–9; AoC, 230n.

[105] 'ad sepeliendum in cimiterio Beati Wilfridi Ripon', juxta murum ecclesiæ, ad finem altaris Sancti Andreæ' and 'altari meæ Sancti Andreæ Apostoli': AoC, 153.

[106] 'ubi corpus Johannis Ely, nuper vicarii præbendæ prædictæ requiescit': ibid.

[107] MR i. 329.

[108] Antoni and Brinklow, *Minster Road, Ripon, North Yorkshire: report on an archaeological watching brief*, 13.

[109] Ibid. 13–14.

been crowded out of the north transept by the Markenfields and, rather than choose an intramural location somewhere farther away from their altar, Ely and Brompton opted for graves within the churchyard but as close as possible to their altar.

Ripon's chantry chaplains, like its vicars, sometimes desired to be buried by their altars. John de Walkingham (d. 1399) wanted to be buried by his altar of the Holy Trinity behind the high altar.[110] Thomas Hawk (d. 1469) wanted to be buried by his altar of the Assumption, and he tasked Christopher Kendale and John Snape with making distributions to poor people who would pray for him after his death.[111] John Birtby (d. 1477) requested burial near his chantry altar of St Andrew, the same altar around which many vicars and members of the Markenfield family wished to be buried.[112] Birtby's close association with the Markenfields is evident in his will. His connection to his patrons might have given him greater confidence that he could be buried by the altar of St Andrew when the vicars of Monkton were apparently unable to find space there.

A variety of objects could form a material link between the dead priest and his altar. John Ely took into account both priests who used the St Andrew altar. He gave his missal to the altar, as well as two sets of vestments, one for use by his successor and the other for the St Andrew chantry chaplain.[113] In a similar way the vicar of Thorpe, Richard de Wakefield (d. 1399), bequeathed some broadcloth to his parochial altar of St John the Baptist.[114] Many of his bequests are to other clerics, and he concluded by leaving the residue of his possessions to chaplains John Ely and Richard Schedwell, 'whom ... I make and ordain my executors in order that they may dispose for my soul just as it should seem best to them to do'.[115] Just as de Wakefield depended on Ely and Schedwell, so too Ely was remembered by Brompton. Vicars did not concentrate all their resources on their parochial altars in the minster. The new common residence had its own chapel dedicated to St Nicholas. In disposing of his possessions in 1471, the vicar John Exilby wrote:

> I leave my breviary to remain forever in the chapel of St Nicholas in the New Bedern of the said collegiate church, under this condition: that my brothers of the said Bedern should pay or cause to be paid six marks to a certain suitable chaplain to celebrate for my soul immediately after my death, and if they

---

[110] MR iv. 168.

[111] AoC, 136.

[112] AoC, 180.

[113] MR i. 330.

[114] MR iv. 167; Eamon Duffy, 'The end of it all: the material culture of the English parish and the 1552 inventories of goods', in Burgess and Duffy, The parish in late medieval England, 381–9 at pp. 381–2.

[115] 'quos ... facio et ordino executores meos vt disponent pro anima mea prout eis melius viderint expedire': MR iv. 167. John Ely ended his career as vicar of Monkton, but Richard Shedwell's position is unknown.

should not desire to do so, the breviary should be sold and disposed of by my executors.[116]

He also bequeathed them his mazer, which was gilded and bound with silver.[117] The bequest of the mazer would have kept him in the memory of his fellow vicars, who would have seen and used it, but more significantly Exilby's will shows that vicars could endow chantries in their chapel rather than depend on the use of an altar in the minster.

The elaborate liturgy of the minster required its clergy to possess a number of different books. On his deathbed a priest might arrange for a colleague or successor to receive some or all of his collection. The books most commonly mentioned were psalters, missals, breviaries and processionals. Liturgical books such as these bound deceased clergy even more tightly to their successors who were already likely to think of them when they stood at the dead man's place in the choir, at his former altar, or near his grave. Often the bequests came with obligations to remember the testator. Robert Laton, chaplain of the St Wilfrid chantry, gave 40s. and a *portiforium* (a portable breviary) to be commemorated for one year.[118] Robert Atkinson asked that his *portiforium* be sold to pay for as many masses as the proceeds of the sale would cover.[119] Some books were even intended to be chained in the choir of the church. William Cawood (d. 1419), canon of Thorpe, bequeathed his psalter 'with the gloss of Cassiodorus, so that it may be chained before the stalls of the prebends of Thorpe and Stanwick ... to remain forever for the use of the ministers of the church'.[120] Here the psalter was within easy reach of John Dene, prebendary of Stanwick, with whom he had founded the St Wilfrid chantry. Some of these books had already passed through the hands of other owners. John Sendale stated that the missal that he left to his new chantry of the Holy Trinity had formerly belonged to Archbishop John Kemp.[121] John Dene (d. 1435) bequeathed to William Scaryngton a *portiforium* that had once belonged to the vicar John Coke.[122] The chantry chaplain Robert Chamber's (d. 1468) bequest of a *portiforium* to Robert Brownfield came with a condition. At the time that Chamber wrote his will,

---

[116] 'lego portiferium meum ad remanendum in perpetuum in capella Sancti Nicholai, infra Novam Bedernam ecclesiæ collegiatæ prædictæ, sub hac condicione, quod fratres mei dictæ Bedernæ reddant vel solvi faciant cuidam capellano idoneo ad celebrandum pro anima mea immediate post decessum meum, sex marcas, et si noluerint, vendatur, et disponatur per executores meos': AoC, 169.

[117] Ibid.

[118] AoC, 178.

[119] AoC, 326.

[120] 'cum glosâ Cassiodori ut sit cathenatum coram stallis Prebendarum de Thorp et Stanewyges, in Ecclesiâ de Ripon, ad utilitatem ministrorum ecclesiæ pro perpetuo reman-surum': TE i. 396.

[121] AoC, 234.

[122] TE ii. 44.

his book was in the hands of the vicar John Exilby, to whom he had given it in pledge for money that he had borrowed. Brownfield would have to redeem the pledge of 6s. 8d. if he wanted to obtain the *portiforium*.[123] In cases where there are no explicit instructions in the will, it is still likely that the recipient of the bequest was expected to remember the dead man either in gratitude for the bequest of a book that he would regularly use or because of a friendship in life that the bequest recognised.

Burial and memory of Ripon's gentry

Gentry families endowed very few perpetual chantries in the minster but spent large sums on monuments and other forms of display. Display, on monuments and in other forms, was a fundamental aspect of gentry culture and crucial to the maintenance of social status.[124] Gentry culture also tended to be very locally focused, more or less so depending on the extent of a family's landholdings.[125] The gentry can be divided into three categories: knight, esquire or gentleman, though in practice the wealthier esquires tended to resemble the knights, and their poorer counterparts were akin to the gentlemen. The lesser category is often described as the parish gentry and the more powerful group the county gentry.[126] The parish gentry focused their commemorative strategies on their parish churches because they had no other options.[127] Knights and their families might have a much wider range of choices, but from the end of the thirteenth century they began to identify more and more with the seat of their power, the manor. At this time many of them founded perpetual chantries in their own manorial chapels. These chapels were another important sign of their status, and chantry chaplains gave them a permanent staff thereby making them more useful to the living and the dead of the household.[128] At the same time, families could invest in their parish churches, converting them into family mausolea and sometimes even colleges that were devoted to commemorating them in ways that resembled the patronal monastic houses in earlier centuries.[129] Some of Ripon's gentry chose the minster as a burial place while others identified with other parish churches or religious houses.

Graves inside the minster clustered around altars, saints' images and other significant locations like the font and the door to the choir. These locations

[123]   AoC, 135.

[124]   Saul, *English church monuments*, 32–3; Peter Coss, *The foundations of gentry life: the Multons of Frampton and their world, 1270–1370*, Oxford 2010, 4–5, 140–1.

[125]   Saul, 'The gentry and the parish', 254–5; Coss, *Foundations of gentry life*, 6.

[126]   Chris Given-Wilson, *The English nobility in the late Middle Ages: the late fourteenth-century political community*, London 1996, 70–2.

[127]   Saul, 'The gentry and the parish', 256.

[128]   Coss, *Foundations of gentry life*, 141.

[129]   Saul, *For honour and fame*, 68; Coss, *Foundations of gentry life*, 140.

were intended to maximise the visibility of the monument and to target a specific audience, thereby soliciting the greatest quantity of the most valuable prayers. Burial by saints' images and altars was intended to win help from the living as well as the very special dead, the saints themselves.[130] Though not originally intended to be family burial churches, the minster and many other medieval churches were adapted to this purpose over time, leading to competition over space wherein political power became manifest in the placement of tombs.[131] Many of these burial places were also sought by the vicars and chaplains of the minster. The general pattern was for the more powerful gentry families and the minster clergy to choose altars as burial places and for other wealthy parishioners, including the lesser gentry, burgesses and wealthy villagers, to ask for burial in the nave. The constant presence and visibility of gentry tombs allowed them to exercise great influence over memory, affirming the power of the living people whose families they represented.[132] To be sure, many of these monuments were very effective as focal points for chantry masses founded by the same families.[133] They could also represent the families who rarely attended the minster, enabling them to be present in memory while absent in body. Because many of the monuments of gentry families were situated by altars, the procession before high mass on Sundays and feast days would regularly encounter them. These same families, as benefactors of the church, were also likely to be remembered in the bidding prayers of the mass.

Very few of Ripon's medieval funerary monuments have survived, and the locations of tombs are known mainly from a few dozen extant wills. There is much better evidence for the locations of the altars than the saints' images, so in effect this means that the graves of the lesser gentry, more usually situated near saints' images, cannot be analysed in the same degree of detail as those of the county gentry buried by altars. While it was common for lesser gentry families to concentrate their bequests on the parish church, the pattern in the parish of Ripon was slightly different because it had so many dependent chapels. The Walworth family's relationship with the Thornton chapel is instructive. In the late fifteenth century the religious life of the Walworth family centred on the chapel of Thornton in the prebend of Studley, where some of their marriages were solemnised and where women from the family were churched after childbirth. They typically made bequests to this chapel but since they could not be buried in or around it they were buried in the minster instead. John Walworth (d. 1459) and his wife Katherine (d. 1470) were buried there, perhaps near the font like their descendant John (d. 1520) and his wife

130 Badham, *Seeking salvation*, 213, 232; Roffey, *The medieval chantry chapel*, 88.
131 Binski, *Medieval death*, 74.
132 Saul, *English church monuments*, 131.
133 Ibid. 129; Roffey, *The medieval chantry chapel*, 105.

Margaret (d. 1521).[134] Their memories were preserved in the Thornton chapel as well as the minster. When she made her will in 1521, Margaret Walworth gave £1 6s. 8d. to buy a chalice for the chapel, provided that 'neighbours of the lordeshipe will be bond that what prest so ever thei have, that he sall syng *Messe* twhyse is a week at Thorneton chapell, to pray for my sall, and my husbande's'.[135] If these conditions were not met, then the money was to be spent on a temporary chantry at the minster.[136] John Walworth's will lists payments to a variety of institutions mentioned in Ripon wills, especially those that were close to Thornton and the family residence at Raventofts Hall. His £4 6s. 8d. to Fountains Abbey 'to be absolvede from all maner of trespaces that ever I dyde to them' and his £3 for a temporary chantry at Ripley owed a lot to his close proximity to both Fountains and Ripley.[137] Robert of Knaresborough – who, with his shrine in Knaresborough, was the nearest saintly neighbour to Wilfrid of Ripon – also features.[138] In its essentials this pattern is often repeated by other gentry families. Their bequests reflect the same connections with local churches and religious houses. Testators with wider horizons often gave money to the four mendicant houses at York or those in Richmond. Many combined a family burial place in the minster with temporary chantries there and in their own chapels.

The county gentry may have shared the parish gentry's preference for long-term liturgical commemoration in their own chapels, but their tombs were more ornate and better placed within the minster. The greater evidence of their commemorative strategies is itself a testament to their exceptional power and their need to represent their status. Having said that, it is worth considering in some detail the histories of fifteenth-century Ripon's most powerful and wealthy families and the manner in which they wished to be remembered. The families which may be classed as county gentry were the Markenfields, Wards, Malories, Nortons and Pigots. Their residences were fairly evenly distributed through the parish and they were all knights, though there was a cadet line of Pigot esquires who were also significant at the end of the fifteenth century. The Markenfields and Wards were long established by that time, but the Malories, Nortons and Pigots were more recent arrivals. Their commemorative strategies reflect a wide array of factors including identification with other religious institutions, adherence to political factions and changing fortunes. There were also the Kendales, who were a parish gentry family who inherited Markington from its ancient manorial lords, the Gyliot family, in the middle of the fifteenth century. The Kendales are an interesting case because they concentrated the memory of their family at the Ladykirk rather than in the minster. These were,

134   *TE* v. 107–8.
135   *TE* v. 107n.
136   Ibid.
137   *TE* v. 108.
138   Ibid.

with the possible exception of the Nortons, the same families whose oaths of fealty bound them to St Wilfrid as Marmion tenants.

The Markenfields of Markenfield

The two Markenfield tombs in the north transept are the grandest of Ripon's surviving medieval monuments. They proclaim the family's status in a variety of ways. The tomb chests are adorned with heraldry that signifies links between the Markenfields and other elite families while the effigies show the knights in their armour and the ladies, at least before they were disfigured in a later era, in their finery. The older tomb belongs to Sir Thomas Markenfield I (d. 1398) and his wife, Denise (née Miniot); Denise was heiress to the estate of Carlton Miniot near Thirsk, which then passed into the hands of the Markenfields.[139] Sir Thomas Markenfield was the head of a long established Ripon family that was rising in prominence during the fourteenth century. At the beginning of the century John Markenfield was a canon of Ripon and York who combined his ecclesiastical career with royal service as Chancellor of the Exchequer.[140] Edward II granted him the right to crenellate his residence at Markenfield in 1310.[141] This was a very desirable privilege for the Markenfields to obtain at a time when knightly families throughout England were fortifying their manor houses and shifting their family burial places from patronal monasteries to their own parish churches.[142] Markenfield itself lay within the Percy fee, and until at least the end of the thirteenth century the Markenfields were buried in the churchyard of Fountains Abbey, a monastery favoured by the Percies. As late as 1271 Roger Markenfield granted the abbey a half acre of land so that he could be buried in its cemetery.[143] Sir Thomas I is the first Markenfield known to have been buried in Ripon Minster.

In the mid-fifteenth century the Markenfields were one of the wealthiest and most powerful families of knights in Yorkshire with an annual income of around £100.[144] They were second only to the great magnate families of the north such as the Nevilles and the Percies. The Lancastrian affinity that had once united the major families of the region unravelled after John of Gaunt's death so that in the middle of the century the conflict between the Nevilles and Percies was the

[139] Walbran, Guide to Ripon, 60; Janet C. Senior, The Markenfields of Markenfield Hall: the rise and fall of a Yorkshire family, Bradford 2009, 25.

[140] Senior, The Markenfields of Markenfield Hall, 18.

[141] CPR Edward II, i. 212.

[142] Saul, For honour and fame, 68.

[143] Abstracts of the charters and other documents in the chartulary of Fountains Abbey in the West Riding of the county of York, ed. William T. Lancaster, Leeds 1915, ii. 520; Senior, The Markenfields of Markenfield Hall, 3.

[144] Pollard, North-eastern England during the Wars of the Roses, 89n.

source of many violent disturbances in Yorkshire.[145] The Nevilles of Middleham had a large concentration of manors to the northwest of Ripon while their rivals, the Percies, had greater influence to the south-east around Knaresborough. The fault line between the supporters of the two families was the boundary of the forest of Knaresborough and the southern edge of the parish of Ripon. From the reign of Henry IV onward the Plumpton family were great supporters of the Percies and built up their base of power around Knaresborough.[146] The Markenfields were the strongest family across the boundary in the parish of Ripon, and by that time they had become staunch supporters of the Nevilles. In 1403 Sir Thomas II fought on the side of the Nevilles against Henry Hotspur Percy's rebellion and in 1417 he went on campaign in France as a man-at-arms with Sir John Neville as his captain.[147] Sir John Markenfield went to France in the service of Richard Neville, earl of Salisbury, in 1431 or 1432.[148] The Plumptons's fortunes were the exact opposite at this time. Sir William Plumpton II was executed in 1405 after joining Henry Percy, first earl of Northumberland, and Archbishop Scrope in rebellion against Henry IV.[149] Later his grandson, Sir William Plumpton III, was steward of Knaresborough and deeply implicated in the violence of the 1440s that pitted the men of Ripon, including the Markenfield, Walworth and Frankish families against Plumpton and the men of Knaresborough.[150] Towards the end of the century it was the Markenfields who suffered misfortune, including the deposition of Richard III who had retained Sir Thomas Markenfield III in 1483.[151]

The Markenfield tombs express the family's chivalric status and its unwavering loyalty to the Neville family, and they were of course intended to be seen. The Markenfields had various audiences and occasions in mind when they positioned their tombs by the altars of the north transept. This transept contained two parochial altars, each with its own chantry by 1370. The outer chapel was dedicated to St Andrew and contained the altar for Monkton prebend. In the early decades of the thirteenth century, Canon Geoffrey de Larder had founded a chantry at this altar, which David de Wollore re-founded in 1370. Although Thomas Markenfield I does not appear among the list of beneficiaries or witnesses at the time of the chantry's re-foundation, de Wollore named him the chantry's patron.[152] Before his death in 1398, Thomas I nominated John de Fulforth as chaplain of the St Andrew chantry to replace the late John Clynt, and his wife Denise afterward approved this

[145] Ibid. 170.

[146] Wilcock, 'Local disorder in the Honour of Knaresborough', 43.

[147] Senior, *The Markenfields of Markenfield Hall*, 27; TNA, E 101/51/2, m 22.

[148] TNA, E 40/695; C 1/12/223.

[149] Dockray, 'Plumpton Family', ODNB.

[150] See Wilcock, 'Local disorder in the Honour of Knaresborough', 39–80

[151] Pollard, *North-eastern England during the Wars of the Roses*, 159.

[152] MR iv. 134.

appointment.[153] In 1410 John de Fulforth resigned the position to become vicar of Alveley and Sir Thomas Markenfield II replaced him with Robert Lytster, alias de Aismunderby.[154] The new chantry priest was probably someone whom Thomas II knew personally as Aismunderby was a village not far from Markenfield. In the same year Thomas II had the minster chapter certify an enrolment of charters relating to the chantry in his patronage.[155] The chantry of St Andrew clearly belonged to the Markenfields regardless of who founded or re-founded it.

The second altar in the north transept was dedicated to St John and was the prebendal altar of Thorpe. A masonry wall, the foundations of which were observed during building work in 1974, originally separated the two altars.[156] This was probably removed to accommodate the tomb of Thomas and Denise Markenfield which, lodged between the altar of St Andrew and the altar of St John, could make a mute but constant appeal to two vicars and two chantry chaplains who used these altars for pious intercession on behalf of their souls. At Easter the parishioners of Monkton and Thorpe took communion at these altars and the Markenfields themselves were obliged to attend on these occasions. In receiving communion they must have taken precedence over all others, while their clothing and the monuments of their ancestors also affirmed their status.

The tomb of Sir Thomas I and Denise is comprised of a large chest with alabaster effigies of the couple. This type of monument was developed to signal high status even among those who could afford tombs and was probably modelled after the saints' shrines of the twelfth century.[157] The sides of the chest are covered in heraldry to indicate family ties and allegiances. The coats of arms lack their original paint, making some of them difficult to identify, but the shield with a saltire at the head of the tomb is undoubtedly meant to be the blazon of the Nevilles (*gules, a saltire argent*). Thomas Markenfield's effigy wears a jupon with his own coat of arms (*argent, on a bend sable three bezants*) and it appears again on the scabbard of his sword. It is depicted twice on the side of the chest, once impaled with Miniot to symbolise the marriage of Thomas and Denise. The arms of the Soothill family (*eagle displayed impaling five fussils in fess*) show the marriage link between Thomas II and Beatrice Soothill.[158] The armour of the effigy and the inclusion of the Neville arms strongly emphasise Thomas Markenfield's role as a warrior. The Scrope of Bolton heraldry (*azure, a bend or*) on both sides of the tomb and that of the Wards of Givendale (*azure, a cross fleury or*) on one side reveal more of Markenfield's affinities. Thomas I

---

[153] *MR* iv. 177–8.

[154] *MR* iv. 159–60.

[155] *MR* i. 184–9.

[156] R. A. Hall, 'Rescue excavations in the crypt of Ripon Cathedral', *YAJ* xlix (1977), 59–63, with appendix by L. A. S. Butler, 'Observations made in the north transept during building work in September 1974', at p. 62.

[157] Saul, *English church monuments*, 154–5.

[158] Senior, *The Markenfields of Markenfield Hall*, 29.

had gone on campaign in France with the Scropes and later testified on behalf of Richard Scrope, lord of Bolton, in the Scrope-Grosvenor heraldic dispute.[159]

The second tomb is that of Thomas III and his wife Eleanor (d. 1490), daughter of another notable Neville retainer, Sir John Conyers.[160] Her family heraldry (*azure, a maunch or*) features on the tomb to symbolise their union. Some of the heraldry from the Thomas I tomb also appears on this monument, including that of Ward of Givendale (*azure, a cross fleury or*), Roos (*azure, three water bougets or*) and Neville (*gules, a saltire argent*). The Markenfields and Wards, two of Ripon's oldest families, had remained friends and had been joined even closer by the marriage of Joan Markenfield and Sir Roger Ward in the middle of the fifteenth century. As with the Thomas I tomb, the location of the Thomas III tomb is significant. John Walbran reported in the late nineteenth century that it had recently been moved from the north-east corner of the St Andrew chapel.[161] In this position it would have precluded the use of the chapel for religious services and covered up the aumbry in the north wall, so the tomb would only have been moved there after the dissolution of the chantries and the chapter of Ripon. When it was moved into the corner of the chapel, two of its sides were cut away so that it would fit more neatly. Originally it had four sides and a correspondingly greater array of heraldry. It could only have stood in the midst of the north transept where it would have imposed itself constantly on the liturgical routine of the minster. Like the older Markenfield tomb, it would have reminded clergy and laity alike to pray for Thomas and Eleanor. At Easter it would have augmented the effect of the tomb of Thomas and Denise. Pilgrims entering the minster *via* the north transept door during the major feasts of St Wilfrid would have confronted the tomb and the Sunday and feast day processions around the altars would have encountered it one or more times every week. None of the other Markenfield monuments have survived, but there must have been more. Thomas III himself articulated as much in his request for burial 'afore the awter of Saynt Androwe in the monastery of Saynt Wilfride in Ripon, emonge the beriall of myn auncestors'.[162] His son Sir Ninian Markenfield (d. 1528) left instructions that he too should be buried in Ripon Minster.[163]

The Wards of Givendale

The Wards had established themselves at Givendale by the early thirteenth century at the latest, and subsequently inherited the manor of Newby when

---

[159] *De controversia in curia militari inter Ricardum le Scrope et Robertum Grosvenor, milites*, ed. N. Harris Nicholas, London 1832, i. 121.

[160] Pollard, *North-eastern England during the Wars of the Roses*, 128-9; Walbran, *Guide to Ripon*, 61.

[161] Walbran, *Guide to Ripon*, 61.

[162] *TE* iv. 124.

[163] *TE* v. 232.

the Newby family was extinguished in the male line.[164] Over the centuries many of the other families around Ripon met the same fate as the Newbys. The Markenfields and the Wards were unique as families that had been established around Ripon from before the thirteenth century and were still there in the sixteenth. Givendale, site of the Wards' manor house, was such an important settlement that one of the prebends of the parish of Ripon bore its name. The prebendal altar for Givendale was in the inner chapel of the south transept. It was dedicated to St Mary, and was also used by the chaplain and Guild of the Assumption. The Ward family had long enjoyed the right to a domestic chapel dedicated to St Thomas at Givendale. The licence granted to William Ward and his heirs had the standard, two-tiered requirements that permitted the Wards to attend the minster very rarely and required other parishioners who used the chapel to attend on a greater number of major feast days.[165]

The Wards could, like the Markenfields, have created a family mausoleum in the minster. They never did so because they had something that the Markenfields did not: their own priory of Cistercian nuns at Esholt. They had been its patrons since about 1184.[166] Sir Roger Ward (d. 1453), a retainer of the earl of Northumberland, ordered his body to be taken to the nunnery of Esholt and buried there.[167] Roger's widow, Joan (d. 1474) later asked to be buried at the same nunnery.[168] She had fully adopted the symbols of family identity, using the manorial chapel at Givendale for her second marriage and choosing the traditional family mausoleum of her first husband rather than being buried with her second husband or her natal family, the Markenfields. Among the names of the known prioresses of Esholt there are two with the surname Ward: Maud (c. 1392) and another Joan in the last decades of the fifteenth century.[169] The only Ward known to have requested burial at the minster was the younger Joan Ward (d. 1474), who was Lady Joan's daughter. They both died in the early part of 1474 and their wills were both proved at York on the same day. The younger Joan Ward wanted to be buried by one of the minster's Holy Trinity altars, and she made notable bequests to the nuns of Esholt and to the chapel of Skelton near the manor of Givendale.[170] The heraldry of the Wards of Givendale (*azure, a cross fleury or*) represented them at Ripon in their absence. It appears not only on both Markenfield tombs but also on the late fifteenth-century stone screen that separates the choir from the crossing of the church. In the 1480s, around the time that the screen was constructed, Sir

---

[164] Gowland, 'The manors and liberties of Ripon', 62.

[165] *MR* iv. 40.

[166] Esholt was definitely a separate religious house by 1184, having earlier been granted by the Wards to Sinningthwaite Priory: Janet Burton, *The monastic order in Yorkshire, 1069–1215*, Cambridge 1999, 131–2; T. M. Fallow, 'Esholt Priory', in Page, *VCH, York*, iii. 161–3 at p. 161.

[167] *TE* ii. 165.

[168] *TE* ii. 165n.

[169] Fallow, 'Esholt Priory', iii. 162–3.

[170] Borthwick Institute, probate register 4, fo. 7.

Christopher Ward was retained by Henry Percy, 4th earl of Northumberland.[171] The friendship between the Ward and Markenfield families had a long history and was not broken by their service to different lords at the end of the Wars of the Roses.

The Malories of Hutton Conyers and Studley

The Malory family's rise was founded on the extinction of three established Ripon families, two of which were very old. These were the Nunwick, Conyers and Tempest families with lands at Nunwick, Hutton Conyers and Studley respectively. The lordship of Studley in particular changed hands relatively frequently over the years. At the end of the twelfth century it belonged to the Aleman family, then the le Gras family inherited the manor in the middle of the next century, and the Tempests only acquired it when Richard Tempest, the second son of Sir Richard Tempest of Bracewell in Craven, married the heiress Isabelle le Gras.[172] His descendant Sir William Tempest died in 1444 and was ultimately succeeded by his daughters, Isabelle and Denise.[173] Through her marriage to William Malory, Denise Tempest brought the manors of Studley and Linton to the Malory family.[174] Earlier generations of Malories had already accumulated lands and lordships in Nunwick prebend by marriages to heiresses from the Nunwick and Conyers families.[175] The Malories evidently sought to consolidate their new standing by establishing a family mausoleum at Ripon, the parish church for Nunwick and Studley. The burial practices of the Markenfields in the north transept provided them with a model to imitate. There are no surviving Malory tombs at Ripon, but Leland wrote that there was one in a chapel in the south transept and others in the churchyard clustered around the south transept door.[176]

The first documented Malory burial in the south transept is that of William Malory (d. 1475) who asked to be buried 'before the altar of St Mary'.[177] Whether or not his request corresponded to a tradition established by his predecessors is difficult to determine, in part because of the renovation of the south transept after the collapse of the crossing tower in 1450. Six years after the death of Sir William Tempest the south-east corner of the central tower broke loose and crashed down onto the choir and south transept. The

---

[171] Pollard, *North-eastern England during the Wars of the Roses*, 126–7.

[172] *Memorials of the abbey of St Mary of Fountains*, ed. John Richard Walbran, James Raine and J. T. Fowler (Surtees Society, 1863–1918), ii. 311–12.

[173] Gowland, 'The manors and liberties of Ripon', 66n.

[174] *Memorials of Fountains*, ii. 314.

[175] Ibid.; Gowland, 'The manors and liberties of Ripon', 65.

[176] *Itinerary of Leland*, v. 142–3.

[177] 'coram altare B. Mariæ': *Memorials of Fountains*, ii. 315.

four piers upon which the tower rested had been subsiding at different rates since the thirteenth century, and attempted repairs before 1450 were not adequate to prevent the collapse.[178] The eastern arcade of the south transept was thoroughly renovated after the fall of the central tower.[179] Work there was probably completed before the replacement of the choir stalls began in the early 1480s, and Archbishop Rotherham's 1482 indulgence for building works at Ripon was the first issued by a new archbishop since 1450 that did not mention the central tower.[180] William Malory's request for burial in the south transept in 1475 is a strong indication that the works had been completed. Walbran recorded the heraldry of the fifteenth-century ceiling of this transept before it was replaced in the nineteenth century, writing that the 'arms of the See of York, Fountains Abbey, the families of Pigot of Clotherholme, and Norton of Norton that adorned the late wooden ceiling of the south transept, showed who were the chief contributors to this work'.[181] The Malory arms do not feature, but may once have been found in less durable media or on screens that separated the chapels from the transept.

Members of the Guild of the Assumption of the Blessed Virgin Mary had selected the area around the St Mary altar in the south transept as their burial place since at least 1390, well before the foundation of the guild's chantry in 1416.[182] The chantry ordination makes no mention of the Malories who only joined its beneficiaries when John Harrison of Ripon bequeathed the Assumption chantry two cottages in 1505.[183] In particular, he named Sir John Malory and his wife Elizabeth, Sir William Malory and his wife Joan, Richard Radcliff and his wife Agnes, Sir Richard Hamerton and his wife Elizabeth, and the chaplain John Hutton.[184] These were significant family members and close associates from the last quarter of the fifteenth century. The William Malory who was married to Joan had been a Marmion tenant since the death of his father in 1475, and died in 1488.[185] His mother was from the Hamerton family and she had previously been married to one of the Radcliffs.[186] The Radcliffs were esquires who later founded the St George chantry in the minster. Elizabeth Malory, widow of Sir John Malory, nominated John Hutton as chaplain of the St John the Evangelist chantry in the minster in 1487.[187] Prior to this appointment, John Hutton had been the chaplain of the Malory's

---

[178]   Harrison and Barker, 'Ripon Minster', 63–4.

[179]   Ibid. 59–60.

[180]   MR ii. 162.

[181]   Walbran, Guide to Ripon, 39.

[182]   TE i. 137.

[183]   AoC, 320–1.

[184]   AoC, 321.

[185]   AoC, 247.

[186]   Memorials of Fountains, ii. 316.

[187]   AoC, 282.

manorial chapel at Hutton Conyers.[188] The Malories resided at both Hutton Conyers and Studley, and had even acquired licences for a new oratory at Studley in the 1450s and 1460s.[189] They established their own chantry in the minster, dedicated to St Wilfrid, at some time in the later fifteenth century, retaining the right to nominate its chaplains.[190]

The Malories placed funerary monuments where they would constantly be able to solicit prayers. The tomb of William Malory (d. 1475) may have been the one that Leland saw in a chapel in the south transept. Like the north transept, the south transept had two altars and at least one chantry, so there were three priests who might regularly see Malory's tomb and pray for him. The Malory graves outside the door of the south transept were still marked and identifiable in Leland's time. Processions entering or leaving the building by the south transept door would have encountered these monuments, and the Palm Sunday procession was likely to have passed close by to them on its circuit around the building. Likewise all canons and chaplains crossing the churchyard from Annsgate, where a number of them had their residences, would have encountered the Malory monuments. It is possible that the second altar in the south transept was the prebendal altar of Studley, dedicated to St Wilfrid, and that this altar was the site of the Malories' St Wilfrid chantry. If so, then there was an added level of significance to the south transept as a burial place.

The Nortons of Norton Conyers

The old Conyers family had held two manors near Ripon: Hutton Conyers, to the south of Nunwick, and Norton Conyers further north near Wath and Melmerby. Richard Norton (d. 1420) acquired the manor of Norton Conyers around the year 1400, either by marriage or purchase.[191] Richard was a prominent lawyer who served as justice of the peace for the North Riding in 1399, became sergeant-at-law in 1401, and royal chief justice in 1413.[192] The Nortons expanded their landholdings and local alliances through marriages in subsequent generations. Sir John Norton (d. 1520) married Margaret Ward, and their daughter Joan married William Malory.[193] John Norton was a lawyer like his ancestor Richard, and first served as justice of the peace for the North Riding in 1485.[194] Although they held the manor of Norton Conyers within the parish of Ripon, the Norton family preferred to make the parish church

---

[188] Ibid.

[189] *Memorials of Fountains*, ii. 314–16.

[190] MR iii. 20.

[191] Gowland, 'The manors and liberties of Ripon', 65; William Page (ed.), *VCH, North Riding*, London 1914–68, i. 393.

[192] C. L. Kingsford, rev. Keith Dockray, 'Norton, Richard (d. 1420)', *ODNB*.

[193] *Memorials of Fountains*, ii. 314.

[194] Pollard, *North-eastern England during the Wars of the Roses*, 166.

of Wath, another one of their manors, their family burial place rather than to share the minster with the other major families.[195] They were, in fact, parishioners of Wath rather than Ripon. When John Norton and Anne Radcliff obtained a licence to wed in the Norton manorial chapel of St Cuthbert in 1493, the curate of Wath performed the ceremony.[196] A chaplain said prayers and masses for the Nortons in this same chapel after Richard Norton's trustees, including his neighbour John Pigot, acquired the necessary mortmain licence for 40 marks in June 1421.[197] The foundation provided a residence and garden for the chaplain together with an annual salary of 8 marks.[198] Shortly before his death in 1420, Richard Norton was party to the foundation of a new chantry in Ripon Minster. Richard and his late wife Katherine were beneficiaries, together with the members of the St Wilfrid guild, of the chantry dedicated to Wilfrid and established at the altar of St Thomas the Martyr.[199] After the tower collapse, the Nortons were among the benefactors who funded the repair of the south transept.[200] Their heraldry and the financial support that it represented helped them to assert their lordship within the parish of Ripon even though they were buried at Wath. Their stake in the Thomas the Martyr chantry was no doubt given to them in exchange for Richard Norton using his powerful connections to help obtain the mortmain licence. The social connections that came with guild membership were also advantageous to the Nortons as they expanded their holdings from Wath into the parish of Ripon.

The Pigots of Clotherholme

Sir Ralph Pigot (d. 1404) gained the manor of Clotherholme in 1359 when he married Joan, heiress of John Clotherholme.[201] The Pigots established themselves at their new manor between the River Laver and Nunwick roughly four decades before the Malories and Nortons superseded the neighbouring Conyers family. They afterwards became very active and visible benefactors of Ripon. Ralph was co-founder of a chantry for the Guild of SS Mary, Wilfrid and All Saints in the Ladykirk around 1380, and in his will he asks for his body 'to be buried in the church of St Peter the Apostle in Ripon'.[202] Within two generations the link between the Pigots and the minster had become fixed. Sir Ralph I's grandson Ralph (d. 1466) wanted to be buried 'in the place where

[195] H. B. McCall, *Richmondshire churches*, London 1910, 147, 150.
[196] *TE* iii. 357.
[197] *CPR Henry V*, ii. 392–3.
[198] Ibid. ii. 393.
[199] *MR* iv. 194–5.
[200] Walbran, *Guide to Ripon*, 39.
[201] Gowland, 'The manors and liberties of Ripon', 61.
[202] 'sepeliendum in ecclesiâ B. Petri Apostoli Ripon': *MR* iv. 137; *TE* i. 331.

my ancestors were previously buried by habit and custom'.[203] He endowed a temporary chantry 'at the auter owre the nedill of Seynt Wilfride in the body of the college kirk of Saynt Petyr in Rypon'.[204] St Wilfrid's needle was located in the Anglo-Saxon crypt, so this altar may have been either in the crossing or at one of the crypt's entrances. His instructions were for the temporary chantry to be at this altar for four years, and at the Pigot chapel of Clotherholme for an additional twenty years.[205] This domestic chapel was as crucial to family identity as the minster. Sir John Clotherholme originally endowed the chapel in 1351, but seeing the inevitable end of his family line, he added the family of his future successor, Sir Ralph Pigot, to the list of chantry beneficiaries in 1359.[206] It is impossible to know whether the Clotherholme family was buried at Ripon. Whether or not they were, the rapid establishment of a Pigot mausoleum there helped them to assert the legitimacy of their lordship at Clotherholme. The Pigot's status as Marmion tenants lent them further credibility as a leading family within the parish. In the second half of the fifteenth century the Pigots were among the most prominent families in the county.[207]

After the death of Sir Ralph II, Lady Margaret Pigot (d. 1485), his widow, lived for nearly twenty more years. Lady Margaret opted not to remarry after her husband's death and had been veiled as a symbol of her vow of chastity in 1469.[208] She made bequests to each of the four mendicant houses in York for a trental, but the bulk of her bequests were local.[209] Her detailed will itemises a vast array of personal bequests to servants and relatives not to mention payments to benefit two of Ripon's hospitals, the bridge over the River Ure, and the minster fabric.[210] One of her executors was Thomas Labray, vicar of Nunwick and formerly her chaplain at Clotherholme.[211] Her son Sir Ralph Pigot III was one of the earl of Northumberland's retainers in the 1480s and one of the wealthiest knights in Yorkshire, but when he died without heirs in 1503 his estates were divided between his nieces Margaret, Joan and Elizabeth.[212] Leland reported that Ralph III was buried 'On the northe syde of the Quiere' in Ripon Minster.[213] The Pigot requests for burial are generally vague, so Leland's observation is crucial. Only John Pigot (d. 1488) gave much

---

[203] 'in loco ubi antecessores mei antea ex more et consuetudine sepulti fuerunt': *TE* iii. 157.

[204] *TE* iii. 157–8.

[205] The priest was to receive £4 annually from properties enfeoffed to Richard and John Pigot and Sir John Norton: *TE* iii. 158.

[206] *MR* iv. 35–6, 251.

[207] Pollard, *North-eastern England during the Wars of the Roses*, 89n.

[208] *TE* iii. 340.

[209] *AoC*, 277.

[210] Ibid.

[211] *AoC*, 278.

[212] *TE* iv. 213–14n; Pollard, *North-eastern England during the Wars of the Roses*, 126–7.

[213] *Itinerary of Leland*, v. 143.

detail, writing that he wanted to be buried 'in the said collegiate church of Ripon, before the pietà image of the Blessed Mary'.[214] This pietà, showing Mary cradling the crucified Christ in her arms, was somewhere in the nave. This John Pigot, esquire, was never lord of Clotherholme, and as such his place of burial was more likely to be an outlier, and the rest of the Pigot graves may in fact have been near Sir Ralph III's grave. The north side of the choir was the typical location for the Easter sepulchre, so it is possible that one of the Pigot graves was used as its base. Proximity to the Easter sepulchre was so desirable that it was worth the sacrifice of visibility entailed with having a flat tomb rather than effigies.[215] In Ripon the location came with the added benefit of proximity to Wilfrid's shrine. The Pigots were a very visible presence elsewhere in Ripon Minster, displaying their heraldry (*sable, three mill picks argent*) on every phase of new construction from the tower collapse to the rebuilding of the nave. All the minster clergy would have seen the Pigot arms on the stone screen as they processed into the choir, and those seated in the north choir stalls would have had a clear view of the Pigot coat of arms carved in stone on the south wall of the choir itself. Their heraldry can even be found on one of the piers of the north nave aisle arcade, which was probably built around five years after the last Ralph Pigot had died and the family's lands had been redistributed to the husbands of his nieces. The other Ripon families may have displayed their heraldry in stained glass, but none of them had it carved in stone in as many different places as the Pigots.

Slightly different priorities are evident in the arrangements made by the cadet branch of the Pigot family. Richard Pigot (d. 1483) was a successful lawyer, acting as sergeant-at-law and as legal counsel to the earl of Warwick in the 1460s and the duke of Gloucester from 1471.[216] As an esquire from the junior branch of the Pigot family, he needed to purchase the manor of Little Barton to establish himself in landowning society in 1460.[217] Richard was active throughout the kingdom during his career and named Clerkenwell in London as his preferred place of burial.[218] If he happened to die in the north of England, then the venerable old abbey of St Mary's in York was his choice.[219] His posthumous distributions and endowments were calculated to have the maximum impact in Yorkshire and London immediately after his death. He set aside 100 marks for the funeral, twenty of which were to be distributed to the poor, and he wanted 1,000 masses said on his behalf 'the daye of my deth, or on the morow after, or as sone after as it may be possible'.[220] He made

---

[214] 'in ecclesia collegiata Ripon' prædicta, ante Beatam Mariam pietatis': AoC, 264.

[215] Badham, *Seeking salvation*, 212.

[216] Pollard, *North-eastern England during the Wars of the Roses*, 135–6.

[217] Ibid. 83.

[218] *TE* iii. 285.

[219] Ibid.

[220] Ibid.

bequests to the friars in London and in the north at York, Richmond and Northallerton, and donated 100 marks to St Mary's Abbey in York to fund commemorations that he had already agreed with them.[221] He also granted twenty marks to the fabric of Ripon Minster 'for the tyme that I was there'.[222]

The John Pigot, esquire, who died in 1488 bequeathed four tenements in Annsgate to the Guild of Holy Cross, to be received after the death of Katherine his wife, so that the guild would pray for their souls forever.[223] It is not entirely clear how this John fits into the Pigot family. He cannot be Richard Pigot's brother, whom Richard refers to as already dead in his own 1483 will, and the only son that he mentions is also called Richard.[224] In any case, John's bequest of property to the guild was no doubt intended to establish a perpetual chantry without acquiring the mortmain licence required to alienate property. Some of the guild members could hold the property in trust while using its revenues to pay for the chaplain whom John requested.[225] It is known from other sources that this was in fact how the guild hired chaplains. John Pigot's bequest might have increased the number of Holy Cross chaplains from one to two, and one of the properties in Annsgate might have been the guild hall and residence of the chaplains. In any case, this expedient spared John the cost of the mortmain licence so that he had more money to hire palmers to go on pilgrimage for him to the Marian shrines of Doncaster and Walsingham, the Holy Blood of Hales and the shrine of Thomas Becket in Canterbury.[226]

The Kendales of Markington

On Monday 23 May 1457 John Kendale of Markington, gentleman, came before canons William Scrope and John Clere to acknowledge that he held the manor of Markington and two messuages in Wallerthwaite from the chapter as a Marmion tenant. He swore fealty to the chapter and was admitted to his inheritance.[227] He was just in time to bear St Wilfrid's relics around the parish boundary, since 23 May was Rogation Monday in 1457. John inherited the manor following the death of his aunt Isabelle on 9 April, the day before Palm Sunday. Isabelle and her sister Alice Kendale had been daughters and co-heiresses of Nicholas Gyliot of Markington.[228] The Gyliot family, who had been Marmion tenants and lords of Markington since at least 1229, was one

---

[221] *TE* iii. 285-6.
[222] *TE* iii. 285.
[223] *AoC*, 266.
[224] *TE* iii. 286.
[225] Kreider, *English chantries*, 79-80.
[226] *AoC*, 265.
[227] *AoC*, 207.
[228] Ibid.

more ancient Ripon family that became extinct in the male line during the fifteenth century.[229]

Alice Kendale was already a widow when she died in the summer of 1451, naming her sons John and Christopher the chaplain as executors.[230] She made her will in the presence of her vicar, John Exilby, meaning that Markington was in the prebend of Thorpe.[231] For her immediate spiritual wellbeing Alice made arrangements for her funeral in Ripon and for the four orders of friars in York to perform a trental. She did not ask to be buried in the minster but rather in the churchyard of the Ladykirk.[232] Her late husband, Hugh, must have been buried there already because when John died in 1469 he requested burial at the Ladykirk by the graves of his parents.[233] Beyond this request John Kendale's will is fairly sparse, and he left most of the arrangements to his wife and brother. The Kendales were the last significant new family to inherit one of the many manors of the parish of Ripon. The Malories had gained part of Studley not many years before, but they were also knights with much greater landholdings than the Kendales. Before the 1450s, the Markenfields had already surrounded the parochial altars of Thorpe and Monkton with their monuments, so the Kendales may have thought that the Ladykirk was a more promising place for family burials than the minster. The association between the chapel and Kendale family identity was part of the reason that Christopher Kendale, in his capacity as the chapter court's commissary, held a session of the court there when it heard the matrimonial case of his niece, Margaret.

The fortunes of families and institutions in the parish were always changing. Men and women died, families became extinct in the male line of succession. John of Gaunt's old affinity disintegrated into feuding between Neville and Percy, Ripon and Knaresborough. The endowments of perpetual chantries waned and were replenished by new benefactors. The minster's crossing tower fell and was rebuilt, the nave was dismantled and replaced. Religious fraternities came and went. All attempts to be remembered forever needed to contend with the ceaseless changing of the world, and all were intended to help the souls of the dead reach a state of changeless perfection in the company of the saints. Tombs, perpetual chantries and anniversaries were intended to ease the torments of souls in purgatory by preserving their memory. They could at the same time benefit the living by making more masses accessible to more people and generally improving clerical provision in the parish. Funerary monuments in particular helped to affirm the status of the living by glorifying their ancestors. The placing of these monuments was a significant factor in

---

[229] MR i. 62.

[230] AoC, 207–8.

[231] AoC, 209.

[232] AoC, 208.

[233] AoC, 227.

how well they could preserve memory, and the best locations were desired by many and only available to few. Many of Ripon's vicars and chaplains wished to be buried near their altars. These same altars were the preferred burial places of some of Ripon's gentry families, whose monuments doubled as their representatives during most of the year when they heard mass in their own chapels. As old families were replaced by new ones during the fourteenth and fifteenth centuries, intramural burial at the minster became important to newcomers as a way of displaying lordship and demonstrating their arrival. The more immediate counterpart to burial in the minster was the oath of fealty to St Wilfrid, which confirmed the succession of one Marmion tenant by another, even if their heraldry and surnames were different.

Conclusion

This book has considered the social production of time, focusing on religious practices and memorial culture within the vast parish of Ripon during the fifteenth century. The minster was the most powerful influence, dividing the day with its bells, the week with its Sunday high masses and the year with its calendar. The spiritual authority invested in the chapter bolstered this power by enabling it to enforce proper observance. Yet the minster was not the only force that shaped time in Ripon and the surrounding area. Lay elites used important feast days as opportunities to display their status, various types of founders endowed their own masses inside and outside the minster, and for much of the year many people followed their own routines in the numerous chapels of the parish. The families and other groups powerful enough to take hold of these opportunities could use them to reinforce their power. Furthermore, ritual and attendance at the minster fluctuated according to the day and season, so it is only within this context that its potential to commemorate the dead can properly be understood. The same applies to the dual nature of the parish and the privileged religious practices of the gentry. While many of the demands imposed by the liturgical calendar were universal, the special character of the ritual year in Ripon was determined by their combination with the feasts of the minster's own saint.

St Wilfrid, apostle of the north of England, was the spiritual patron and lord of late medieval Ripon. His lordship was symbolised by his heraldry, displayed alongside that of the knights and archbishops who sponsored the rebuilding of the nave in the early sixteenth century, and it was manifested in the oaths of fealty that the knights and gentlemen who were Marmion tenants swore to him when they inherited their lands. This special form of tenure integrated new lords into parish society when old families became extinct in the male line of succession. Even if they no longer carried the relics of the saint at Rogation, their oaths were still timed to correspond with Ripon's major annual procession. In their place other men of good standing in the parish bore the relics of their patron, who protected their lands and livelihoods from disease, bad weather and demonic influence. The saint's power was at work in the chapter court, which defended his rights in the liberty and preserved his peace, sentencing the invaders of the liberty to humiliating public penance. In exchange for his patronage, the minster clergy honoured Wilfrid by celebrating his three feast days and requiring all parishioners, regardless of their rank, to attend. The parishioners of Ripon, like pilgrims from farther afield, could seek help from Wilfrid at his image, head and shrine. Access to the head and shrine may have been restricted to Wilfrid's feast days, but his image in the nave was always approachable. The dead as well as the living appealed to Wilfrid for his help, with many parishioners making gifts to the shrine in their wills and some even asking to be buried near his image. Wilfrid was prepared to help his faithful adherents in all seasons.

The minster church itself, complete with its institutional structure and enormous parish, was another component of Wilfrid's enduring legacy. Possession of Wilfrid's relics was a significant feature of the contest for primacy between England's two metropolitans. York and Canterbury both claimed them, but York had the feast days, pilgrimage church and contact relics to support their claim. In shaping the cult of St Wilfrid at Ripon, the archbishops of York set the stage for its late medieval parish structure. To preserve the collegiate church that housed Wilfrid's shrine, the archbishops kept the tithes of Ripon's six prebends concentrated in the hands of the canons of Ripon, rather than permitting the division of the large parish into several smaller and more manageable ones. Thereafter the establishment of a great number of chapels during the thirteenth and fourteenth centuries created smaller congregations within the parish of Ripon. These chapels were paid for by their founders and all the chapter's rights, privileges and tithes were preserved. During much of the year these chapels acted as the real parish churches for Ripon's many different groups of parishioners. The religious practices of all Ripon's parishioners, including the gentry, should be interpreted within this context.

Ripon's gentry practised a very conventional type of religion adapted to the unusual circumstances of the parish: their manifest fear of purgatory, veneration of the saints and concentration on display fit neatly into Carpenter's definition of gentry religion. In the fifteenth century the knights, esquires and even some of the lesser gentry families had their own chapels. Many of these were used by other parishioners on a regular basis. The Ripon chapter permitted and indeed encouraged this from as early as the thirteenth century because the parish was unmanageable otherwise. Whether or not the use of these chapels constituted a withdrawal from the communal religion of the parish depends on how the community in question is defined. If the whole parish of Ripon is thought of as a community, then the only conclusion is that the gentry were absent from its liturgy most of the time. If instead the parish was many smaller communities, some made up of the populations of the areas around each lord's manor – in other words the local group of parishioners together with the lord, lady and their household – then the gentry remained an integral part of it. The same definitions of community can be applied to the villagers of Skelton or Aldfield with similar results. In fact, if there was to be a community of the whole parish, it could only really have existed on the major feast days when all parishioners were supposed to attend the minster. The chapel licences show that in this respect the gentry had the privilege of attending the minster even less often than the other parishioners who used their chapels. They were also more capable than most of being represented in their absence, both by displays of heraldry and by the tombs of their ancestors. When they attended on the great feast days their presence in the minster church brought these symbols and memorials into play to reinforce their status.

On Sundays and feast days the liturgical emphasis was on the mass, but there were a number of other sacraments and non-sacramental ceremonies that marked important stages in the lives of Ripon's parishioners from birth to death. A thorough analysis of the parish must also take account of these rites of passage, including baptism, churching, marriage, vows of chastity and extreme unction. The circumstances of these rituals, especially where and how they took place, lend weight to the interpretation of the parish as divided into many smaller units though still tied to the minster in significant ways. Baptism was the most significant of these. Ripon's parishioners were all baptised in a single font located in the nave of the minster. Pateley Bridge, a separate parish in all but name, was the only exception to this rule. Ripon Minster took a slightly more relaxed approach to marriage, allowing some marriages to be solemnised outside of the minster though only on the condition that the ceremony was performed by the vicar within whose prebend the chapel stood. The late medieval English custom of treating marriage as a process gave Ripon's parishioners a somewhat wider scope to contract their marriages among friends and family first and then later solemnise it within the minster or a chapel. Nevertheless, the minster clergy were anxious that this final solemnisation occur. Without it their knowledge of the marital status of parishioners would have been insufficient to enforce morality by prosecuting fornication and adultery. The churching ceremony that purified and readmitted a woman to her church following childbirth concerned the minster clergy if the woman regularly attended the minster, but otherwise they were content to permit women to be churched by their own chaplains in their own chapels. The widow's vow of perpetual chastity was administered by a bishop, so it did not concern Ripon's clergy though they would, like everyone else, have been able to recognise a vowess from the veil and mantle that symbolised her changed status. Guild members, when they wore their guild livery, likewise displayed their membership of an organisation that guaranteed their moral quality by regulating their behaviour.

The annual pattern of saints' feasts gave the villages and guilds their own moments in time; they were the calendar equivalents of the chapels and altars maintained by these groups. Many of the most important feast days of the guilds and villages took place during the six months between midsummer and Christmas. This portion of the year was largely free of obligatory feasts, and villagers may not have attended the minster more than a few times during this period. Instead, their religious practices were focused on the local chapels whose patronal feasts were the crowning moment of the village calendar. During the fifteenth century, even chapels very close to the minster were the focal points of smaller congregations. Those known to have had patronal feasts officiated by a priest from the minster, or in some cases from Fountains Abbey, were the hospital of St John the Baptist (24 June), St Swithun, Skelton (2 July), St Mary Magdalene in Stonebridgegate (22 July), St Lawrence, Aldfield (10 August) and St Michael-on-the-Mount (29 September). The minster clergy also celebrated masses for guilds based in the minster, using the guild's altar for the occasion. The guild holidays were the Assumption of the Blessed Virgin (15

August), Exaltation of Holy Cross (14 September), St Wilfrid (translation, 24 April) and Corpus Christi (moveable). Only the last two occurred within the Christmas to midsummer portion of the year, but guild members living close to the minster probably attended more regularly than the inhabitants of distant settlements. By and large the phase of the year from Christmas to midsummer contained the major feast days when attendance at the minster was obligatory and the many smaller social groupings of the parish were brought together.

At Ripon Minster the feast days that drew the largest crowds were Christmas, Epiphany, Candlemas, Palm Sunday, Holy Thursday, Holy Friday, Easter, Ascension, Pentecost, All Saints and the feasts of St Wilfrid. All of them, except for Epiphany, Palm Sunday and Holy Thursday were feasts when ordinary parishioners were required to attend the minster. The rituals of these feast days incorporated the many smaller groups of parishioners into a single parish whose spiritual lords were the minster clergy and whose heavenly patron was St Wilfrid. These feast days offered a spectacle unmatched by any guild or chapel in the parish. The ritual performance of the liturgy, with its organ music and polyphonic singing, outclassed anything to be found elsewhere in the parish. Beyond the liturgy of mass and office there were the edifying entertainments provided by the players hired at Christmas and Easter. Normal spatial prohibitions were relaxed to allow lay participation in the adoration of the cross on Good Friday and the opening of the Easter sepulchre on Easter morning. Processions in the minster were also very grand, especially on Christmas, Palm Sunday, Easter, Ascension and Corpus Christi. The greatest of all processions was the Rogation procession on the three days before the feast of the Ascension, the beating of the bounds that secured the parish border by ingraining it in the memory of Ripon's parishioners. The single most powerful symbol of parish identity was St Wilfrid, whose relics were the focal point of the procession. If the people of Ripon felt that they were part of a community that encompassed the whole parish, this community had Wilfrid as its head.

Wilfrid's lordship was of the greatest importance to the clergy of the minster, who derived their own authority from it. For them, the major feast days of the Ripon calendar were like the sacrament of baptism: a matter of rights to be preserved. The Easter obligations of Ripon's parishioners comprised two more sacraments – confession and communion – that remained under the minster's control. If the clergy did not enforce their rights they would lose them, and if they did not preserve the borders of their territory it could be diminished by encroaching neighbours. It was equally important for them to properly honour their patron on his feast days lest he withdraw his blessings. Laypeople similarly sought the saint's help in return for venerating him with gifts and the observance of his feasts. The timing of Wilfrid's feasts made them an integral part of the agricultural year that defined the lives of many of Ripon's parishioners. The Rogation procession with his relics in May not only protected the boundaries from being forgotten but also protected the crops, livestock and people of the parish from malign forces. Wilfrid's feasts in April and October, with their summer and winter fairs respectively, were ideal occasions for the marketing of livestock, and the fairs continued to serve their secondary purpose of honouring the saint by attracting pilgrims to his shrine. In between the summer and winter fairs was the feast of Wilfrid's nativity, which inaugurated the harvest season at the beginning of August. The timing of the feast situated it, like the patronal feasts of the guilds and chapels, out of the way of the big universal feasts of the first half of the year. The link between the date of the feast and that of St Peter *ad vincula*, or Lammas, associated Wilfrid with one of his favourite saints as well as making him co-patron of Ripon's harvest season. The feast of Wilfrid's nativity was unique to Ripon, and it appears to have been the most important of his three feasts. It was the only one of them when all the minster clergy wore their ceremonial copes in the high mass procession, a distinguishing feature it shared only with Christmas and Easter. Moreover, the feast of St Wilfrid's nativity was, like Christmas and Easter, one of the few times when Ripon's gentry were required to attend the minster.

Gentry families were the most privileged of any of the groups of Ripon's parishioners. The thirteenth-century chapel licences show that founders of high status were not required to go in person to the minster on nearly as many feast days as the rest of the parishioners who used the same chapels. By the fifteenth century all the greater gentry families had their own chapels and some, like the Malories, had more than one. The wealthier and more powerful families of knights and esquires appear to have stood further back from the religion of the parish than their counterparts. While new Marmion tenants still pledged their fealty to Wilfrid and the chapter on the days leading up to the feast of the Ascension, they had ceased undertaking the ancient customary duty of bearing Wilfrid's relics around the boundary during the procession. The Pigots, Wards, Malories and even the Kendales were all Marmion tenant families whose patriarchs did not escort the feretory in 1481, leaving this duty to others who were eager to have their local importance confirmed in the wider context of the parish. Thus gentlemen like the Walworths and Richard Frankish shared the burden of carrying the relics with prosperous village husbandmen and yeomen. However, the absence of the greater gentry from the Rogation procession and many of the major feast days in the minster did not threaten their status in society because even in their absence they were constantly represented by displays of their heraldry and the monuments of their ancestors.

To gentry families their lineage and honour were the crucial aspects of their identity. Their chapels were important as signs of their status and places where they could guarantee that their ancestors were posthumously commemorated with masses and prayers. Like the village chapels, these chapels had their own patron saints, yet it was lineage rather than family patron saints that gave the gentry the core of their identities. The most important and recogniseable symbol of this identity was heraldry. In the minster, displays of heraldry on the many parts of the building renovated after 1450 identify the most important families as benefactors of the works. The few surviving funerary monuments use heraldry to identify not just the dead but also their friends, family and patrons. The burial place of a family concentrated the memory of its ancestors in one location and was another potent sign of its identity. Some of the greater gentry families had long-standing burial traditions in places outside of the parish. The Wards, for example, preferred their nunnery at Esholt, and the Nortons continued to use Wath as a burial place even after their sphere of interest extended into the parish. Others, like the Malories and the Markenfields, established their family mausolea in the minster and thus entered a fierce contest with the other elites – lesser gentry, clergy, burgesses – for burial space inside the church.

The most desirable burial places within the building were around the altars and images of the saints. These locations were prized because they enabled the monuments of the dead to beseech the living for prayers. The visibility of monuments was highly important. In particular, who saw the tombs and when they saw them were both crucial to their efficacy in generating prayers and preserving memory. The priests who performed masses at these altars and the people who attended these masses were potential intercessors. The Sunday and feast day processions that asperged the altars before the mass would have encountered these same tombs. The regular contact between procession and monument is almost too mundane to be remarkable, yet it surely guaranteed that certain of the dead would be remembered when many others were forgotten. The status of living knights and their families was dependent on the memory of their ancestors preserved in this way. The constant repetition of chantry masses was similarly powerful and correspondingly expensive to obtain. There were many less expensive options available, but their ability to preserve the memory of the dead and affirm the status of the living diminished depending on how widely available they were. The times and places in which the dead could be remembered were limited, as were the resources available to maintain that memory – as some might have hoped – forever. With the passage of time some of the long-dead were inevitably forgotten in order to remember those who had died more recently. The removal of huge quantities of bones from the churchyard during the rebuilding of the minster nave in the early sixteenth century demonstrates this fact as graphically as any other evidence. At that time many individual churchyard graves were dug up in order to expand the width of the nave and thus, among other things, provide more of the desirable intramural burial places that so many parishioners sought.

St Wilfrid had been dead for over eight-hundred years when the new nave of Ripon Minster was completed in 1522. Now, when the Rogation procession returned to the minster on the feast of the Ascension it met the Holy Spirit in the form of the cloud installed by the young men's guild at the east end of the nave. The lowering of the cloud symbolised the descent of the Holy Spirit again on Pentecost. Like the biblical Apostles, Wilfrid was filled with this same spirit, though it came upon him in the fiery portents of his miraculous birth. The rebuilding of the nave glorified the minster and its patron, and the fabrication of the cloud magnified the spectacle of some of its processions, but little else changed at the time. The years still passed with the daily tolling of bells, the changing seasons marked by feasts and fasts, the processions trooping along the borders of the parish with the relics of their saint. For a little while longer Wilfrid remained the link between Ripon and the remote majesty of heaven, his feast days still dividing the year as regularly as the slow revolution of its stars.

Bibliography

Unpublished primary sources

Kew, The National Archives
C 1/12/223; C 1/168/3; C 43/441/31; C 47/46/452; C 143/185/9; C 143/438/7; C 143/438/23; E 40/695; E 101/51/2; E 178/2609; 179/63/6; E 179/63/12; SC 6/HENVII/1031

Leeds, Brotherton Special Collections
Ripon Cathedral, dean and chapter archives
MS Dep 1980/1 40; MS Dep 1980/1 78; MS Dep 1980/1 183; MS Dep 1980/1 288.3; MS Dep 1980/1 356; MS Dep 1980/1 434

Ripon Cathedral Library
MS 8

York, Borthwick Institute
Probate registers 1–4

Published primary sources

Abstracts of the charters and other documents in the chartulary of Fountains Abbey in the West Riding of the county of York, ed. William T. Lancaster, Leeds 1915
Acts of chapter of the collegiate church of SS Peter and Wilfrid, Ripon, AD 1452 to AD 1506, ed. J. T. Fowler (Surtees Society, 1875)
Bede's Ecclesiastical history of the English people, ed. Bertam Colgrave and R. A. B. Mynors, Oxford 1969
Building accounts of Henry III, ed. H. M. Colvin, Oxford 1971
Calendar of charter rolls, London 1906–27
Calendar of patent rolls Edward II, London 1894–1904
Calendar of patent rolls Edward III, London 1891–1916
Calendar of patent rolls Henry IV, London 1903–9
Calendar of patent rolls Henry V, London 1910–1
The certificates of the commissioners appointed to survey the chantries, guilds, hospitals, etc. in the county of York, ed. William Page (Surtees Society, 1894–5)
De controversia in curia militari inter Ricardum le Scrope et Robertum Grosvenor, milites, ed. N. Harris Nicholas, London 1832
The historians of the Church of York, ed. James Raine, London 1879–94

The itinerary of John Leland in or about the years 1535–1543, ed. Lucy Toulmin Smith, London 1907–10

The Life of Bishop Wilfrid by Eddius Stephanus, ed. and trans. Bertram Colgrave, Cambridge 1927

Manuale et processionale ad usum insignis Ecclesiæ Eboracensis, ed. W. G. Henderson, Durham 1875

Memorials of the abbey of St Mary of Fountains, ed. John Richard Walbran, James Raine and J. T. Fowler (Surtees Society, 1863–1918)

Memorials of the Church of SS Peter and Wilfrid, Ripon, ed. J. T. Fowler (Surtees Society, 1882–1908)

The poll taxes of 1377, 1379 and 1381, ed. Carolyn C. Fenwick, Oxford 1998–2005

The registers, or rolls, of Walter Grey, lord archbishop of York, ed. James Raine (Surtees Society, 1872)

Testamenta Eboracensia: a selection of wills from the registry at York, ed. James Raine (Surtees Society, 1836–1902)

VCH North Riding, ed. William Page, London 1914–68

VCH York, iii, ed. William Page, London 1913

Secondary sources

Antoni, Bryan, and David Brinklow, *Minster Road, Ripon, North Yorkshire: report on an archaeological watching brief* (York Archaeological Trust 1999 Field Reports, xix)

Arnold, John, *Belief and unbelief in medieval Europe*, London 2005

Badham, Sally, *Seeking salvation: commemorating the dead in the late medieval English parish*, Donington 2015

Bartlett, Robert, *Why can the dead do such great things? Saints and worshippers from the martyrs to the Reformation*, Princeton 2013

Binski, Paul, *Medieval death: ritual and representation*, Ithaca 1996

Birkett, Helen, *The saints' Lives of Jocelin of Furness: hagiography, patronage, and ecclesiastical politics*, York 2010

Blair, John, 'Clerical communities and parochial space: the planning of urban mother churches in the twelfth and thirteenth centuries', in T. R. Slater and Gervase Rosser (eds), *The church in the medieval town*, Aldershot 1998, 272–94

— *The Church in Anglo-Saxon society*, Oxford 2005

Bossy, John, 'The mass as a social institution, 1200–1700', *P&P* c (Aug. 1983), 29–61

Brown, Peter, *The cult of saints: its rise and function in Latin Christendom*, Chicago 1981

Burgess, Clive, '"For increase of divine service": chantries in the parish in late medieval Bristol', *Journal of Ecclesiastical History* xxxvi (1985), 46–65

— 'A service for the dead: the form and function of the anniversary in late medieval Bristol', *Transactions of the Bristol and Gloucestershire Archaeological Society* cv (1987), 183–211

— '"By quick and by dead": wills and pious provision in late medieval Bristol', *EHR* cii (1987), 837–58

— '"A fond thing vainly invented": an essay on purgatory and pious motivation in late medieval England', in S. J. Wright (ed.), *Parish, church, and people: local studies in lay religion, 1350–1750*, London 1988, 56–84

— and Eamon Duffy (eds), *The parish in late medieval England*, Donington 2006

Burton, Janet, *The monastic order in Yorkshire, 1069–1215*, Cambridge 1999

Carley, James, 'The provenance of the Morgan Golden Gospels (Pierpont Morgan Library, MS M.23): a new hypothesis', in Kathleen Doyle and Scot McKendrick (eds), *1000 years of royal books and manuscripts*, London 2013, 53–67

Carpenter, Christine, 'Religion of the gentry', in Daniel Williams (ed.), *England in the fifteenth century*, Woodbridge 1987, 53–74

— 'Gentry and community in medieval England', *Journal of British Studies* xxxiii (1994), 340–80

Cassidy-Welch, Megan, *Monastic spaces and their meanings: thirteenth-century English Cistercian monasteries*, Turnhout 2001

Colvin, Howard, 'The origin of chantries', *Journal of Medieval History* xxvi (2000), 163–73

Coss, Peter, *The foundations of gentry life: the Multons of Frampton and their world, 1270–1370*, Oxford 2010

Crouch, David, *Piety, fraternity and power: religious guilds in late medieval Yorkshire*, York 2000

— 'The origin of chantries: some further Anglo-Norman evidence', *Journal of Medieval History* xxvii (2001), 159–80

Dobson, R. B., 'Yorkshire towns in the late fourteenth century', *Publications of the Thoresby Society* lix (1986), 1–21

Dockray, Keith, 'Plumpton Family (*per. c.*1165–c.1550)', *ODNB*

Donahue, Charles, *Law, marriage, and society in the later Middle Ages: arguments about marriage in five courts*, Cambridge 2007

Draper, Peter, *The formation of English gothic: architecture and identity*, New Haven 2006

Duffy, Eamon, *The stripping of the altars: traditional religion in England, 1400–1580*, 2nd edn, New Haven 2005

— 'The end of it all: the material culture of the English parish and the 1552 inventories of goods', in Burgess and Duffy, *The parish in late medieval England*, 381–9

Duncan, Sandra, 'Prophets shining in dark places: biblical themes and theological motifs in the *Vita Sancti Wilfridi*', in Higham, *Wilfrid: abbot, bishop, saint*, 80–92

Dyer, Christopher, *An age of transition? Economy and society in England in the later Middle Ages*, Oxford 2005

Fallow, T. M., 'Esholt Priory', in Page, *VCH, York*, iii. 161–3

French, Katherine L., *The good women of the parish: gender and religion after the Black Death*, Philadelphia 2008

Geary, Patrick, *Furta sacra: thefts of relics in the early Middle Ages*, Princeton 1978

Gent, Thomas, *The ancient and modern history of the loyal town of Rippon*, York 1733

Gilchrist, Roberta, *Medieval life: archaeology and the life course*, Woodbridge 2012

Gilyard-Beer, R., 'Bedern Bank and the Bedern Ripon', *YAJ* lviii (1986), 141–5

Given-Wilson, Chris, *The English nobility in the late Middle Ages: the late fourteenth-century political community*, London 1996

Gowland, Tom S., 'The manors and liberties of Ripon', *YAJ* xxxii (1936), 43–85

— 'Ripon Minster and its precincts', *YAJ* xxxv (1943), 270–87

Graves, C. Pamela, *The form and fabric of belief: an archaeology of the lay experience of religion in medieval Norfolk and Devon* (British Archaeological Reports, cccxi), Oxford 2000

Hall, R. A., 'Rescue excavations in the crypt of Ripon Cathedral', *YAJ* xlix (1977), 59–63

— and Mark Whyman, 'Settlement and monasticism at Ripon, North Yorkshire, from the 7th to the 11th centuries AD', *Medieval Archaeology* xl (1996), 62–150

Hallett, Cecil, *The cathedral church of Ripon: a short history of the church and a description of its fabric*, London 1901

Hanna, Ralph, 'Some Yorkshire scribes and their context', in Denis Renevey and Graham D. Caie (eds), *Medieval texts in context*, Abingdon 2008, 167–91

Harrison, Stuart, and Paul Barker, 'Ripon Minster: an archaeological analysis and reconstruction of the 12th-century church', *Journal of the British Archaeological Association* clii (1999), 49–78

Harrison, William, *Ripon millenary: a record of the festival; also a history of the city, arranged under its wakemen and mayors from the year 1400*, Ripon 1892

Harvey, John, *The perpendicular style, 1330–1485*, London 1978

— *English mediaeval architects: a biographical dictionary down to 1550*, Gloucester 1984

Hayward, Paul A., 'St Wilfrid of Ripon and the northern Church in Anglo-Norman historiography', *NH* xlix (2012), 11–35

Hearn, M. F., 'Ripon Minster: the beginning of the Gothic style in northern England', *Transactions of the American Philosophical Society* lxxiii (1983), 1–196

Heffernan, Thomas J., *Sacred biography: saints and their biographers in the Middle Ages*, Oxford 1988

Higham, N. J. (ed.), *Wilfrid: abbot, bishop, saint: papers from the 1300th anniversary conferences*, Donington 2013

Horrox, R. E., 'Medieval Beverley', in K. J. Allison (ed.), *VCH, East Riding, VI: The borough and liberties of Beverley*, Oxford 1989, 2–62

Hughes, Jonathan, *Pastors and visionaries: religion and secular life in late medieval Yorkshire*, Woodbridge 1988

Hutton, Ronald, *The rise and fall of Merry England: the ritual year, 1400–1700*, Oxford 1994

— *The stations of the sun: a history of the ritual year in Britain*, Oxford 1996

Imesch, Kornelia, 'The altar of the Holy Cross and the ideal of Adam's progeny: "ut paradysiace loca possideat regionis"', in Edelgard E. DuBruch and Barbara I. Gusich (eds), *Death and dying in the Middle Ages*, New York 1999, 73–106

James, M. R., 'Twelve medieval ghost stories', *EHR* xxxvii (1922), 413–22

James, Mervyn, 'Ritual, drama, and social body in the late medieval English town', *P&P* xcviii (Feb. 1983), 3–29

Jennings, Bernard (ed.), *A history of Nidderdale*, 2nd edn, Pateley Bridge 1983

Jones, Glanville R. J., 'The Ripon estate: landscape into townscape', *NH* xxxvii (2000), 13–30

Kerr, Neil R., *Medieval manuscripts in British libraries*, Oxford 1962–92

Kingsford, C. L., 'Norton, Richard (d. 1420)', rev. Keith Dockray, *ODNB*

Kreider, Alan, *English chantries: the road to dissolution*, Cambridge, MA 1979

Kümin, Beat, *The shaping of a community: the rise and reformation of the English parish, c. 1400–1560*, Aldershot 1996

Lambert, T. B., 'Spiritual protection and secular power: the evolution of sanctuary and legal privileges in Ripon and Beverley, 900–1300', in T. B. Lambert and

David Rollason (eds), *Peace and protection in the Middle Ages*, Durham 2009, 121-40

Landes, David S., *A revolution in time: clocks and the making of the modern world*, Cambridge 1983

Le Goff, Jacques, *Medieval civilization, 400-1500*, trans. Julia Barrow, Oxford 1988

— *À La Recherche du temps sacré: Jacques de Voragine et la Légende dorée*, Paris 2011

Leach, Peter, and Nikolaus Pevsner, *The buildings of England: Yorkshire West Riding: Leeds, Bradford, and the North*, New Haven 2014

Lefebvre, Henri, *The production of space*, trans. Donald Nicholson-Smith, Oxford 1991

— *Rhythmanalysis: space, time, and everyday life*, trans. Stuart Elden and Gerald Moore, London 2004

Lepine, David, '"Their name liveth forevermore?": obits at Exeter Cathedral in the later Middle Ages', in Caroline M. Barron and Clive Burgess (eds), *Memory and commemoration in medieval England*, Donington 2010, 58-74

McCall, H. B., *Richmondshire churches*, London 1910

McKay, William, 'The development of medieval Ripon', *YAJ* liv (1982), 73-82

McKinnell, John, 'For the people/by the people: public and private spaces in the Durham sequence of the sacrament', in Frances Andrews (ed.), *Ritual and space in the Middle Ages*, Donington 2009, 213-31

McSheffrey, Shannon, 'Place, space, and situation: public and private in the making of marriage in late-medieval London', *Speculum* lxxix (2004), 960-90

Mayo, Janet, *A history of ecclesiastical dress*, London 1984

Miller, Edward 'The occupation of the land: Yorkshire and Lancashire', in Thirsk, *Agrarian history of England and Wales*, iii. 42-52

— 'Farming practices and techniques: Yorkshire and Lancashire', in Thirsk, *Agrarian history of England and Wales*, iii. 182-94

Moorhouse, Stephen A., 'Boundaries', in S. A. Moorhouse and M. L. Faull (eds), *West Yorkshire: an archaeological survey to AD 1500*, Wakefield 1981, ii. 265-89

Morris, Richard, *Churches in the landscape*, London 1989

Murray, Alexander, 'Medieval Christmas', *History Today* xxxvi (1986), 31-9

Nelson, Janet T., 'Queens as Jezebels: the careers of Brunhild and Balthild in Merovingian History', in Derek Baker (ed.), *Medieval women* (Studies in Church History, subsidia i, 1978), 31-77

Norton, Christopher, *St William of York*, York 2006

— 'Richard Scrope and York Minster', in P. J. P Goldberg (ed.), *Richard Scrope: archbishop, rebel, martyr*, Donington 2007, 138-213

Orme, Nicholas, 'The other parish churches: chapels in late medieval England', in Burgess and Duffy, *The parish in late medieval England*, 78-94

Penman, Michael A., 'Christian days and knights: the religious devotions and court of David II of Scotland, 1329-71', *Historical Research* lxxv (2002), 249-72

Pfaff, Richard, *New liturgical feasts in later medieval England*, Oxford 1970

— *The liturgy in medieval England: a history*, Cambridge 2009

Phythian-Adams, Charles, *Local history and folklore: a new framework*, London 1975

— 'Ritual constructions of society', in Rosemary Horrox and W. Mark Ormrod (eds), *A social history of England, 1200-1500*, Cambridge 2006, 369-82

Pollard, A. J., *North-eastern England during the Wars of the Roses: lay society, war, and politics, 1450-1500*, Oxford 1990

Poole, Reginald L., 'St Wilfrid and the see of Ripon', *EHR* cxxxiii (1919), 1-24

Richmond, Colin, 'Religion and the fifteenth-century English gentleman', in Barrie Dobson (ed.), *The Church, politics, and patronage in the fifteenth century*, Gloucester 1984, 193–208

Roffey, Simon, *The medieval chantry chapel: an archaeology*, Woodbridge 2007

Rosser, Gervase, 'Communities of parish and guild in the late Middle Ages', in S. J. Wright (ed.), *Parish, church, and people: local studies in lay religion, 1350–1750*, London 1988, 29–55

— *The art of solidarity in the Middle Ages: guilds in England, 1250–1550*, Oxford 2015

Rubin, Miri, *Corpus Christi: the eucharist in late medieval culture*, Cambridge 1991

Saul, Nigel, 'The gentry and the parish', in Burgess and Duffy, *The parish in late medieval England*, 243–60

— *English church monuments in the Middle Ages: history and representation*, Oxford 2009

— *For honour and fame: chivalry in England, 1066–1500*, London 2011

Schmitt, Jean-Claude, *Ghosts in the Middle Ages: the living and the dead in medieval society*, trans. Teresa Lavender Fagan, Chicago 1998

Scott, G. Gilbert, 'Ripon Minster', *Archaeological Journal* xxxi (1874), 309–18

Senior, Janet C., *The Markenfields of Markenfield Hall: the rise and fall of a Yorkshire family*, Bradford 2009

Stancliffe, Clare, 'Dating Wilfrid's death and Stephen's *Life*', in Higham, *Wilfrid: abbot, bishop, saint*, 17–26

Stocker, David, 'The quest for one's own front door: housing the vicars choral at English cathedrals', *Vernacular Architecture* xxxvi (2005), 15–31

Swanson, R. N., *Church and society in late medieval England*, Oxford 1989

Tanner, Norman P., *The Church in late medieval Norwich, 1370–1532*, Toronto 1984

Thacker, Alan, 'The cult of saints and the liturgy', in Derek Keene, Arthur Burns and Andrew Saint (eds), *St Paul's: the cathedral church of London, 604–2004*, New Haven 2004, 113–22

— 'Wilfrid, his cult, and his biographer', in Higham, *Wilfrid: abbot, bishop saint*, 1–16

Thompson, A. Hamilton, 'Collegiate Church of St Peter and St Wilfrid, Ripon', in Page, *VCH, York*, iii. 367–72

Thirsk, Joan (ed.), *The agrarian history of England and Wales, III: 1348–1500*, Cambridge 1991

Vauchez, André, *Sainthood in the later Middle Ages*, trans. Jean Birell, Cambridge 1997

Walbran, John Richard, *A guide to Ripon, Fountains Abbey, Harrogate, Bolton Priory, and several places of interest in their vicinity*, 12th edn, Ripon 1875

Walker, Simon, 'Yorkshire justices of the peace, 1389–1413', *EHR* cviii (1993), 281–313

Wander, Stephan, 'Westminster Abbey and the apostolic churches of northern France', *Studies in Iconography* iv (1978), 3–22

Watson, Sethina, 'City as charter: charity and the lordship of English towns, 1170–1250', Caroline Goodson, Anne E. Lester and Carol Symes (eds), *Cities, texts, and social networks, 400–1500: experiences and perceptions of medieval urban space*, Farnham–Burlington, Vt 2010, 235–62

Werronen, Stephen, 'Ripon and the Scottish raids, 1318–1322', *NH* xlix (2012), 174–84

— 'The hospital of St Mary Magdalene and the archbishops of York, c. 1150–1335', *Nottingham Medieval Studies* lviii (2014), 115–36

Whyman, Mark, 'Excavations in Deanery Gardens and Low St Agnesgate, Ripon, North Yorkshire', *YAJ* lxix (1997), 119–63

Wilcock, Ruth, 'Local disorder in the Honour of Knaresborough, *c.* 1438–1461 and the national context', *NH* xli (2004), 39–80

Wilson, Christopher, 'Ripon: the cathedral', in Peter Leach and Nikolaus Pevsner, *The buildings of England: Yorkshire West Riding: Leeds, Bradford, and the North*, New Haven 2014, 637–58

Winchester, Angus J. L., *The harvest of the hills: rural life in northern England and the Scottish Borders, 1400–1700*, Edinburgh 2000

Wolf, Kenneth Baxter, *The life and afterlife of St Elizabeth of Hungary: testimony from her canonization hearings*, Oxford 2011

Wollasch, Joachim, 'Les Obituaires, témoins de la vie clunisienne', *Cahiers de civilisation médiévale* xxii (1979), 139–77

Wood-Legh, Kathleen, *Perpetual chantries in Britain*, Cambridge 1965

Woolgar, C. M., *The senses in late medieval England*, New Haven 2006

Unpublished dissertations

Douglas, Mark, 'The archaeology of memory: an investigation into the links between collective memory and the architecture of the parish church in late medieval Yorkshire', PhD, Durham 2003, <http://etheses.dur.ac.uk/1260/>

Miller, Jeffrey A. K., 'The building program of Archbishop Walter de Gray: architectural production and reform in the archdiocese of York, 1215–1255', PhD, Columbia 2012

Web-based sources

'Masters of the rolls (1286–2012)', *ODNB*

Index